Frederick George Lee

The Christian Doctrine of Prayer for the Departed

Frederick George Lee

The Christian Doctrine of Prayer for the Departed

ISBN/EAN: 9783742856760

Manufactured in Europe, USA, Canada, Australia, Japa

Cover: Foto ©Lupo / pixelio.de

Manufactured and distributed by brebook publishing software (www.brebook.com)

Frederick George Lee

The Christian Doctrine of Prayer for the Departed

THE CHRISTIAN DOCTRINE OF
PRAYER FOR THE DEPARTED

By the Rev. FREDERICK GEORGE LEE
D.C.L., F.S.A.
VICAR OF ALL SAINTS', LAMBETH

With Copious Notes and Appendices

STRAHAN & CO., PUBLISHERS
56 LUDGATE HILL, LONDON
1872

LONDON:
PRINTED BY VIRTUE AND CO.,
CITY ROAD.

Dedicated

WITH RESPECTFUL REGARD

TO

MRS. STAVELEY

OF OLD SLENINGFORD HALL, NEAR RIPON

AS A SMALL ACKNOWLEDGMENT OF HER MANY KINDNESSES

TO ME AND MINE

TRUSTING THAT THE DOCTRINES SET FORTH IN

THIS TREATISE

MAY, AFTER LOSSES AND SEPARATIONS

POINT OUT A SOURCE OF COMFORT AND CONSOLATION

TO ALL WHO SORROW WITH CHRISTIAN HOPE FOR THOSE WHO SLEEP

BELIEVING IN

THE RESURRECTION OF THE FLESH

AND

THE COMMUNION OF SAINTS

AND LOOKING FORWARD IN FAITH TO THE

BREAKING OF THE EVERLASTING DAY

AND TO THE

FINAL RESTITUTION OF ALL THINGS

"THOSE who depart out of this life full of grace and love, but still indebted for the sufferings which divine justice has reserved to them, suffer for them in the next. And this is the reason why the Church has offered prayers, alms, and sacrifices for the faithful departed who were in communion with her, believing that they receive comfort and aid thereby. The Council of Trent bids us believe thus much on the subject of the souls in Purgatory, not defining in what their sufferings consist, or in any way diving into such matters, but rather demanding great circumspection where so little is revealed, and blaming those who pronounce as certain what must at present be vague and undetermined. Such is the holy and innocent doctrine the Catholic Church teaches regarding satisfaction, which is imputed to us as a great offence. If, after this explanation, Protestants still accuse us of not doing justice to the satisfaction of Jesus Christ, we will once more repeat that our Blessed Lord has paid for us the full and entire ransom for our redemption, and that we believe nothing to be wanting to it, because it is an infinite ransom; and that these pains and sufferings we speak of as reserved to us, do not in the least proceed from any want of perfection in His Infinite Satisfaction, but from a certain law of discipline He has framed for us, restraining us by a wholesome fear."—BISHOP BOSSUET's *Exposition of the Teaching of the Universal Church.*

PREFACE

THE materials out of which this treatise has been formed have been accumulating for many years. It has always been a source of great pleasure and satisfaction to the Author to visit and examine our most interesting and instructive old parish churches—amongst the greatest glories of the country. And while he deeply laments that restorations of so many of them have been carried out in anything but a conservative spirit, it is impossible to be otherwise than heartily grateful that the tide of destruction, rapacity, and neglect which rolled over the land both at the Reformation and the Great Rebellion has been now efficiently stemmed. But while this is certainly the case, it is impossible not to regret the utter destruction of many family monuments, the mutilation and removal of others, and the general loss of ancient relics, both architectural and ecclesiological, during the recent Catholic Revival. Much evil has been wrought through ignorance, but more by neglect and want of ordinary care. Particularly has this taken place with reference to early monumental brasses and ancient memorial legends. Many post-Reformation gravestones have likewise perished of late years, and with them some interesting evidence of the vitality of old Catholic usages.

The immediate cause which led to the materials collected being arranged, added to, and put into shape, was the *ex cathedrâ dictum* of His Grace the Archbishop of Canterbury to a distinguished Eastern Patriarch that the Church of England did not authorize nor sanction Prayer for the Dead. A similar opinion was afterwards pronounced by one of His Grace's suffragans, Dr. Ellicott, Bishop of Gloucester. It was felt by several that such individual utterances—apparently meant to circumscribe Christian liberty—were not unlikely to cause perplexity at home, and create grave misapprehension abroad, which was notoriously the case in both instances. Hence this publication. Of course, members of the Church of England may reasonably decline to be committed to the private declarations and personal fancies of individual bishops. For example, God forbid that the opinions and *dicta* of Bale and Cranmer, of Burnet and Hoadley in the past, or of Hinds and Colenso in the present day, should have the smallest weight with members of the National Church or other Catholic Christians. Yet no opportunity should be lost to inform the faithful regarding true principles and undisputed facts. How far the principles of this book are true, and the facts reliable and recognized, must be left to the information, judgment, and charity of the reader.

When ancient services used of old in this Church and realm are carefully compared with those now in the Prayer Book, it is impossible not to regret the loss we have sustained by the change. No doubt our present Burial Service is solemn, dignified, and touching, and full of consolation to the mourners. But it is nevertheless intentionally and eminently selfish. The living rather than the departed are considered throughout it, while the dead are almost entirely forgotten. And what, during the past three centuries, has been the reasonable consequence of this uncharitable forgetfulness? Even this—that our funerals have by degrees become more and more distinctively heathen in their character, and less Christian than ever. Moreover, such a care and regard for the bodies of the dead, believed by Christians to be temples of the Holy Ghost, as was always manifested alike for poor and rich in pre-Reformation times, is now either altogether unknown or most exceptionally rare. The author does not refer to the degrading rites and practices common at certain unconsecrated joint-stock cemeteries, nor to the burial of "town paupers" at so much a hundred, but to recent proceedings which have obtained in certain of the sacred graveyards belonging to our ancient parish churches.

If there is anything calculated to bring down the curse of Almighty God upon us as a Church and nation, it is the scandalous desecration and cold-blooded sacrilege involved in pulling down some of the city churches and selling their sacred sites for commercial purposes and temporal advantages. Yet this has been done again and again, with the full sanction of our bishops, and, as far as the public is aware, without any formal protest on the part of Christians in general. Railway companies, too, and the makers of new roads, have unhappily obtained a sanction from Authority to carry works through several old burying-places. The churchyards of St. Margaret's, Westminster, of St. Mary Somerset, near Doctors' Commons, of Old St. Pancras, of St. Andrew's, Holborn, and of St. Martin's-in-the-Fields, as well as many others in London, have been ruthlessly dealt with in a manner which would have been simply impossible with civilized Pagans before the coming of our Lord. Tons of human bones—in some cases those of bodies not interred more than twenty years—have been carted away and disposed of, the larger to dealers in those substances, the lesser to be crushed and made use of in the manufacture of agricultural manure. Were a record in detail set down of what has taken place in these and other notorious cases, all decent people who still believe in Christianity would stand appalled. In the Author's own personal knowledge, the desecration perpetrated in the churchyard of St. Margaret's, Westminster, when the railway between Victoria and the City was being constructed, was something too horrible to describe. The remembrance of what he insisted on seeing very early one Sunday morning, on going from Belgravia to minister at his own church, still most vividly haunts him like a frightful dream. It would be well if the bishops, the City authorities, and the clerical jobbers, who indirectly conjoin to desecrate the dead, would sometimes take the trouble of personally investigating the results of their combined co-operation. Surely—considering common decency only, and putting Christianity out of the question—it would make them pause ere they again offered such sacrifices to Commercial Necessity, a nineteenth-century Materialism, or Personal Gain.

In the case of St. Benet's, Gracechurch Street, recently demolished, those Christian corpses which had been buried within its sacred walls were removed, or were supposed to be removed. In one instance the mortal remains of a personal friend and relation of the present Rector of St. Ethelburga's in Bishopsgate Street, the late Rev. Dr. Gaskin, who for forty years had been Secretary to the S.P.C.K., were placed at the disposal of his surviving relative. Dr. Gaskin, sometime Rector of St. Benet's, believing, as he was frequently heard to remark, that "there my bones will rest until the Day of Judgment," desired to be buried in that, his own church. He was a dignified old man, six feet in height. When the Rector of St. Ethelburga's examined the coffin delivered up as Dr. Gaskin's, it was found to be scarcely five feet eight inches in length, including a new wooden shell of rough deal planks; and, as the coffin-plate had been torn away, it was no doubt that of some other individual. "In order," writes the Author's informant, "to avoid a scene at the re-interment in Stoke Newington churchyard, where many had collected, I let the ceremony go on, feeling that any attempt to recover the real Dr. Gaskin was too late."

With regard to the deep and serious loss which so many in London and our great cities experience from the present non-use of the Burial Service—a service practically unknown in all probability by ninety-nine out of every hundred of our people, the Author would venture respectfully to point out to his brethren of the clergy how desirable it would be that, both for rich and poor, the bodies of their departed relatives should invariably be brought into the church for the introductory portion of that service to be used over them. A parochial guild for assisting in this work might with no great difficulty be formed in every parish. Still further, would it not be well, at least once a-year, on some day within the Octave of All Saints'—the day immediately following that festival, for example—to hold a special service in memory of the dead? The Communion at Funerals,* formally put forth under Queen Elizabeth, frequently

---
* Vide Appendix No. VII.

used for members of noble and gentle families in the past, might be made available for all in the present. A bier or hearse, covered with a suitable pall, might be placed, flanked with standards for tapers, at the foot of the altar; a sermon suitable to the solemnity, preceded by the Bidding Prayer with a special mention and remembrance of individuals passed away, might be preached after the Creed. The Psalms *Quemadmodum* and *De profundis*, as well as the *Dies iræ*, might be suitably and legitimately introduced, and thus something practical be done as regards the wants of the departed and the obvious duty of the quick. One such service as this, rendered with care, devotion, recollectedness, and solemnity, would do far more to impress the doctrine of Christian charity for the dead and the truth of the Communion of Saints on ordinary people than twenty homilies. For such a service there are abundant precedents.*

* Vide Nichol's "Progresses of Queen Elizabeth," vol. iii. p. 115; Nichol's "Progresses of James I.," vol. ii. p. 495; Ibid., vol. iv. p. 601; Ibid., vol. iv. p. 1043; "The Weekly Journal or Saturday Post," for March 18, 1721, *in loco;* "The Daily Journal," for August 13, 1722, *in loco;* "The Gentleman's Magazine," vol. vii. p. 765; Ibid., vol. xxx. p. 540; Peck's "Desiderata Curiosa," vol. ii. pp. 252—256, London, 1779; Bishop Montague's "Visitation Articles," Cambridge, p. 76; Kennet's "Register," p. 765 (for the observance of Obit Sunday, at St. George's, Windsor, in 1662); Sandford's "Genealogical History of the Kings of England," p. 472, London, 1677; Gunton's "History of Peterborough Cathedral," pp. 77—79; Collier's "Ecclesiastical History,"

Even if there were not, when a special day of late years has been so commonly set apart to thank God for a bountiful harvest—a blessed innovation of the Catholic Revival, now universally adopted on all sides, and formally sanctioned by Convocation—surely such a modest restoration as that faintly sketched out above would soon be tolerated by Authority, and eventually become popular with all.* The Harvest Thanksgiving Feast is a public religious testimony that our people, deliberately rejecting the daring speculations of quack philosophers, hold that the great Creator Who made the law can suspend its operation, and that seed-time and harvest, sunshine and shadow, drought or plenty, punishments and rewards, come not by chance, but are from Him, and

---

vol. ii. pp. 259, 260; Strype's "Annals," lib. i. cap. 10; Ibid., cap. 15; Kennett's "Parochial Antiquities," *in loco;* Calderwood's ,'Altare Damascenum," p. 650; "The Ecclesiologist," vol. v. p. 132.

* Another obvious want is a suitable public Form for the Burial of Infants who have been baptized. Our ordinary service is neither applicable nor suitable to such cases; and few amongst both clergy and laity can have done other than experience this. When, however, as is now the case, Special Psalms have been appointed by our bishops for special occasions, it will no doubt soon be the lot of the Church of England to obtain something more appropriate for public use at the funerals of infants than is at present possessed. It is a question whether any bishop might not at once draw up such a service, and any priest under him use it. There would be nothing in the Act of Uniformity to forbid it, any more than the use of other current services not found in the Book of Common Prayer—if it were composed of Psalms, versicles, responses, and prayers taken out of the Holy Scriptures.

are bestowed ever as He wills and ordains. A service commemorating the dead would be an equally public avowal of our practical belief in the Communion of Saints, as well as the expression of a firm conviction that death, though the end of our time of probation, is but the door of Eternity; and would give the lie to the deadly dogma of Indifferentism, now current and so popular, which is summed up in that dark declaration of the self-satisfied sceptic—" Let us eat and drink, for to-morrow we die."

In truth, when, as a National Church, we have duly measured our loss through the influence of enfeebled statements in our public services regarding Prayer for the Departed, we shall be better able to effect a needful change, and complete a constructive reformation, as most necessary for the times in which we live. If this volume should in any degree contribute to the promotion of such an object, the Author's aim and hope will have been more than satisfied.

It now remains for him publicly to acknowledge his obligations to Dr. Littledale, not only for having drawn his attention to the very early Jewish inscriptions in the Crimea, containing Prayers for the Dead, but also for providing him with examples of the most remarkable of those existing, which are embodied in a note at pp. 33 and 34. He is also specially indebted to an essay on the general subject from the pen of the Rev. Malcolm MacColl, M.A., Rector of St. George's, Botolph Lane, from which a lengthy quotation will be found in the twelfth chapter. Mr. De Lisle, of Garendon Park, Sir Alfred Slade, and Sir Charles L. Young, have likewise afforded him acceptable information.

As regards the catena of post-Reformation inscriptions provided in Appendix No. XI., more than four-fifths have been copied by the Author from monumental memorials personally inspected from time to time during the past twenty years; collected, in the first instance, for use in the preparation of a Paper on "Christian Epitaphs," which he had the honour of reading before the Oxford Architectural Society in the year 1853. For the rest he is indebted to the Rev. Thomas Hugo, M.A., F.S.A., Rector of West Hackney; to the Rev. Prebendary Walcott, B.D., F.S.A., Precentor of Chichester Cathedral; to the Rev. J. T. Fowler, M.A., F.S.A. of the University of Durham; to John Gough Nichols, Esq., F.S.A., of Holmwood Park, Dorking; to H. W. King, Esq., of Tredegar Square; to W. Consitt Boulter, Esq.,

F.S.A., of Hull; and to several correspondents of *The Church Times;* to each and all of whom he gratefully returns his thanks.

F. G. L.

6, Lambeth Terrace, London,
    Nov. 16, 1871.

TABLE OF CONTENTS.

		PAGE.
I.—THE COMMUNION OF SAINTS		1
II.—THE RATIONALE OF PRAYERS FOR THE DEPARTED		12
III.—PRAYERS FOR THE DEPARTED USED BY THE JEWS		22
IV.—TESTIMONY OF THE APOSTOLIC WRITINGS TO THE USE OF PRAYERS FOR THE DEPARTED		38
V.—TESTIMONY OF THE LITURGIES TO THE USE OF PRAYERS FOR THE DEPARTED		48
VI.—TESTIMONY OF ANCIENT FATHERS TO THE USE OF PRAYERS FOR THE DEPARTED		66
VII.—THE PRACTICE OF THE ANGLO-SAXON CHURCH		81
VIII.—THE FAITH AND PRACTICE OF THE MEDIÆVAL CHURCH		89
IX.—THE DOCTRINE OF PURGATORY		105
X.—THE PRACTICE OF PRAYING FOR THE DEPARTED OBSCURED IN THE SIXTEENTH CENTURY		133
XI.—POST-REFORMATION DOCTRINE AND PRACTICE		151
XII.—THE CHRISTIAN DUTY OF PRAYING FOR THE DEPARTED		182

APPENDICES.

I.—INHUMATIO DEFUNCTI (SECUNDUM USUM SARUM)		197
II.—MISSÆ PRO DEFUNCTIS (SECUNDUM RITUM ROMANUM), FOLLOWED BY THE OLD ENGLISH MASSES FOR THE DEAD		211
III.—THE OFFICE FOR THE DEAD, ACCORDING TO THE ROMAN RITE (TRANSLATED INTO ENGLISH)		228
IV.—THE ORDER FOR THE BURIAL OF INFANTS, ACCORDING TO THE ROMAN RITE (TRANSLATED INTO ENGLISH)		263

CONTENTS.

	PAGE
V.—MISSA IN CEMETERIO (FROM EGBERHT'S PONTIFICAL)	269
VI.—EXTRACT FROM THE COMMUNION SERVICE IN EDWARD VI.'S FIRST PRAYER BOOK; TOGETHER WITH THE CELEBRATION OF THE HOLY COMMUNION WHEN THERE IS A BURIAL OF THE DEAD.—A.D. 1549	270
VII.—CELEBRATIO CŒNA DOMINI IN FUNERIBUS.—A.D. 1560	272
VIII.—VARIOUS FORMS OF BIDDING THE BEADS	274
IX.—GRACES USED AT THE COLLEGES OF OXFORD AND CAMBRIDGE, AND ELSEWHERE, COMMEMORATING BENEFACTORS AND THE FAITHFUL DEPARTED	277
X.—IN COMMENDATIONIBUS BENEFACTORUM	296
XI.—MONUMENTAL INSCRIPTIONS CONTAINING PRAYERS FOR THE DEPARTED.—A.D. 1550—1870. INDEX OF NAMES TO THE MONUMENTAL INSCRIPTIONS	298
XII.—JUDGMENT OF SIR HERBERT JENNER FUST, DELIVERED IN THE COURT OF ARCHES, NOV. 19, 1838	341
XIII.—A FUNERAL SERMON—OUR DUTY TO THE DEPARTED	356
GENERAL INDEX	363

CHAPTER I.

THE COMMUNION OF SAINTS.

THE doctrine of the Communion of Saints is that dogma peculiar to Christianity from which flows a knowledge of the practical duties bearing on our relations as Christians either to other.

Saints are those who have been formally "sanctified in Christ Jesus"[*] by the operation of Holy Baptism; men of holiness, "born of God,"[†] who have been gathered out of the general body of mankind, and enrolled under the banner of the Cross. Thus sanctified, they are called to serve Almighty God fervently and constantly, by the addition of grace to grace, and by the constant practice of those duties which have been ever and always enjoined upon the followers and servants of our Blessed Saviour, even from the day of Pentecost. The divine operation effected through the sacrament of regeneration, in

[*] 1 Cor. i. 2.   [†] 1 John v. 1.

those who have duly and rightly received it, is the commencement of a true and real separation from the unregenerate. And though the work of grace thus effected is by no means completely wrought out, yet when that which has been in the first instance bestowed is properly, fairly, and faithfully used, and nothing to the contrary be manifest, it may be reasonably and hopefully presumed that all who have thus been supernaturally made regenerate are in some sense holy, and deserve the name of " saints." For the sacred Scriptures certainly warrant the practice.[*]

The apostles, in the adoption of this particular term, did but follow the custom of the elder dispensation; for the Psalms tell of "the congregation" and "the assembly of the saints," of "Aaron, the saint of the Lord;" the prophets speak of "the saints of the Most High;" while on the first Good Friday, at the awful death of the Redeemer of mankind, we read that "the bodies of the saints which slept arose." So then it is manifest that they who depart hence, and are no more seen, not only do not lose the character for holiness they possessed when in the body, but have acquired, or are about to acquire, greater security, that by the favour and grace of God it shall

---

[*] 1 Cor. i. 2; vi. 11; xiv. 33; 2 St. Peter i. 5; 2 Cor. vii. 1.

in due course be theirs in perfection for ever and ever.

From this it follows that there is a true and real distinction between the "saints that are in the earth"* and the saints in heaven, both as regards their capacities, graces, and existing advantages, privileges, and benefits; just as the church militant and the church triumphant—though but One Church —differ both in their relations either to other, as well as in their relations to Almighty God.

In regard to the last-mentioned point, the saints, as we know, have communion with their great Creator and Father† (Κοινωνία μετὰ τοῦ Πατρός). Of old "Abraham believed God, and it was imputed unto him for righteousness: and he was called the friend of God."‡ Under the Gospel dispensation, so many divine gifts and graces have been bestowed upon the faithful, who are called "the sons of God,"§ that they actually become "partakers of the divine nature." ‖

The saints likewise enjoy communion with Jesus Christ, the eternal Son of God (Κοινωνία τοῦ Υἱοῦ). As St. John, the beloved apostle, explicitly declares, "Our communion is with the Father and the Son."¶

* Psalm xvi. 3.
† 1 St. John i. 3.
‡ St. James ii. 23.
§ 1 St. John iii. 1.
‖ 2 St. Peter i. 4.
¶ 1 St. John i. 3.

This communion, while supernatural, is yet most real and true; for our Blessed Lord has taken upon Him our nature, our sins, and the curse due unto them; while we, on the other hand, by divine mercy and favour, having received of His fulness, are solemnly called to the fellowship of His sufferings, in order that we may become conformable to His death.*

Furthermore, the saints have communion with God the Holy Ghost (Κοινωνία Πνεύματος), as is manifest from the concluding words of St. Paul's Second Epistle to the Corinthians, "The Grace of our Lord Jesus Christ, and the Love of God, and the Fellowship (κοινωνία) of the Holy Ghost be with you all."† It is by the gifts and graces communicated through the Holy Spirit that those who are called out of the world into the church are truly sanctified. God is our Father by creation, but we are still more intimately united to Him by adoption, and it is by the specific operations of "the Spirit of His Son" that we are enabled to call Him, "Abba, Father."‡ "If a man love me," was the gracious statement and promise of our Blessed Saviour, "he will keep my words: and my Father will love him, and we will come unto him,

---

* St. John i. 16; Phil. iii. 10.
† 2 Cor. xiii. 14—κοινωνία, fellowship, partnership, intercommunion.
‡ Gal. iv. 6, 7.

and make our abode with him."* And where God the Father and God the Son are, there too is God the Paraclete; for "If any man have not the Spirit of Christ, he is none of His."† St. Paul, therefore—summing up the practical point of our Christian belief—most reasonably asks, "Know ye not that ye are the temple of God, and that the Spirit of God dwelleth in you?"‡

Still further, the saints of God in the church of His Son enjoy a true and real communion with the holy angels—those unfallen spirits who dwell in the light and glory of their adorable Creator and Lord. The joyful mysteries and details of the Incarnation explicitly inform us of this. An angel foretold the birth of St. John the Baptist. Gabriel, from the right hand of God, announced to Mary the conception of the Redeemer of mankind, and nine months afterwards a company of the heavenly host sang their *Gloria in excelsis* at His birth in time. An angel touched the water of the Pool of Bethesda, thus endowing it with miraculous powers. In our Blessed Saviour's agony in the garden, an angel appeared to strengthen Him. Again, "The angel of the Lord descended from heaven, and came and rolled back the

---

* St. John xiv. 23.   † Romans viii. 9.   ‡ 1 Cor. iii. 16.

stone from the door"[*] of the sepulchre where our Lord had been laid. After His ascension, two others stood by the apostles in white apparel, who declared that the second coming of their ascended Lord should be in like manner.[†] So too an angel opened the prison doors where the apostles were confined; and it is formally revealed that the angels shall separate the righteous from the wicked at the last great day. In truth, "Are they not all ministering spirits, sent forth to minister for them who shall be heirs of salvation?"[‡] Their services, likewise, ordained and constituted in a wonderful order, are such as that they take a deep and lively interest in our condition, progress, or lapse. They joy over the repentant sinner.[§] They lift up their holy hands in intercession for us in our time of weakness and hour of trial.[||] They guide and guard us in danger and temptation. The angels of our little ones, in fine, do always behold the Father's face in heaven.[¶]

[*] St. Matt. xxviii. 2.
[†] Acts i. 11.
[‡] Heb. i. 14.
[§] St. Luke xv. 10.
[||] Gen. xxxii. 26; xlviii. 16; Zech. i. 12; Tobias xii. 12. The following invocatory prayer is still used in many parts of England:—
"Matthew, Mark, Luke, and John,
Bless the bed I lie upon,
Four corners to my bed,
Four angels at my head;
One to sing and one to pray,
And two to carry my soul away;
And if I die before I wake,
I pray to God my soul to take
For Jesus Christ our Saviour's sake.
Amen."

[¶] St. Matt. xviii. 10.

The saints on earth, undergoing their probation, also enjoy a true and real communion with all the saints living in the same church, no matter how widely separated they may be either from the other. Those who walk in the light and love of God have fellowship one with another.* For the unity of the Spirit causes all that is conferred upon the general community to be common to every member. Thus the divine fruit of the sacraments belongs to the faithful in general.† Such are links by which the saints of every country are bound together in a spiritual and supernatural bond. Baptism, the only door by which men are admitted into the church, creates new links in the golden chain. The other sacraments strengthen those links, more especially that which is commonly

---

* 1 St. John i. 7.

† Every pious and holy action undertaken by one appertains to all, and becomes profitable to all. This is confirmed by St. Ambrose, who commenting on Psalm cxix. 63, "I am a companion of all them that fear thee," observes, "As we say that a member is a partaker of the entire body, so do we say that it is united to all who fear God." Therefore our Lord taught us to say, "our," not "my bread." This communion of all good things is illustrated in Scripture by a comparison borrowed from the members of the human body, in which there are many members; each performing its own, not all the same, functions. And these members are so well adapted and connected together, that if one suffers, the rest sympathize; or if one is in a healthy state, the feeling of pleasure is common to all. So is it in the church. Although the members are various, of different nations, rich and poor, freemen and slaves, yet having been once initiated by baptism, all become members of the one body, of which Jesus Christ is the Head.

called "*The* Sacrament," viz., the Holy Communion of our Lord's Body and Blood. Through Christ, there present, every member coming with due and proper disposition partakes beneficially of that spiritual food.

> "A sumente non concisus,
> Non confractus, non divisus,
> Integer accipitur.
> Sumit unus, sumunt mille;
> Quantum iste, tantum ille,
> Nec sumptus consumitur."*

The saints on earth, undergoing their probation, likewise enjoy a true and real communion † with all the saints who have departed this life, whether the latter be waiting for the consummation of the number of the elect, or have been graciously admitted into the actual presence of God. This is clear from St. Paul's statement regarding actual intercommunion in his Epistle to the Hebrews: "Ye are come unto Mount Sion, and unto the city of the living God, the heavenly Jerusalem, and to an innumerable company

---

* Lauda Sion Salvatorem.

† The clause "Communionem Sanctorem" is not found in the most ancient versions of the Apostles' Creed, whether Oriental or Western. They are wanting in the Creed of Aquiloia, as well as in that commented on by St. Augustine in his treatise, "De Fide et Symbolo." Nor are they in the Creed of the Church of Jerusalem, as set forth by St. Cyril. The doctrine expressed in this clause is a reasonable and legitimate development, however, from that which immediately precedes it.

of angels, to the general assembly and church of the first-born, which are written in heaven, and to God the judge of all, and to the spirits of just men made perfect, and to Jesus the mediator of the new covenant."[*]

Moreover, death cannot and does not remove the foundation of the communion of saints, which stands in true but mystical union betwixt Christ and His church. Death has no power over the conjunction between the Head and the members, or over the reality of that blessed intercommunion, its influence, or its results. Death, which is merely the separation of soul and body, mars not the real and abiding communion between the faithful in Christ; but in some respects renders it more real, more divine, more lasting. He who has departed this life in the faith and fear of God, fortified by the sacraments of the church, and duly prepared for his passage across the valley of the shadow of death, gains by the change; for in the land beyond Jordan he finds that there is neither fear nor temptation nor sorrow nor loss. There the communion of saints remaineth intact and perfect. Here on earth the faithful hold visible and external communion with the sinner, the hypocrite, and the

---

[*] Heb. xii. 22, 23.

nominal Christian—each receiving the sacraments, each joining in common prayer, and each professing the same faith. Hereafter the communion of saints will be completed and perfected; so that all members of Christ will be more intimately joined together, both in will and work, than was ever their lot in the time of their temporary separation. Nevertheless, the communion or partnership exists as well while some of the faithful are undergoing their probation as when that probation is at an end; for there can be no real and efficient partnership where some members take no interest in the welfare of their fellows, and do nothing to promote each other's spiritual advantage. A communion of saints in which there is no charitable interchange of offices is no communion at all. It becomes a mere empty phrase or formal term, without reality, without object, without life.

While, therefore, the faithful on earth pray daily that the kingdom of God may come—that the consummation of all that is holy and pure and just and true may speedily be accomplished—the saints under the altar cry, "How long, O Lord! how long?" sending up their intercessory orisons for the whole church of the redeemed.

It will be consequently concluded that this our true

belief in the communion of saints should ever excite us to pureness of heart and holiness of living. At the same time, we should be constantly reminded of our bounden duty to render heartiest gratitude to Almighty God for so obvious and rich a blessing. We should likewise be excited to the deepest love, reverence, and devotion for the saints, whether living, departed, or crowned. In the natural order, nearness of relationship implies hearty affection. Yet amongst relations no communion which is temporal can be compared with that which is spiritual and eternal amongst the grace-won children of the Crucified. And our love will naturally and properly grow deeper for those of the One Family of Christ who, having passed from our sight and knowledge, are safe in the keeping of the Most High, whether they be waiting for the eternal rest and perpetual peace of His heavenly mansions, or, walking in white raiment, are already crowding the steps of the great white throne, purified from every—even the smallest—stain, sanctified and crowned.

CHAPTER II.

THE RATIONALE OF PRAYERS FOR THE DEPARTED.

A PIOUS and reverent care for the dead is one of the common instincts of humanity. Nations which have believed in a state of existence after death —and this has been the conviction of all save the most debased and barbarous—have likewise shown a reverence for the departed, not only in sentiment but in deed.* Burials have almost invariably taken place with respect for the bodies of those whose souls have passed away; and funeral rites have outwardly expressed this sincere conviction in no unmistakable manner. The most ancient custom amongst primitive

---

* Vide Homer, Odyss., xi. 72; Herodotus, lib. v. 92; Horace, Odes, i. 23; Plin., Epistles, vii. 27; Virgil, Æn. iii. 300; Euripides, Hecuba, 536; Ovid, Fast., ii. 566. As regards the care of the ancient Greeks for their dead, vide Euripides, Hippolyto, v. 1458; Pliny, Nat. Hist., lib. xiii. c. 1; Virg., Æneid, ix. v. 486; Homer, Iliad. r. v. 211; Æneid, vi. v. 417; Eurip., Troad., v. 446; Ovid, Metamorph., lib. iv. v. 154; Eurip., Alcest., v. 608; Troad. v. 256; Ovid, Metamorph., lib. viii. v. 528; Virg., Æneid, iv. v. 672; Euripid., Alcest., v. 430; Æneid, xi. v. 187; Odyss. ♂. v. 71; Iliad, ψ. v. 252.

nations was to bury the dead out of sight;* though some embalmed the bodies of the departed, while others committed them to the funeral pyre. The practice of interment, however, was almost universal in the East. Moreover, both amongst the Egyptians and Ethiopians this custom obtained, as it did also in the case of the Jews—a fact evident from the records of their history in Holy Scripture.

Now in this care for the departed many have traced a dim and uncertain belief, on the part of those who have exercised it, both in the immortality of the soul and in the resurrection of the flesh. They have looked upon the separation of soul and body as only taking place for a time, not for ever; and have held a faith, founded on a true and almost universal tradition, that in a distant future soul and body should be reunited.† This tradition, coming down from our

---

* Vide Cicero, De Legibus, lib. ii.; Terentius, Andrœa, act i. scene 1; Martial, lib. iv. epig. lxxv.

† The mythology of the Egyptians taught that there was a specific region for the departed, corresponding to the Greek *Hades* and the Latin *Tartarus*, which was termed "Amenti." Here was a tribunal to determine the final destiny of departed souls—here their transmigration was authoritatively arranged. The Egyptians divided the whole world into three zones—the Zone of the Earth, or that of trial; the Zone of the Air, or that of temporal punishment; and the Zone of Everlasting Repose. Some souls, after having passed their time of probation in the Zone of the Earth, were sent to the Zone of temporal punishment to suffer for a while, either as a prelude to their return to the Zone of Probation, to animate a new body, or as a preparation for their removal to the Zone of Everlasting Rest. All this is set forth

first parents, as might have been expected, was more carefully preserved, and less corrupted, by the children of Abraham than by any other race. It had been cherished by the patriarchs, as the words of Job testify, accepted by the leaders and teachers of the people of Israel; until in the later age of the Evangelical prophets it developed and expanded into a definite system of dogma, which necessitated a corresponding practice on the part of those who accepted the same. And this practice is found current amongst the Jews from the time of the Maccabees unto the present day. From our Blessed Saviour and His apostles it received neither criticism nor condemnation; while several exhortations and injunctions found in the writings of the apostles, not only indirectly support the practice, but in certain instances appear very pointedly to enjoin it. That all the most ancient liturgies contain prayers for the departed will, in due course, be shown. And if, as may be reasonably assumed, the practice of praying for the dead existed in the Jewish Church, immediately before the advent of our Blessed Saviour, and had come down from times

---

with singular lucidity in a work by Cardinal Angelo Mai, entitled "Catalogo de Papiri Vaticani," &c., published at Rome in 1825. In the fifth illustration at the end of the book is a curious and striking representation of the judgment of a soul.

long anterior, it will at once be seen how entirely impossible it is for those who repudiate and neglect the practice, or regard it as an innovation, to account of its universal acceptance by the whole family of Christians in the earliest ages of the church, or to specify when such an innovation first became current, and when the legitimate successors of the apostles first formally sanctioned it. The fact that, both in East and West, the church universal has constantly enjoined the duty, is a consideration of the highest value and of the greatest weight.

Furthermore, the doctrine that in the state immediately after death the souls of the faithful are being prepared for the mansions of heaven, is interwoven with some of the most important and fundamental articles of the Christian faith. For those souls which, summoned to the judgment-bar of Christ, have been found to have departed this life in unrepented, deadly sin, there is nothing but an eternal alienation from God Almighty and all that is good. "They that have done evil [shall go] into everlasting fire."* On the other hand, amongst those who, by the favour and grace of the Most High, have succeeded in making their calling and election sure, how many

---

* Creed of St. Athanasius.

pass away stained and defiled with lesser sins, sins which do not merit eternal condemnation, but which, nevertheless, have to be removed ere the soul can look for the eternal peace and heavenly light of the home of God! for "there shall in no wise enter into it anything that defileth."[*] All wounds, whether of body or soul, are not deadly; every small offence does not actually and completely cut off the latter from God's favour,[†] nor absolutely drive away from us the Holy Spirit, our Counsellor and Guide.[‡] To us,

---

[*] Revelation xxi. 27.

[†] "As in this life the measure of our sanctification and purity is the measure of our likeness to God, the sight of Him in Paradise 'as He is,' requires perfect purity, for 'there is no fellowship between light and darkness,' nothing of human impurity shall enter into His kingdom, and 'without holiness no man shall see the Lord.' Therefore neither secret nor open, habitual or actual evil, may cleave to the soul; so long as it retains any moral defect, any vestige of sin and its consequences, it cannot really attain to the beatific vision of God, and, if the cleansing process is not completed in this life, it must be carried on in the interval between death and resurrection. God disciplines us that we may be partakers of His holiness, and 'whom He loveth He chastiseth,' so long as the soul requires this means of purification."—*First Age of the Church*, by Döllinger, Oxenham's translation, p. 248, second edition. London, 1867.

[‡] "Prayers for the dead, on the face of the question, whether they be lawful or unlawful to Christians, provide an escape from the terrible and overpowering thought of the everlasting damnation of the incalculable majority of mankind, dying in sin, in carelessness, in ignorance, or in a very imperfect religious condition. Once the mind grasps the doctrine that the condition of souls between death and judgment is one of gradual purification for all who do not resolutely set their wills to do evil and resist God, and that the intercessions of the living can aid this process, it becomes possible to reconcile our notions of God's mercy with His justice. But take this doctrine away —even on the hypothesis that it is false, and we find the inevitable

and to all, God is patient, longsuffering, and merciful. Yet how many are there who pass from our sight and knowledge, called away suddenly by accident to the particular judgment-bar, without preparation for death, or careful repentance for past omissions and failings! Neither aliens nor rebels nor reprobate, yet still stained with the marks of past transgressions, they must be fittingly prepared, by patient waiting and painful preparation in the land on the other side of Jordan, for the glories and joys of the Heavenly Jerusalem beyond. Ere they stand before God and walk in white raiment, all the stains must be removed, even the least; for He, their Creator, Saviour, and Sanctifier, is of purer eyes than to behold iniquity. And only the spotless, cleansed and clean, appear in His very presence and bow before His footstool.

This being so, no one could, at the same time, maintain that a soul, tainted with small sins, sins of infirmity and human weaknesses, would be punished

---

result to be the denial of everlasting punishment for continuous and wilful sin, the negation of hell, the gradual assertion of the harmlessness of sin itself (which is alleged by extreme Universalists to be only a 'lower form of good'), and thus the destruction of God's attribute of justice and of man's perception of right and wrong, to the obvious encouragement of every sort of license and recklessness. The Universalist sects (amounting in America to millions) which have split off from the Church and from the elder Nonconformists owe their origin to the discontinuance of Prayers for the dead."—*Richard F. Littledale, LL.D.*

throughout eternity because of such. It follows, therefore, that in the world to come, there must be some relaxation of sin. And this fact, as it may be plainly gathered from our Blessed Lord's teaching in Holy Scripture, is equally implied and set forth in the common belief of the Church Universal. We are taught, as documents and writers of authority hereafter to be cited will show, that the One Family of Christ is divided into three parts: (α) the church militant here on earth, (β) the church patient or waiting in the place of departed spirits, beyond the grave, and (γ) the church triumphant in heaven. Now all the members who go to make up these three distinct and yet united portions are by God's favour—and first and specially by the grace of new birth in the sacrament of the font—fellow-members of Holy Church and coheirs of the eternal promises. Our love, therefore, as St. Thomas Aquinas points out, should embrace them all.* For the charity of Jesus,

---

* "Love, which is the bond uniting the members of the church, extends itself not only to the living, but to the departed who die in charity. For charity is the life of the soul, as the soul is the life of the body. And 'charity,' as St. Paul declares to the Corinthians (1 Cor. xiii. 8), 'never faileth.' Charity, moreover, never forgets. Similarly also the dead live in the memories of living men. The intention of the living, therefore, can be directed towards them; and so the suffrages of the living avail the dead in two ways: first, by reason of the union of charity; and, secondly, by reason of intention directed towards them.

our Head and Lord, bands us in true communion with the whole body. We share with others, and others, in a measure, share with us, the woes and sorrows as well as the joys and consolations, common to the whole band. The doctrine of "the Communion of Saints" is with us a reality and a fact. Implying a communication of certain good works and charitable offices, it sets forth the actual duty of an active mutual interest, either for the other, in all the members of Christ. On behalf of the saints of God, purified, sanctified, and crowned, we rejoice and praise Him, because of His mercy and their triumphs. We know, likewise, that from the height of their glory and the splendour of their eternal home, they, members of the church triumphant, look down upon the strangers and pilgrims who are wending their way homewards, and intercede for success in the journey, and for an eventual triumph. We, of the militant church here, as did the Jews of old, invoke the saints to praise the Lord of Heaven,* and ask them still to lift up holy hands, as near to and favoured by God,

---

The suffrages of the living do not avail the dead as to change their state from misery to felicity, or the converse. But they do avail for the diminution of punishment, or the like, which does not change the state of the dead." — *St. Thomas Aquinas*, "On the Incarnation," sec. 471.

* Psalm cxlviii. 1; cxlix. 5.

on our behalf, who are still in the conflict, it may be weak and wayward, stumbling and falling, but rising again; sometimes overcome, but anon conquering, and ever hoping for the end of the conflict and for the breaking of the eternal day.

And, whether the hand of death has fallen heavily upon us, or we be still amongst those whose warfare is not yet ended, the saints of the church triumphant continually ask for our eventual triumph. They pray ever that we may succeed in overcoming our foes, while it is called day, before the night cometh, when no man can work. And for the patient or waiting part of the One Family of Christ, for the faithful departed, they ask light, refreshment, and rest, when it pleases God—the work of cleansing being finished—to be merciful and loving and pitiful, and to take them into His very presence.

And what is asked for on behalf of the faithful departed by the saints who are reigning with Christ, has been the subject of the militant church's sacrifice and prayers from the beginning.* Whenever the children of

---

* The following are from the Roman Catacombs:—
EXVPERI REQ.
IN PACE . Q. V.
ANN. xxiii. ET. M. iii. D. vi.

"Exuperius, who lived 23 years, 3 months, and 6 days, mayest thou rest in peace."

(Cemetery of Callistus, Rome.)

the spiritual Israel were gathered together to intercede for their brethren in the faith, those who had gone before them in the sleep of peace were ever and always remembered. Death, no doubt, was a true separation; but, on the other hand, the spiritual bonds of religion were not broken by death. Upon them, as regards their intercommunion, Death hath no power. Forged by the command of the Lord of Life, these bonds bind the souls of the faithful together, and unless rusted by sin, or rudely snapped by the reprobate, their hold is complete both for time and eternity.

From which considerations, to be amplified in detail hereafter, the duty of prayer for the departed, as well as the rationale of that duty, may be sufficiently gathered.

DOMITI
IN PACE.
LEA FECIT.

"Domitius, may you rest in peace. Lea inscribed this."
(Cemetery of Callistus, Rome.)

KALEMERE DEVS REFRI-
GERET SPIRITVM TVVM
VNA CVM [*spiritu*] SORORIS TVAE
HILARE.

"O Calemera, may God refresh thy soul, together with the soul of thy sister, Hilara."

[The above, given by Lupi at p. 137 of his "Dissertation on the Epitaphs of the Martyrs under Severus," contains a representation of our Lord as the Good Shepherd, the Lamb of the Flock, and the Phœnix—emblem of the Resurrection.]

CHAPTER III.

PRAYER FOR THE DEPARTED USED BY THE JEWS.

THE plain testimony of the patriarch Job on behalf of the doctrine of the Resurrection of the Body indicates how vastly superior was the knowledge of the patriarchs to that which existed amongst the most elevated of heathen philosophers. "I know that my Redeemer liveth, and that He shall stand at the latter day upon the earth: and though after my skin worms destroy this body, yet in my flesh shall I see God: whom I shall see for myself, and mine eyes shall behold, and not another; though my reins be consumed within me."* This statement, as is evident, mainly touches the doctrine of the Resurrection of the Body. But its importance does not rest there. A belief in the separate and continuous existence of the soul appears to have been current and contemporaneously held: for both amongst the Jews of old,

* Job xix. 25—27.

as well as with heathen nations,* the prevalence of a belief in ghostly apparitions is undoubted. Moreover, a conviction that immediately after death retribution for sins committed in the body surely followed, was likewise a very ordinary and widespread doctrine of both.

This may be specifically illustrated from the case of Enoch. It is recorded in the Book of Genesis that "Enoch walked with God, and he was not, for God took him."† Here, then, it is formally declared that Enoch was with God. St. Paul's comment in the Epistle to the Hebrews re-states, amplifies, and gives point to the simple record of Moses. "Enoch was translated that he should not see death; and was not found, because God had translated him: for before his translation he had this testimony, that he pleased God."‡ It is clear, therefore, from this important gloss, that the patriarchs neither doubted the existence of a future state, nor rejected the doctrines of the Immortality of the Soul and of the Resurrection of the Body. And it is equally clear that current opinion amongst the Jews of St. Paul's time supported and warranted a use of those arguments which were so pertinently and forcibly pressed upon them

---

* Æneid, book vi. 325.   † Gen. v. 24.   ‡ Heb. xi. 5.

by the apostle. Of the patriarchs, he declared that "they were strangers and pilgrims upon earth," seeking, not an earthly but a heavenly country; and he maintained, as a consequence of this faith and conviction, that "God is not ashamed to be called their God: for He hath prepared for them a city."* In truth, the whole of this part of St. Paul's epistle contains most forcible reasoning against the current scepticism of the Sadducees, and furnishes abundant proof of the kind of facts which the Jews of that period were willing to admit, and on which the apostle, in part, founded the arguments of his epistle.

And that St. Paul's statements, acquiesced in by those to whom he wrote, were justified by the ancient traditions of God's chosen people, is apparent from the records of their history.† For example, the care with which the bodies of the patriarchs were buried, though only directly indicating a belief in the Resurrection of the Body, yet indirectly set forth a belief in a future state. So with regard to the account of the death and burial of Jacob.‡ "He gathered up his feet into the bed, and yielded up the

---

* Heb. xi. 13—16.
† Gen. xxiii.; xxv. 8—10; xxxv. 29.
‡ Gen. xlix. 29—33; l. 1—14.

ghost, and was gathered unto his people."* From this it is clear that the inspired writer believed him to have "yielded up the ghost" to "the God of the spirits of all flesh."† Furthermore, the following passage from the Book of Ecclesiastes, throws light on the belief of the Jews: "When they shall be afraid of that which is high, and fears shall be in the way, and the almond-tree shall flourish, and the grasshopper shall be a burden, and desire shall fail: because man goeth to his long home, and the mourners go about the streets: or ever the silver cord be loosed, or the golden bowl be broken, or the pitcher be broken at the fountain, or the wheel broken at the cistern. Then shall the dust return to the earth as it was: and the spirit shall return unto God who gave it."‡ So, too, a previous passage from the same book: "All are of the dust, and all turn to dust again. Who knoweth the spirit of man that goeth upward, and the spirit of the beast that goeth downward to the earth?"§ Thus much as regards ancient traditions and the belief of the patriarchs.

But there is one event recorded, of great moment

* Gen. xv. 15; xxv. 8.
† Numbers xvi. 22; xxvii. 16.
‡ Ecclesiastes xii. 5—7. See also Isaiah lvii. 16; and Zech. xii. 1.
§ Ecclesiastes iii. 20, 21.

and importance, in the First Book of Samuel, which throws light on the traditional faith of the Jews at that period, and which deserves consideration. The passage is consequently quoted at length :—

"Now Samuel was dead, and all Israel had lamented him, and buried him in Ramah, even in his own city. And Saul had put away those that had familiar spirits, and the wizards, out of the land.

"And the Philistines gathered themselves together, and came and pitched in Shunem: and Saul gathered all Israel together, and they pitched in Gilboa. And when Saul saw the host of the Philistines, he was afraid, and his heart greatly trembled.

"And when Saul inquired of the Lord, the Lord answered him not, neither by dreams, nor by Urim, nor by prophets.

"Then said Saul unto his servants, Seek me a woman that hath a familiar spirit, that I may go to her, and inquire of her. And his servants said to him, Behold, there is a woman that hath a familiar spirit at En-dor. And Saul disguised himself, and put on other raiment, and he went, and two men with him, and they came to the woman by night: and he said, I pray thee, divine unto me by the familiar spirit, and bring me him up, whom I shall name unto thee. And the woman said unto him, Behold, thou knowest what Saul hath done, how he hath cut off those that have familiar spirits, and the wizards, out of the land: wherefore then layest thou a snare for my life, to cause me to die? And Saul sware to her by the Lord, saying, As the Lord liveth, there shall no punishment happen to thee for this thing. Then said the woman, Whom shall I bring up unto thee? And he said, Bring me up Samuel. And when the woman saw Samuel, she cried with a loud voice: and the woman spake to Saul, saying, Why hast thou deceived me? for thou art Saul. And the king said unto her, Be not afraid: for what sawest thou? And the woman said unto Saul, I saw gods ascending out of the earth. And he said unto her, What form is he of? And she said, An old man cometh up; and he is covered with a mantle. And Saul perceived that it was Samuel, and he stooped with his face to the ground, and bowed himself. And Samuel said to Saul, Why hast thou disquieted me, to bring me up? And Saul answered, I am sore distressed; for the Philistines make war against me, and God is departed from me, and answereth me no more, neither by prophets, nor by dreams: therefore I have called thee, that thou mayest make known unto me what I shall do. Then said Samuel, Wherefore then dost thou ask of me, seeing the Lord is departed from thee, and is become thine enemy? And the Lord hath done to him, as he spake by me: for the Lord hath rent the kingdom out of thine hand, and given it to thy neighbour, even to David: because thou obeyedst not the voice of the Lord, nor executedst his fierce wrath upon Amalek, therefore hath the Lord done this thing unto thee this day. Moreover the Lord will also deliver Israel with thee into the hand of the Philistines: and to-morrow shalt thou and thy sons be with me: the Lord also shall deliver the host of Israel into the hand of the Philistines. Then Saul fell straightway all along on the earth, and was sore afraid, because of the words of Samuel: and there was no strength in him; for he had eaten no bread all the day, nor all the night." *

Now with regard to this remarkable and supernatural occurrence, carefully considered in all its details, it is evident that its features and details were no mere delusion, no simple exercise of the fancy or imagination of those who witnessed them, but stern reality; and amongst other mysterious events we find the express record of a prophecy which was exactly

* 1 Samuel xxviii. 3—20.

fulfilled on the following day. The form which appeared to Saul is spoken of as "Samuel himself;" and this conviction, evidently current amongst the Jews, is definitely expressed by the author of the Book of Ecclesiasticus, who, in praise of Samuel, declares that "after his death he prophesied, and showed the king his end, and lifted up his voice from the earth." *

Thus it may be readily inferred that the common traditional belief of the Jews was that the spirits of those who had departed out of this life were detained in some hidden abode, waiting for the Great Day; a belief which would reasonably follow from their reception of the respective doctrines of the Immortality of the Soul and the Resurrection of the Body.† And if this was so, if the spirits of men lived after death and

---

* Ecclesiasticus xlvi. 20.

† "Many of them that sleep in the dust of the earth shall awake, some to everlasting life, and some to shame and everlasting contempt. And they that be wise shall shine as the brightness of the firmament; and they that turn many to righteousness, as the stars for ever and ever." (Daniel xii. 2, 3.)

"Thy dead men shall live, together with my dead body shall they arise. Awake and sing, ye that dwell in dust: for thy dew is as the dew of herbs, and the earth shall cast out the dead." (Isaiah xxvi. 19.)

"Their worm shall not die, neither shall their fire be quenched; and they shall be an abhorring unto all flesh." (Isaiah lxvi. 24.)

"Thus saith the Lord God unto these bones; Behold, I will cause breath to enter into you, and ye shall live: and I will lay sinews upon you, and cover you with skin, and put breath in you, and ye shall live; and ye shall know that I am the Lord." (Ezekiel xxxvii. 5, 6.)

their eventual state lay in the future, then it would be reasonable, charitable, and righteous for the living to intercede and pray for the departed. When obscure and imperfect tradition eventually gathered such force as that the realities of a future state were seen and appreciated by the ancient people of God, then—unless there existed some express injunction to the contrary, which is nowhere put on record[*]—the duty which was enjoined by Judas Maccabeus, and practised by his followers, may be accepted as in harmony with the will of God.

That such a duty was enjoined, and such a practice was current, is evident from the records of the same in the Second Book of Maccabees. We there read that certain of the soldiers of Judas Maccabeus had been slain in his wars with heathen nations. When their comrades charitably came to take up the dead bodies to bury them, it was discovered that the slain

---

[*] "We find by the History of the Maccabees, that the Jews did pray and make offerings for the dead; which appears by other testimonies, and by their form of prayer still extant, which they used in the captivity. Now it is very considerable that since our Blessed Saviour did reprove all the doctrines and traditions of the Scribes and Pharisees, and did argue concerning the dead and the resurrection, yet He spake no word against this public practice, but left it as He found it; which He, who came to declare to us all the will of His Father, would not have done if it had not been innocent, pious, and full of charity."—*Liberty of Prophesying*, Bishop Jeremy Taylor. Book i. sec. 20, p. 345.

had secreted certain things consecrated to the idols of the Jamnites "under their coats"—an act distinctly forbidden by the Mosaic law. "Then every man," we read, "saw that this was the cause wherefore they were slain." The Almighty had thus testified His hatred of their offence by permitting them to fall in battle. "All men, therefore," continues the sacred narrative, "praising the Lord, the righteous Judge, who had opened the things that were hid, betook themselves unto prayer, and besought Him that the sin committed might wholly be put out of remembrance. Besides that, noble Judas exhorted the people to keep themselves from sin, forsomuch as they saw before their eyes the things that came to pass for the sins of those that were slain. And when he had made a gathering throughout the company to the sum of two thousand drachms of silver, he sent it to Jerusalem to offer a sin-offering, doing therein very well and honestly, in that he was mindful of the resurrection: for if he had not hoped that they that were slain should have risen again, it had been superfluous and vain to pray for the dead, and also in that he perceived that there was great favour laid up for those that died godly, it was an holy and good thought. Whereupon he made a reconciliation for the dead that they might be delivered from sin." *

It is evident from this record of events that the duty of prayer for the departed was clearly recognized by God's ancient people at least a hundred and sixty years before the coming of our Blessed Lord, while the allusion to its obvious bearings on the doctrine of the Resurrection of the Body seems to indicate that such prayer for the dead was a common and acknowledged practice of that period.† This, of course, is in perfect harmony with what may be seen to have been the progress of doctrinal development evidenced in the writings of the sacred writers and prophets of Israel,‡ in regard both to a future

---

* 2 Maccabees xii. 39. This Book is regarded as belonging to the Canon of Scripture by the Apostolical Canons, by Tertullian, St. Cyprian, St. Hilary, St. Ambrose, St. Augustine, and by the Third Council of Carthage. Other ancient authorities regard it as "apocryphal"—meaning that it was not in the Hebrew Canon as compiled by Esdras. None have doubted that it is a genuine book, and even Protestants generally have allowed that it is historically worthy of credit, which, as regards the remarks in the text, is all that is required.

† Josephus plainly testifies to the belief current in his day as to the value and importance of prayer for the departed, when he assures his readers that the Jews refused to pray for those who had committed suicide. This marked exception clearly proves that they were willing and ready to pray for those who died in other ways. Vide "Wars of the Jews," chap. xci.

‡ Vide Deut. xxxiii. 6.—"Let Reuben live, and not die"—which is looked upon by SS. Ephrem, Cyril, and Epiphanius, as a prayer for the soul of Reuben. A similar interpretation is that which is common amongst the Jews of the present day. Vide also Psalm cxlix. 5.

state and the important dogma of the Resurrection of the Flesh.

And when it is found that no condemnation of this practice was made by our Blessed Saviour; but that, on the contrary, much of His teaching and that of His apostles was based on such a belief of a future state as would have involved the practice, the universality of such prayers in the ancient Liturgies of the Christian Church, borrowed no doubt from the Jews, who buried their dead with pious intercessions and hopeful petitions for peace,* is

---

* (a) "Thou who raisest to life again the departed, have mercy upon him who lieth here."

(β) "Thou who art our succour and defence, redeem the soul of thy servant, who putteth his trust in thee."

(γ) "Thou, the light of the living, and the glory of those who sleep, raise him up again in thy mercy."

(δ) "Thou, our strength and shield, protect thy servants, and give them everlasting life."

Leo Allatius remarks that the Jews pray and give alms for the dead, not only on the day of the funeral and the Sabbaths, but also specially upon the tenth moon of September, when a solemn service is performed, and doles are distributed, to incite the receivers to pray for the departed. "De utriusque Eccl. Orient. et Occid. de Purgatorio consensione," p. 913.

(ε) Translations of Hebrew inscriptions on grave-stones in the Crimea, from an essay by Dr. Chwolson, in the *Mémoires de l'Academie Imperiale des Sciences de St. Petersbourg*, vol. ix. No. 7. St. Petersburg, 1865:—

STONE III.

"This is the tombstone of the grave of Parlak, four thousand and ninety —— may he enter into peace and rest on his couch —— after the Creation." (A.D. 179.)

STONE IV.

"And this is the tombstone of Hillel, son of Rabbi Moses, his rest be in Paradise in glory. [He died] in the year 4216, may his soul be bound fast in the bundle of life with the Everlasting, our God, and the place of his rest be in glory."

STONE IX.

"This is the gravestone of Buki, son of Izchak, the Priest, his rest be

readily accounted for, and the similarity of the existing ritual prayers of the Jewish people to those of the early Christians becomes specially deserving of notice.

The following petition, used in their Burial Service, is said to have come down from the time of our Blessed Saviour, and certain of its phrases are found sculptured on memorial stones in the ancient Jewish cemetery at Prague:—

"O Lord God of Life, God of the Living, Thou art our supporter, our succour, and our shield and defence: Thou sustainest the living, Thou comfortest the dying: Thou raisest in Paradise, [he died] at the time of the deliverance of Israel, in the year 702 after our exile." (A.D. 6.) *This is important for the date.*

STONE XII.

"And this is the stone, which I have set up at his head, upon the grave of Rabbi Joseph, son of Rabbi Elijah, who died in the year 4280 after the Creation [A.D. 369], 1065 after our exile. May his soul abide in happiness."

There are several more, but these contain all the varieties of expression in prayer. The commonest is, "May his soul be fast bound in the bundle of life," &c. (Vide 1 Sam. xxv. 29.) One such inscription is of A.D. 197.

(ζ) Inscriptions from the Jewish Catacomb in the Vigna Randanini, at Rome, published by F. Raffaelle Garrucci, in 1862:—

"—— Rabbi Jacob Ben-Hezekiah —— may his soul be joined to the bundle of the living, and live with the righteous of the world to come. Amen. Amen." (Date, 4914 of Creation.)

"Here lieth Rmoanos (?) Amen. A holy child. May thy repose be in peace."

(ἐν εἰρήνῃ ἡ κοίμησίς σου.)
[This is the commonest prayer, and is of constant occurrence in the catacomb.] So in several other Greek ones; and the Latin "Dormitio tua in bonis" also occurs.

"Here lieth Eutychianus, a devout co-ruler. May his rest be happy with the righteous."

"Dormitio tua inter dicaeis."

up again the departed. Have mercy upon all Thy people whom Thou didst choose of old. Redeem the posterity of Thy faithful servant Abraham, whether they have departed this life or are still in the flesh. Raise them up again, Thou who delightest in life; write their names in Thy Book, and grant them life everlasting." *

Another prayer from the Jewish Ritual † is added, the language of which is solemn, devout, and dignified, and in perfect harmony with the subject of its supplication. It occurs in the "Form for Evening Service for the New Year:"—

"Blessed art Thou, O Lord our God, and the God of our ancestors, the God of Abraham, the God of Isaac, and the God of Jacob, the great, the almighty, and tremendous God, the most High God, who bestoweth gracious favour, possessor of all things, who remembereth the piety of the Patriarchs, and will in love send a Redeemer to their posterity for the sake of His Name. Remember us unto life, O Lord the King, who delighteth in life, and write us in the Book of Life, for Thy sake, O God of Life. O King, Thou art our Supporter, our Saviour, and our Shield. Blessed art Thou, O Lord, the Shield of Abraham. Thou, O Lord, art mighty for ever; it is Thou who revivest the dead and art mighty to save; who sustainest the living with beneficence, and with great mercy comfortest and quickenest the departed, sup-

---

* For examples of these prayers, vide "Jewish Liturgy.—Order of Readings," 8vo. Amsterdam, 1723. "Occasional Prayers of the Jews," 4to. Berlin, 1866. "Spanish Jews' Occasional Prayers," 8vo. Amsterdam, 1617—18; and another edition of the same work, 8vo, Amsterdam, 1695.

† The above form is taken from the "Authorized Service Book of the English Jews."

portest the fallen, and healest the sick. Thou settest at liberty those who are bound, and wilt accomplish Thy faith unto those who sleep in the dust. Who is like unto Thee, O Lord of mighty acts, or who can be compared unto Thee, O King, who killest and restorest to life, who givest rest to the departed, and causest everlasting salvation to spring forth?"

Another form, taken from the recognized and most ancient Hebrew Ritual of the Spanish Jews,* is that formally appointed to be used at funerals for the soul of the person being buried. It is asserted to be very ancient, and to have come down, unmutilated, for at least fifteen centuries :—

"Have pity on him, O Lord, living God, Master of the Universe, with whom is the source of life, that he may always walk in the way of life, and that his soul may repose for ever and ever with those elected unto life everlasting. May God the all-merciful, according to the abundance of His mercy, pardon all his iniquities: may his good works be ever remembered, and may he be admitted into His presence amongst the number of the faithful."

Further on the person departed is thus addressed by the rabbi, or minister, who officiates :—

"May the gates of heaven be thrown open to you, may you look upon the city of peace and the tabernacles which are secure:

---

* This Ritual is that which is commonly followed by the Jews of the whole of Europe; and, by custom and common consent, has become the universal ritual of the ancient people of God. Vide "The Talmudical Dissertation on Benedictions," chap. iii.; and "The Jewish Prayer Book," 8vo., printed by M. Phillips, 23, Little Alie Street, Goodman's Fields.

May the Angels of Peace hasten to welcome you with joy: May the High Priest receive and conduct you: May your soul go to the double cave of Abraham, and hence upon the wings of the Cherubim to the Garden of Eden: May Michael the great angel fling open to you the gates of Paradise: May he present your soul as an offering unto God, and may the Angel of the Covenant, who redeemeth, go before you to the pleasant places where the children of Israel dwell!"

From the statements, facts, and documents thus quoted, combined with a knowledge that our Blessed Saviour nowhere condemned a practice which was certainly current during the period of His sojourn upon earth, it may be reasonably concluded, not only that the Jews regularly and commonly practised the duty of praying for the departed,* but that such a practice was in accordance with the will of Almighty God, who had vouchsafed to be their guide, and who, when the times were accomplished, sent His only-begotten Son to seek and to save those who were lost.

---

* A still more interesting and uncommon form, given to me by my friend Mr. De Lisle, of Garendon Park, who copied it from a Jewish cemetery in Germany, is even more like the ordinary Christian formula than those already quoted. It runs as follows:—

"The prayers of the faithful are earnestly desired on behalf of . . . . who departed this life on . . . ."

CHAPTER IV.

TESTIMONY OF THE APOSTOLIC WRITINGS TO THE USE OF PRAYER FOR THE DEPARTED.

IF, as has been shown, there be after death not simply a heaven and a hell, but a third place, where the souls of the faithful, departed in God's faith and fear, are detained until they are duly prepared for the Beatific Vision, it will reasonably follow that it is of obligation on the part of the faithful who are still in the flesh to offer up prayers that God, in His time and way, may grant unto them peace, rest, and eternal light, and may in due course give them the full fruition of their desires and hopes. And this, though it be not definitely set forth, may be gathered from various passages bearing on the subject in the apostolic writings.

These writings imply a knowledge of that revelation regarding a future state which it had pleased our Blessed Saviour to make to his apostles, and parts of which are recorded in the Sacred Gospels.

For example. In the Sermon on the Mount, the following solemn utterance occurs: "Agree with thine adversary quickly, whiles thou art in the way with him; lest at any time the adversary deliver thee to the judge, and the judge deliver thee to the officer, and thou be cast into prison. Verily I say unto thee, Thou shalt by no means come out thence, till thou hast paid the uttermost farthing"*—a passage which Tertullian, St. Cyprian, Origen, and St. Jerome† interpret as descriptive of the hidden place where the souls of the faithful are detained until they are duly cleansed and prepared for the presence and home of God. And this interpretation appears to be completely borne out by the parable of the Rich Man and Lazarus,‡ which, in regard to the special subject under consideration, demands careful attention. Lazarus, it will be noted, is not said to be in heaven. "He was carried by the angels into Abraham's bosom." Now Abraham had not yet entered into heaven.§ He was, however, so near the place of

---

* S:. Matt. v. 25, 26.
† Tertullian, De Anima, c. 17; St. Cyprian, Epistolæ, lib. iv. No. 2; Origen, Hom. in Lucam, No. xxxv.; St. Jerome, Com. in Matt., cap. v.
‡ St. Luke xvi. 19—31.
§ The terms of this parable were

punishment that, though there was a great gulf fixed between his resting-place and the hell in which the rich man "lifts up his eyes being in torments," he could hear the prayer of Dives and respond to his urgent petition. That petition was not that he, the rich man, should be sent on a message of mercy to his relations still in the flesh, for he was in hell; but that Lazarus, who was with Abraham in the hidden place, should be despatched on this errand. Thus it may be gathered that our Blessed Saviour, in framing this parable, so adapted its circumstances and teaching to the current and common belief of those to whom it was addressed, using language, sentiments, and metaphors easily and readily comprehended, that it might effect His gracious purpose towards those to whom, and for whose benefit, it was spoken, and serve at the same time to bring out still more clearly for His immediate disciples the distinctive teaching and more definite revelations of His most holy religion.

The same doctrine regarding the future state is manifested, likewise, in the case of the penitent thief.* Hanging on a cross to the dying Redeemer's

evidently selected by its Divine Author in such a manner as to harmonize with the ordinary conception of a future state current at the period at which it was spoken. Ancient Jewish tradition, least incorrupted, no doubt clearly upheld exactly those ideas of that state which are here so plainly enunciated.

* St. Luke xxiii. 39—43.

right hand, he prayed to Him, "Lord, remember me when Thou comest into Thy kingdom." He does not pray to be taken to that kingdom, but only to be remembered by the Saviour when He has attained to the same. Heaven was the kingdom and home of Christ. This had been His with the Eternal Father and Blessed Paraclete before the worlds were. Thither He would go. But for himself the malefactor asked that he might be remembered, and have a home in the hidden place of departed spirits. And this petition, because of his amazing faith, hope, and charity, his Lord promptly granted: "Verily I say unto thee, To-day shalt thou be with me in paradise." Now it appears clear, as well from the statement itself, as from the words addressed by our Saviour to Mary Magdalene in the garden after His resurrection,[*] that the paradise here promised to the thief was neither heaven nor hell. It was not heaven, for our Lord's statement was, "I am not yet ascended to my Father;" it could not be hell, for hell is not a place of pleasure, and yet our Lord had made the promise, "To-day shalt thou be with me in paradise." St. Peter, in the third chapter of his first general epistle, throws great light on this point in the following

[*] St. John xx. 17.

passage: "For Christ also hath once suffered for sins, the just for the unjust, that He might bring us to God, being put to death in the flesh, but quickened by the Spirit.* By which also He went and preached unto the spirits in prison,† which sometime were disobedient, when once the longsuffering of God waited in the days of Noah."‡ Here then is a categorical statement regarding the place of departed spirits, as set forth by Christ's apostle,

---

* This word signifies the soul of Christ, not God the Holy Ghost. Vide Bp. Horsley's Sermons, vol. ii. No. 20, on the Descent of Christ into Hell, *in loco.*—"Cum articulus sit, Christum ad inferos descendisse, et non possit intelligi ratione Divinitas, secundum quam est ubique; nec ratione corporis secundum quod fuit in sepulchro; restat quod intelligatur ratione animæ: quo supposito, videndum et qualiter anima Christi descendit ad Infernum."—*Durand,* "Com. in Sentent. Theol." lib. iii. dist. 22, quæs. 3.

† Vide on this point Iren. Adv. Hæres, lib. iv. cap. 45; St. Clem. Alex. Strom., lib. vi. cap. 6, p. 763; St. Cyril Alex., Com. in Ioan., cap. xvi. 16; Suarez, Com. in Tertium partem D. Thomæ, tom. ii. disp. 43, sec. 8. Justin Martyr, in his dialogue with Trypho the Jew, quoted a passage from Isaiah, as follows: "The Lord God of Israel remembered his dead, which slept in the land of the grave, and descended unto them to present unto them His 'Salvation.'" This passage, however, is not found in the Hebrew text, though it is also used by St. Irenæus.

‡ 1 St. Peter iii. 18—20. From this passage it appears clear that even after our Blessed Lord had suffered for our sins, and had already paid the price of His precious bloodshedding for the redemption of mankind, there were still some souls to whom the merits of their Redeemer's full, perfect, and sufficient sacrifice upon the altar of the cross had not as yet been applied, and who were in an actual state of suffering in the other world, in fact, "in prison." Such souls were neither in heaven nor hell. Heaven is not a prison. To hell, the place of the damned, our Saviour went not, for preaching can neither effect reformation nor improvement with such.

which appears to put on record the fulfilment of old promises and pledges made in God's Name and behalf by certain of the Jewish prophets, and likewise to throw more light on contemporary statements of the apostles. Thus wrote Hosea regarding the work of the Messiah: "I will ransom them from the power of the grave; I will redeem them from death: O death, I will be thy plagues; O grave, I will be thy destruction: repentance shall be hid from mine eyes."* And thus Zechariah: "As for Thee, also, by the blood of Thy covenant I have sent forth Thy prisoners out of the pit wherein is no water."† Isaiah had set forth to the same effect two hundred years before, the work, office, and benedictions of the expected Redeemer: "I the Lord have called thee in righteousness, and will hold thine hand, and will keep thee, and give thee for a covenant of the people, for a light of the Gentiles; to open the blind eyes, to bring out the prisoners from the prison, and them that sit in darkness out of the prison-house"‡—words which had their fulfilment in the work done, as St. Paul declares, by our Blessed Lord between the

---

* Hosea xiii. 14.
† Zechariah ix. 11.
‡ Isaiah xlii. 6, 7; vide also Isaiah li. 14, and lxi. 1, in which the loosing of the bound prisoners by the Messiah is distinctly promised.

period of His death upon the cross and His rising to life again on the first Easter morning.

Furthermore: It appears certain from the apostolic writings that the dead can be benefited by the living, and that the state of the righteous, or faithful departed, between their death and the general judgment-day is one in which progression and improvement are possible. St. Paul's statement regarding the resurrection of the body, and the arguments by which he supports that doctrine, are worthy of remark as bearing on the general subject: "Else what shall they do which are baptized for the dead, if the dead rise not at all? Why are they then baptized for the dead?"* Now, whatever may have been the custom here referred to, it is clear that in some mode or another those in the flesh, by being baptized on behalf of the departed, held that they conferred upon them a favour or advantage. And it will at once be

---

* 1 Cor. xv. 29.—"St. Paul mentions one peculiar custom, that of vicarious baptism for the dead. He urges many arguments for the resurrection, that else those who are baptized for the dead would do something quite foolish and senseless. The practice must, therefore, have been a common one. Probably it was done for those who had an intention of being baptized, but had died without fulfilling it. A surviving relative would then be baptized for the dead, in order to give a public testimony to the church that he had died a member of it in mind and desire, and so to obtain for him the prayers of the church, which else were not offered for those who die unbaptized."—*The First Age of the Church*, by Dr. Döllinger (Oxenham's translation, 2nd edition, p. 321. London: 1867).

TESTIMONY OF APOSTOLIC WRITINGS. 45

noted that the same line of argument is adopted here by the apostle as was used by the author of the Book of Maccabees, who appeals to the regard which the living entertain for the dead as a proof of the dogma of the Resurrection of the Body.

Again: One of the latest writings of the Apostle St. Paul contains a distinct and definite prayer for a certain Onesiphorus: "The Lord give mercy unto the house of Onesiphorus; for he oft refreshed me, and was not ashamed of my chain: but, when he was in Rome, he sought me out very diligently, and found me. The Lord grant unto him that he may find mercy of the Lord in that day: and in how many things he ministered unto me at Ephesus, thou knowest very well."* At the end of the same epistle, amongst both general and personal congratulations, St. Paul greets "the household of Onesiphorus,"† omitting special mention of its head, thereby affording a strong presumption that he was no longer in the flesh, and therefore no more a subject for such greeting. The remarkable prayer offered for him, consequently, that he might find mercy of the Lord "in that day,"‡ that is, the "day of the Lord," "the great

---

* 2 Tim. i. 16–18.
† 2 Tim. iv. 19.
‡ "Who shall be punished with everlasting destruction from the presence of the Lord, and from the glory of His power; when He shall come to

and terrible day," the day of the great and general judgment, may be reasonably taken as a definite prayer for the departed, because similar expressions, corresponding exactly to this, are found in other portions of the writings of the first followers of our Lord.*

Here we see then that it was evidently far from the apostle's intention to limit the work of God in the soul to the narrow period of man's probation below. Death, as his teaching so clearly declares, does not stop the influence of grace. The weak, those who were cut off in their weakness, will go from strength to strength, panting for God as the hart desireth the water-springs, until, their time of cleansing, purifica-

---

be glorified in His saints, and to be admired in all them that believe (because our testimony among you was believed) *in that day* (ἐν τῇ ἡμέρᾳ ἐκείνῃ)." (2 Thess. i. 9, 10.)

* (α) "Waiting for the coming of our Lord Jesus Christ: who shall also confirm you *unto the end* (ὃς καὶ βεβαιώσει ὑμᾶς ἕως τέλους ἀνεγκλήτους ἐν τῇ ἡμέρᾳ τοῦ Κυρίου ἡμῶν Ἰησοῦ Χριστοῦ) that ye may be blameless in the day of our Lord Jesus Christ." (1 Cor. i. 7, 8.)

(β) "The very God of peace sanctify you wholly; and I pray God your whole spirit and soul and body be preserved blameless *unto the coming* of our Lord Jesus Christ. Faithful is He that calleth you, who also will do it." (1 Thess. v. 23, 24.)

(γ) "That ye may be sincere, and without offence *till the day* of Christ." (Phil. i. 10.)

(δ) "I give thee charge in the sight of God, who quickeneth all things, and before Christ Jesus, who before Pontius Pilate witnessed a good confession; that thou keep this commandment without spot, unrebukeable, *until the appearing* of our Lord Jesus Christ (μέχρι τῆς ἐπιφανείας τοῦ Κυρίου ἡμῶν Ἰησοῦ Χριστοῦ)." (1 Tim. vi. 13, 14.)

All of which passages indicate that the time of sanctification extends, and the work of sanctification goes on, until the great Day of Judgment.

tion, and preparation past, they appear every one of them in Sion. Those who silently cry to their Lord and Hope " out of the deep " will find that the path of the just is as the shining light that shineth more and more unto the perfect day. Those who, with the creeping years, are nearing the consummation of that happiness, purchased for them by the precious blood of God's dear Son, and won by themselves through a ready co-operation with the will of the Most High, will not forget others of the One Family who are still in the background, amid the shadows and darkness of the great deep out of which they cry. Those who, by the merciful goodness of their Creator, are being prepared for the glories of heaven, as well as the souls of the martyrs under the celestial altar, ever send up their sweet plaint because of what seems to be their waiting, and are bidden be patient until the beautiful breaking of the everlasting day. And the saints of the Old Testament, as we know, cannot be made perfect until the work of the new creation is finally consummated,* and God becomes all in all.

Thus much may be reasonably gathered from Holy Writ, more especially from the teaching of the Apostles.

* "God having provided some better thing for us, that they without us should not be made perfect." (Heb. xi. 40.)

CHAPTER V.

TESTIMONIES OF THE LITURGIES TO THE USE OF PRAYERS FOR THE DEPARTED.

EVERY fresh investigation, each new discovery, leads the student of Christian antiquity to rank the various ancient Liturgies in the highest position as sure witnesses and unerring guides of the faith and practice of the early church. The Liturgies of St. James, St. Mark, and St. Clement are known to have been in existence and use[*]—in the main as they have come down to us—from the early part of the third century; while portions of them, especially those most sacred and essential parts common to all, in great probability had the apostles themselves for their authors. It has been recently shown that St. Paul quoted from the Liturgy[†] of St. James, and some critics have dis-

---

[*] As regards the Liturgy of St. Clement, some writers have affirmed their belief that it has never been used, but, as others consider, on inadequate grounds, and with no direct and sufficient evidence on the point.

[†] "Liturgical Quotations," No. xv. of "Essays on Liturgiology," by J. M. Neale. London, 1867.

covered in the works of Hermas* passages parallel with the exact and express language of that venerable and precious document, as also in the first and second Epistles of St. Clement† and elsewhere.

This being so, the testimony of the Liturgies, whether those of the Catholic Church or of ancient heretical sects which broke off from her communion in generations long gone by, becomes of the greatest importance in serving to determine the plain historical fact that prayers for those departed in God's faith and fear were universally used in the first ages of the church;‡ and that this devout and holy custom was, as a matter of course, current with many of the earliest separated communities, unless their avowed ground of separation was based on the denial of some Christian doctrine, to which prayer for the dead was intimately allied, or from which its practice was necessarily deduced.

Here then are set forth such extracts from those

---

* "Shepherd of St. Hermas," lib. iii. 3; "First Epistle of St. Clement," xxxiii.—xxxv.

† "Second Epistle of St. Clement," ii. 11.

‡ Vide the Greek "Anthologium," 4to. Venice, 1621. The author would specially commend to the Liturgical scholar Dr. Henry Denzinger's "Ritus Orientalium, Coptorum, Syrorum, et Armenorum," etc. (Wirceburgi, 1863), in two volumes, from which he has gained considerable assistance, and to the writer of which he is under obligations. Also Dr. Daniel's "Codex Liturgicus," in 4 vols. Lipsiae, 1847—1854.

Liturgies as bear upon the subject. However much their language may differ in detail, the substance of all is identical, and each one provides a practical testimony on the question of Prayer for the Departed, which is of marked and deep interest:—

1.—LITURGY OF ST. JAMES.*

"Remember, Lord, the God of the spirits and all flesh, the orthodox whom we have commemorated, from righteous Abel unto this day. Give them rest there in the land of the living, in Thy kingdom, in the delight of paradise, in the bosom of Abraham, Isaac, and Jacob, our holy fathers, whence pain, and sorrow, and groaning is exiled, where the light of Thy countenance looks down, and always shines. And direct, O Lord, in peace the ends of our lives, so that they may be Christian and well-pleasing to Thee, and blameless; collecting us under the feet of Thine elect, when Thou wilt and as Thou wilt, only without shame and offence: through Thine only-begotten Son, our Lord and God and Saviour Jesus Christ: for He alone hath appeared on the earth without sin."

2.—THE LITURGY OF ST. JAMES. (Now used by the Christians of St. Thomas.)†

"We implore of Thee, O Almighty Lord, to unite us without delay to the company of the first-born, who are written in heaven. We remember them so that they also may remember us before Thee, and may communicate with us in this spiritual sacrifice for

---

* "Liturgy of St. James," folio, Paris, 1560, and 8vo, Antwerp, 1560. MS. copy taken from the Liturgical Notes of the late Rev. W. H. Mill, D.D. The original MS. is in the Bodleian Library.

† This has been compared with a

the preservation of those who live, for the consolation of all who are in trouble, and for the repose of the faithful departed, our fathers, brethren, and rulers, by the grace and through the mercies of Thy only Son, and of Thy all-holy, good, adorable, life-giving, and consubstantial Spirit . . . .
Remember, O Lord, all the orders ecclesiastical, which in the orthodox faith have gone before us, and now rest in the sleep of peace; likewise for all whom they offered, and for those who are now named. O Lord, the Lord God of spirits and of all flesh, remember all those who in the true faith have gone from us, give rest to their bodies, souls, and spirits, and deliver them from the condemnation which never endeth. Make them glad in that place which the light of Thy countenance visiteth, blotting out their misdeeds, and not entering into judgment with them; for there is none innocent before Thee, save only Thine only-begotten Son, by whose hands we also hope to find mercy and remission of our sins, both for them and for ourselves, for His sake." *

3.—LITURGY OF ST. JAMES. (Bishop Rattray's version.)

" Remember, O Lord, the God of spirits and of all flesh, those whom we have remembered, and those also whom we have not remembered, from righteous Abel even unto this day. Do Thou give them rest in the region of the living, in the bosom of our holy fathers, Abraham, Isaac, and Jacob, whence sorrow, grief, and lamentation are banished away, where the light of Thy

* Another form, sometimes in use by the same community, runs as follows: "Let us remember the faithful, our fathers and brethren, who have departed this world in the orthodox faith; let us, I ask, beseech the Lord to absolve and forgive them their sins and transgressions, and make them worthy to rejoice for ever, with the righteous and upright who have obeyed the will of God."—Collection of Liturgies, p. 132. Dublin, 1822. Vide also "The Christians of St. Thomas," by G. B. Howard, pp. 233, 234. London 1864.

countenance visits and shines continually. And vouchsafe to bring them to Thy heavenly kingdom. And dispose the end of our lives, O Lord, in peace, that they may be Christian, well-pleasing to Thee, and free from sin, gathering us with Thine elect: through Thy only-begotten Son, our Lord and God and Saviour Jesus Christ. For He alone appeareth without sin upon the earth, through whom and with whom Thou art blessed and glorified together with Thy Holy Spirit, now and ever, world without end. Amen." *—*The Ancient Liturgy of the Church of Jerusalem, &c.*, 4to. pp. 119. London, 1744.

4.—LITURGY OF ST. MARK.†

"Give rest to the souls of our fathers and brethren who have heretofore slept in the faith of Christ, O Lord our God, remember-

---

* The original MS. of this version, lettered "Common Prayer Book," is preserved in the Diocesan Library at Brechin. It is quarto in size, and contains 147 pages.—Below is an extract from the Communion Office now in use by the Scottish Episcopalians. It differs from the form drawn up by Archbishop Laud, as well as from that in the first Prayer Book of King Edward VI. :—

"And we also bless Thy Holy Name, for all Thy servants, who, having finished their course in faith, do now rest from their labours.

"And we yield unto Thee most high praise, and hearty thanks, for the wonderful grace and virtue declared in all Thy saints, who have been the choice vessels of Thy grace, and the Lights of the World in their several generations: most humbly beseeching Thee, to give us grace to follow the example of their steadfastness in Thy Faith, and obedience to Thy Holy Commandments; that at the day of the general resurrection, we, and all they who are of the Mystical Body of Thy Son, may be set on His Right Hand, and hear His most joyful Voice, Come, ye Blessed of My Father, inherit the kingdom prepared for you from the foundation of the world.

"Grant this, O Father, for Jesus Christ's sake, our only Mediator and Advocate. Amen."—(Ed. Aberdeen, 1862.)

† This is the Liturgy of the ancient Church of Alexandria. Some writers term it the Coptic or Alexandrian Liturgy. An early edition, with which the above version has been compared, was printed at Paris, in 8vo, A.D. 1583.

ing our ancestors, fathers, patriarchs, prophets, apostles, martyrs, confessors, bishops, holy and righteous persons, every spirit who has departed in the faith of Christ, and those whom we remember to-day, more especially the most holy, immaculate, blessed, our Lady, Mother of God, and ever virgin. And to the spirits of all these give rest, O our Master, Lord and God, in the tabernacles of Thy saints, vouchsafing to them in Thy kingdom the good things of Thy promise, which eye hath not seen nor ear heard, and which things it hath not entered into the heart of man to conceive, which Thou, O God, hast prepared for those who love Thy Holy Name. Grant rest to their souls, and vouchsafe to them the kingdom of heaven."

5.—LITURGY OF ST. JAMES, THE BROTHER OF OUR LORD. (Corrupt as regard text.)*

"Look down, O Lord, in Thine infinite compassion upon the souls of the faithful departed, who when upon earth served Thee in the orthodox faith, and, in the place of those who sleep, waiting for the joys of the heavenly paradise, be propitious to them, for the sake of Thine only-begotten Son. Support them when darkness is around, and give them comfort; let Thy light, even the light of Thy presence, fall upon them, and of Thy mercy grant them in the end peace everlasting."

6.—LITURGY OF ST. CLEMENT.†

"Furthermore we offer to Thee [this sacrifice] for all the saints who have pleased Thee from the beginning of the world, the

---

* From a Syriac MS. of the fourteenth century in the Vatican Library. This form is evidently founded on the ancient Liturgy of St. James of Jerusalem, though in other parts it contains expressions which are decidedly of a Monophysite tendency. Vide "Renaudotii Liturgiar. Oriental. Col.," tom. ii. p. 37—39.

† This Liturgy is commonly known

patriarchs, prophets, righteous men, apostles, martyrs, confessors, bishops, priests, deacons, sub-deacons, readers, singers, virgins, widows, laymen, and all whose names thou knowest."

7.—LITURGY OF ST. CLEMENT. (Syro-Jacobite.)*

"At Thy spiritual and holy altar, O Lord, give rest, good memory, and happiness to all the bodies, souls, and spirits of our fathers, brothers, and sisters, whether of the flesh or of the spirit; who, in whatever countries, cities, or states, have departed this life; whether they have been drowned in seas or rivers, or have died in their journeyings, and of whom no memorial remaineth in the churches existing upon earth. Grant those, O Lord, who have departed this life in the orthodox faith, a good memory, in company with the illustrious ones whose names are written in the Book of Life. And to all of those who, having run their race in this world, have appeared perfect and righteous before Thee; and, having been freed from the sea of transgressions, have reached Thy presence, our fathers and brethren of the flesh and of the spirit, grant, O Lord, in that spiritual and mighty bosom, eternal rest. In the dwelling-places of light and gladness give them the spirit of joy. In the tabernacles of shadow and rest grant them the treasures of felicity — whence every

---

as "The Liturgy of the Apostolic Constitutions." The exact age of these latter has long been a vexed question, though generally assigned to the third century. The Liturgy embodied in them—from which the above extract is taken—is no doubt much earlier. Some have held that it had for its compiler the saint whose name it bears. This, on the other hand, has been disputed, and by those, too, who have admitted its high antiquity. Vide "Liturgiarium Orient. Collectio," Renaudot, tom. ii. p. 186. Its peculiarity is that the Lord's Prayer does not occur in it. Vide "Apostolical Constitutions," book viii. chap. xii.

* The prayers for the dead in this Liturgy are full of simple beauty and theological exactness. The above may be compared with similar petitions in the Apostolical Constitutions.

sorrow is excluded, and where the souls of the righteous, without labour, expect the first-fruits of eternal life; and where the spirits of just men, being made perfect, wait for the fruition of their promised reward: in that place where the labourers and the weary turn their eyes towards paradise; and they who are invited to the marriage-supper look for the Bridegroom; when they who have been called to that feast wait until they go up to the same, and earnestly desire the new state of glory: where sorrows are banished away and joys remain, through and for the sake of Thine only-begotten Son, Jesus Christ our Saviour, by whom alone we look to obtain mercy both for ourselves and for them."*

8.—LITURGY OF ST. JOHN CHRYSOSTOM.†

"Furthermore, we offer to Thee this reasonable service on behalf of those who have departed in the faith, our ancestors, our fathers, patriarchs, prophets, apostles, preachers, evangelists, martyrs, confessors, virgins, and every just spirit made perfect through the faith; especially the most holy, undefiled, excellently laudable, glorious Lady, the Mother of God and Ever-Virgin Mary; the holy John the Prophet, Forerunner, and Baptist, and all celebrated apostles, Saint N. [*the saint of the day*], whose memory we also celebrate, and all Thy saints, through whose

---

* This Liturgy, Syro-Jacobite, is based upon that of St. James of Jerusalem, *i.e.*, the Hierosolymitan, or, as Dr. Daniel terms it, the Antiochene. Renaudot and other competent critics deny that it is the work of St. Clement.

† "Missa Divina, Græce et Latine, Sti. Ioannis Chrysostomi." 4to. Venet., Sabio, 1528. This is the second edition of the Greek text, and the first Latin edition. It is without any pagination. Another had been published at Rome, in quarto, two years earlier. This Liturgy is used by all the Greeks of the Oriental and Western Churches, also by the Georgians, Mingrelians, and Bulgarians, though in each case rubrical directions and later prayers have been added or introduced.

prayers look down upon us, O God. And remember all those who are departed in the hope of the resurrection to eternal life, and give them rest, where there is no sorrow nor mourning, and where the light of Thy countenance, O Lord God, shines upon them."

9.—The Nestorian Liturgy.

"And we beseech Thee, O Lord, and supplicate before Thee, to remember through this oblation, the fathers, the patriarchs, prophets, apostles, martyrs, confessors, bishops, doctors, priests, and deacons,[*] and all of those of our ministry who have departed this life, and all our brethren in Christ, and all who have departed from this world in the true faith, whose names are known unto Thee. Pardon and forgive them in whatsoever they have sinned or transgressed against Thee, seeing that they were by nature inclined to evil, and, as men, clothed with iniquity. And through the prayers and supplications of all who have been approved before Thee, turn Thee unto us, and have mercy upon us, and upon Thy servants and people who are now standing before Thy holy altar, and make us all meet to be partakers in that portion and inheritance unto which the saints in light have attained."[†]— "The Nestorians and their Rituals," G. P. Badger, vol. ii., pp. 281, 282. London, 1852.

---

[*] Compare this with the Liturgy of St. Clement, as given by Renaudot and Asseman.

[†] This form is taken from the Liturgy ordinarily in use amongst the Nestorians. There are two others occasionally adopted, from one of which, that called after Theodore of Mopsuestia, a corresponding extract is given next in order. Some of the early, and certain of the latter, parts of the ordinarily-used Nestorian Liturgy, are founded upon what is termed "The Liturgy of the Apostles." Critics are not agreed as to the age of this, though it is usually regarded in its chief portions as of the latter part of the third century. Vide "Dissertatio de Nestorianorum Liturgiis," Renaudot, tom. ii. p. 566.

TESTIMONIES OF THE LITURGIES. 57

10.—LITURGY OF THEODORE OF MOPSUESTIA.* (Nestorian form still occasionally used.)

"O Lord our God, graciously receive from us this sacrifice of thanksgiving, the reasonable fruit of our lips and our bounden duty, that this remembrance may be good before Thee of the ancient just men, holy prophets, blessed apostles, martyrs, confessors, bishops, doctors, priests, deacons, and all the sons of the holy church universal, who have departed out of this life in the true faith; so that by Thy grace, O Lord, Thou mayest bestow upon them forgiveness of all their sins, which in this world, attacked by temptation, they may have committed, for there is no one without sin."

11.—LITURGY OF ST. IGNATIUS. (Syro-Jacobite or Monophysite.)†

"Because of Thy great goodness, O Lord, receive peacefully and calmly the spirits and souls of Thy servants and worshippers,

---

* "Renandotii Liturgiar. Oriental. Collectio," tom. ii. 616—625.

The translation of this passage has been compared with an original Syriac MS. of the above Liturgy.

The following Litany occurs in the Nestorian Service for the "Burial of a Priest:"—

"Let us pray. Peace be with us.

"Pray for our brother, the priest, the son of our faith, who has departed out of this world, that God who approved of him, and took him away in the true faith, may guide him to the haven of all the righteous, so that when He shall awaken and raise up all who sleep in the dust, and when the righteous and just shall attain a good end, He may call him and exalt him to His own Right Hand. R. Amen.

"And write his name in the Book of Life. R. Amen.

"And number him with His Elect. R. Amen.

"And mingle him, through the grace of Christ, with the assembly of those who praise Him, and with all the just and righteous, who were approved before Him for ever and ever. R. Amen."

On casting earth into the grave in the form of a cross, the people cry out three times,

"Give rest to the soul of this Thy servant in the place where the righteous dwell."

† A Liturgy based on that of St.

who out of this present life have departed to Thee; but especially receive those for whom, and on whose behalf, this sacrifice is now offered and completed. Remember them; give them repose, and place them in the mansions of light, in the homes of blessed spirits, in the heavenly Jerusalem, in the Church of the First-Born which is written in heaven. And giving unto them a good memorial and a most blessed repose, because of Thy great love to mankind, grant them that life which knows not old age; give them the good things which pass not away, and the joys which are endless. May they obtain mercy through Thy clemency, and rest through Thy mercy. Hide them under the shadow of Thy wings, and condemn them not because of their offences; for in Thee and Thine only-begotten Son they have ever put their trust."*

12.—LITURGY OF ST. GREGORY ABULFARAGIUS.† (Syro-Jacobite, or Monophysite.)

"And because Thou, O Lord, art the righteous rewarder both of quick and dead, and in Thy hands are the souls of the faithful, we pray Thee, on behalf of all who, having passed out of this transitory life, have departed in the orthodox faith, to remember them of Thy mercy, to hear our prayers on their behalf, and to

James of Jerusalem, wholly distinct, in its main characteristics, from the Petrine.

* The concluding sentences of this quotation are in the original somewhat obscure, and vary slightly in different MSS. as to their text. This is evident from a comparison of the works of Le Brun, Asseman, and Renaudot.

† This Liturgy is based on that of St. James of Jerusalem, which latter has three chief branches—(1) that used in the Isle of Sicily, partly assimilated to the Liturgy of St. Peter; (2) that of St. Cyril, having certain features in common with the Liturgy of Alexandria; and (3) the Syriac Liturgy of St. James—the direct source of that of St. Gregory Abulfaragius, differing materially from that of Jerusalem, from which the above quotation is taken. Vide Renaudot, tom. ii. pp. 343—469.

pass not over these our humble supplications which we make to Thee for them. In Thy royal likeness they were created, therefore of Thy mercy, O Lord, spare them, and of Thy clemency forgive them. Lead them to Thy habitations and guide them to Thyself, joining them with the number of Thy heavenly host, where Thine only-begotten Son is hymned with honour and glory in repeated song. According to His never-failing word, we trust in Thy mercy, O Lord, for the remission of all sins, both for them and for ourselves."

13.—LITURGY OF ST. BASIL, *ex versione Andreæ Masii.* (Copto-Jacobite.*)

"O Lord, remember also in like manner those of the priesthood, and those of the laity likewise, who have already fallen asleep. Vouchsafe to grant to all their souls rest in the bosom of our holy fathers Abraham, Isaac, and Jacob. Bring them in and gather them together in a green place by the waters of consolation in the paradise of joy, where, in the brightness of Thy saints, sorrow and misery and sighing are for ever banished away."

14.—LITURGY OF JOHN BAR MADAN. (Syro-Jacobite.)†

"O God, spare those who in true faith, and in the orthodox creed, have been set free from this temporal life, and according to

---

* There are said to be a large number of ancient Liturgical fragments, called after St. Basil—most of which appear to have been formed after the original model of the Liturgy of St. James. The anaphora or canon does not vary greatly, though both the introductory and concluding parts differ to a very remarkable extent; while those portions in which the dead are commemorated, though different in language, are identical in sentiment.

† This, though owning distinctive Monophysite peculiarities, is based on the Syriac Liturgy of St. James, and is extremely like other Syro-Jacobite Liturgies, more especially those of St. Celestine, Dionysius, and Michael of Antioch. Vide "Liturgiarum Orientalium Collectio," 1847.

Thine equitable sentence have returned to Thee, their first Almighty cause; yea, spare them and be merciful. Regard them as of the number of Thine elect, cover them with the glorious cloud of thy saints; place them on Thy right hand with the Lamb, and bring them into Thine holy habitation. Cause them to reach the blessed home of Thy kingdom. Grant that they may be invited to Thy banquet, and bring them into the land of joy and rejoicing, where grief and misery have no place, and sighing and suffering are for ever ended. Deal with them in mercy, O Lord, because of the frailties of the flesh, in the terrible hour of Thy judgment, and examine them not severely when they stand before Thee."

15.—LITURGY OF ST. JAMES OF BOTNA. (Syro-Jacobite.)

" O Lord, give rest to the souls of those whom we commemorate, and write their names in the Book of Life. Make them worthy of the joys to be had in paradise. Place them in the home of the righteous, unite them to the company of the pious; cause them to arrive in the harbour of life, where is the habitation of rest, and where sorrows, weaknesses, sighs, and wretchedness for ever flee away; where the saints enjoy blessedness, and where the pious have rest. For the sake of Jesus Christ cast out neither any of them nor of ourselves, for He is the spotless One upon earth, our Mediator and Redeemer."

16.—LITURGY OF MALABAR. (Ancient form.)

" Let us remember also our fathers and our brethren who have departed out of this world in the orthodox faith. Let us pray, I say, to the Lord that He may absolve them, and may forgive them their offences, and may vouchsafe that they, with all just and righteous men who have obeyed the divine will, may rejoice for ever and ever in the light and love of the Omnipotent, the All-charitable, and the Eternal."

17.—LITURGY OF THE CHURCH OF ABYSSINIA.*

"From the throne of Thine unconceived glory, vouchsafe, O Lord, to look with the eye of pity and compassion on the souls of the faithful departed, the works of Thine own hands. Be merciful unto them, O Great King, and forgive their past transgressions, putting away the remembrances of former sins, because of Thine own dear Son. Leave them not desolate in a place of darkness and terror, but lift up their eyes to the land of paradise, and satisfy their longings with the waters of Thy comfort. Protect them from the incursion of their foe, and shield them by the hand of Thy Omnipotence. Call them, in their day of rejoicing, to delight in the glories of Thy heavenly mansions, where light, and peace, and joy eternal are for ever and ever. We ask this both for quick and dead because of Thine only-begotten Son, in whom continually we place our hope and trust."†

18.—LITURGY OF THE CHURCH OF ARMENIA.

"Remember, O Lord, and have mercy upon the souls of the faithful departed, and be Thou propitious to them. Grant them

---

* The germ of this Liturgy—which, to judge from the above extract, is remarkable for its orthodox beauty, though in other portions interpolations have been made—is the ancient Liturgy of St. Mark. Another form is as follows: "Give rest to our fathers and brethren, who have slept and departed from us in the orthodox faith . : . O Christ our God, remember all those who are in thy celestial kingdom, and grant to them light and rest."—"Abyssinian Liturgy" (in some expressions of which it appears that the holy gifts are offered to the Son instead of to the Father).

† Ludolphus, La Croze (a Benedictine monk who renounced his order), and other writers, assert that the Christians of Abyssinia possess no less than nine various versions of their Liturgy, each one differing in some respect from the others, but all containing substantially those parts which are common to the Liturgy of St. Mark. Vide Renaudot's "Canon Universus Æthiopum," and Dr. Neale's "Ancient Liturgies." London, 1859.

rest and life, and place them amongst Thy saints in the kingdom of heaven, making them worthy of Thy mercy."

19.—Liturgy of St. Peter.*

"Remember also, O Lord, the souls of Thy servants and handmaidens N. and N., who have gone before us with the sign of the faith, and sleep the sleep of peace: To them, O Lord, and to

---

* The Roman form is identical in this part with that of the ancient church of Salisbury, and with the Bangor, York, Hereford, and other old English national rites, except that the word "animarum" occurs after, "Memento etiam Domine," in the Sarum canon. The text of the Ambrosian Liturgy here—with the exception that the rubrics of the Roman form are wanting—is the same. Vide Daniel's "Codex Liturgicus," tom. i. p. 92.

The following prayers are taken from the "Sacramentarium Leonianum," in "Liturgia Romana Vetus," of L. A. Muratorius, reprinted from the Vatican Codex. Venice, 1748:—

"Omnipotens sempiterne Deus, qui contulisti fidelibus tuis remedia vitæ post mortem: præsta, quæsumus, propitius, et placatus, ut anima famuli tui . . . . . a peccatis omnibus expiata, in tuæ redemptionis sorte requiescat. Per.

"Hostias tibi, Domine, humili supplicatione deferimus; ut anima famuli tui . . . . per hæc pia placationis officia, perpetuam misericordiam consequatur. Per.

"Hanc igitur oblationem, quam tibi offerimus pro anima famuli tui . . . . quæsumus, Domine propitius accipias; et miserationum tuarum largitate concedas, ut quidquid terrena conversatione contraxit, hic sacrificiis emundetur, ac mortis vinculis absolutis, transitum mereatur ad vitam. Per."—Muratorius, lib. i. p. 451.

Vide also the various forms of prayer for the departed in the Gregorian Sacramentary: "Orationes in agenda mortuorum, quando anima egreditur de corpore;" "Orationes post lavationem corporis;" "Orationes post sepultum corpus." Likewise, "Missa unius defuncti;" "Missa pro defuncto nuper baptizato;" "Missa in anniversario unius defuncti;" "Missa plurimorum defunctorum," etc.—Muratorius, lib. ii. pp. 214—221.

The following is taken from the Mozarabic Liturgy, which belongs to the Ephesine branch in the Liturgical tree:—

"Dicat Presbyter.—Vivant in vobis, Jesu Domine, apostoli tui Jacobi prædicamenta doctrinæ, quibus docemur illum beatum esse qui inlatus tentationis valuerit æquanimiter supportare quo dum præsentia mala

all who rest in Christ, we pray Thee, grant a place of refreshment, of light, and of peace. Through the same Christ our Lord. Amen."

20.—LITURGY OF ST. XYSTUS, PATRIARCH OF ROME. (Christians of St. Thomas.)*

"Be Thou, O Lord, one who giveth rest, and Propitiator to all the faithful dead, who have been saved by the death of Thy only-begotten Son.

"And being saved from death by Thee, O Lord, and being delivered from the grave, and shapen forth from the dust; may the grace of Thy only Son prevail upon us, by whose hands we also trust to find mercy, and remission of sins for His sake, both for us and them.

"And with the renewal of the general resurrection make us and them in Thy grace, O Lord, meet for the joy which is in Thy spiritual kingdom; so that herein, as in all things, Thy all-glorious and blessed Name may be glorified and praised by all, with that of our Lord Jesus Christ, and Thy Holy Spirit."

21.—LITURGY OF ST. DIONYSIUS, BISHOP OF ATHENS. (Christians of St. Thomas.)†

"Remember, O Lord, all the faithful and true dead, who sleep potentissime toleraverimus, in pace et charitate nunc et in æternum tecum sine fine vivamus. R. Amen.

"Dicat Presbyter.—Quia tu es vita vivorum, sanitas infirmorum, ac requies omnium fidelium defunctorum in æterna sæcula sæculorum, R. Amen."—Ed. Alex. Leslie, Romæ, 1755.

* Vide "Renaudotii Liturgiar. Orient. Collect.," tom. ii. p. 138, who gives ten pages further on, at p. 148,

"A Liturgy of St. Peter, Prince of the Apostles" (Jacobite), not unlike the above, and containing equally distinctive teaching as regards Prayers for the Departed. This latter, as Renaudot maintains, appears to be a compound of the Roman Mass (unreformed and unaltered) and the Liturgy of St. John Chrysostom.

† Vide "Renaudotii Liturg. Orien. Coll.," tom. ii. p. 202.

in Thy hope; and give rest in Thy mercy to those who have been redeemed by the blood of Thy only-begotten Son.

"And, looking upon them in love, pardon their offences, O Lord, and remit their faults, for the sake of the body and the blood of Thy only-begotten Son hidden in their members, by whose hands we also hope to find mercy and remission of sins for His sake, both for us and for them."

Though the list here given of ancient Liturgies which contain prayer for the departed is considerable, yet it does not comprise one half of those precious documents existing—all remarkable for the independent and yet concurrent testimony they so clearly bear to the public practice of the early Christians in this particular. Sufficient examples, however, both from the most ancient and leading Liturgies—those from which all others have had their origin and root—as well as from those of a later period, used by some of the earliest and most ancient heretical sects, have been provided, so that this catena of authority may be at once seen to be pertinent and weighty; and may serve to show how clearly the practice in question was enjoined on the faithful by the example and authority of the public authorized form for celebrating the Holy Eucharist. In fact, there can be little doubt that whatever influence the *Disciplina arcani* had in other particulars, in this the concurrent practice of the church was such that no question could have arisen as to the legality and propriety of the custom.

Renaudot ably and fully states the case in the following striking passage. His conclusion appears inevitable:—

"Si quidquid antiquissima omnium ecclesiarum traditione stabilitum apud Christianos, et observatum est, commemoratio defunctorum fuit, ad altare Dei inter sacrorum mysteriorum celebrationem. Illam consuetudinem sua ætate ubique observatam, jam à veteri disciplina omniumque consensu confirmatam testatur Augustinus pluribus in locis, consentientesque habet veteres Patres omnes. Officia quoque antiquissima, non ea modo quæ huc usque usurpantur sed Gottica, Gallicana, Mosarabica Ambrosiana; Græcæque Liturgiæ, commemorationis illius formas exhibent, quæ cum Orientalibus, Copticis, Æthiopicis Syriacis cujuscumque ritus Liturgiis, perfecte consentiunt, nihil ut sit, de quo dubitari, aut in quo novitatem suspicari minùs queat."*

* P. 104, vol. ii., Renaudot.

CHAPTER VI.

TESTIMONY OF ANCIENT FATHERS TO THE USE OF PRAYERS FOR THE DEPARTED.

HAVING shown at some length that the most ancient Liturgies contain distinct prayers for the departed, together with those which, though of considerable antiquity yet more recent, were founded upon them, and that this was the case whether they were orthodox or heretical, it becomes necessary to gather together the most important portions of that testimony on the subject which may be found in the authentic writings of the Christian Fathers. It was commonly believed in the first ages of the church that the souls of all just men, departed in the faith and fear of Christ, were placed in some special locality, called sometimes "Hades," sometimes "Paradise" or "Abraham's bosom," a locality of rest and refreshment, distinct from heaven, but yet the prelude to, or place of preparation for it. This is the opinion of the Pastor Hermas, of St. Justin Martyr, Pope Pius I., St.

Irenæus, St. Clement of Alexandria, Tertullian, Origen, Victorinus the Martyr, Novatian, Lactantius, St. Hilary, as well as of St. Ambrose, St. Gregory Nyssen, Prudentius the Christian poet, St. Augustine, and St. Chrysostom. More definite ideas as to the duty expected from the living on behalf of the deceased will be referred to in due course. As regards prayers for the departed, what is seen to be so plainly set forth in the "Apostolical Constitutions," here reproduced, is likewise taught with equal definiteness by many an early writer whose authority is weighty and valuable.

The following is the specific prayer for the dead taken from the "Apostolical Constitutions:"—

"We offer unto Thee for all Thy Saints, who have lived well-pleasing in Thy sight from the foundation of the world; for patriarchs, prophets, holy men, apostles, martyrs, bishops, confessors, presbyters, deacons, sub-deacons, readers, singers, virgins, widows, laymen, and all whose names Thou knowest." *

Tertullian makes mention of special oblations for

---

* "'Ετι προσφέρομέν σοι καὶ ὑπὲρ πάντων τῶν ἀπ' αἰῶνος εὐαρεστησάντων σοι ἁγίων, πατριαρχῶν, προφητῶν, δικαίων, ἀποστόλων, μαρτύρων, ὁμολογητῶν, ἐπισκόπων, πρεσβυτέρων, διακόνων, ὑποδιακόνων, ἀναγνωστῶν, ψαλτῶν, παρθινων, χηρῶν, λαϊκῶν, καὶ πάντων ὧν αὐτὸς ἐπίστασαι τὰ ὀνόματα."—*Apostolical Constitutions.* Compare this with corresponding petitions in the Ancient Liturgies.

the departed, made on their birthdays—that is, on the days upon which they began their new birth of everlasting felicity.* And again elsewhere thus writes :—

"Every woman prayed for the soul of her deceased husband, desiring that he might find rest and refreshment at present, and a part in the first resurrection; and offered an annual oblation for him on the day of his death." †

On the other hand, and in a similar manner, he declares that the husband prayed for the soul of his wife, and offered annual oblations for her.‡ These statements are made, as should be noted, so as to indicate that such acts were ordinary and common.

From Tertullian we pass on to St. Cyprian, who frequently alludes to the same custom. On behalf of those who had suffered martyrdom, the Christians made oblations of praise, prayer, and thanksgiving; for others he declares that prayers were commonly

---

* "Oblationes pro defunctis, pro natalititiis, animâ die facium."—*Tertullian.* . "De Col. Mil." c. 3, p. 102. Ed. Paris, 1664.

† "Pro anima ejus orat, et refrigerium interim appostulat ei, et in prima resurrectione consortiem et offert annuis diebus dormitionis ejus."—*Tertullian.* "De Monogam.," c. 10, p. 531. Ed. Paris, 1664.

‡ "Jam repete apud Deum, pro cujus spiritu postules, pro qua oblationes annuas reddas."—*Tertullian.* "Expost. ad Castit.," c. xl.

put up. Those for the martyrs he terms "oblationes" and "sacrificia;"* those for ordinary Christians commemorative prayers. This latter point is evident from what he writes of a certain Geminius Victor, for whom, because, contrary to law, he had appointed a priest to be his executor, no oblation should be made for his rest or sleep, nor any deprecation be used in his name according to the custom of the church.†

Origen declares that the Christians of his day "thought it convenient to make mention of the saints in their prayers, and to excite themselves to good works by the remembrance of them."‡

The writer who passes under the name of Origen, in his commentary on the Book of Job (no doubt a contemporary with or an immediate successor to Origen himself), thus mentions the custom of the faithful in his day: "They made devout memorial of the saints, and their parents and friends who were dead in the

* "Celebrentur hic a nobis oblationes et sacrificia ob commemorationes eorum."—*St. Cyprian.* Epist. xxvii. p. 28. Ed. Oxon., 1682.

"Sacrificia pro eis semper, ut meministis, offerimus, quoties martyrum passiones et dies anniversaria commemoratione celebramus."—*St. Cyprian.* Epist. xxxiv.

† "Non est, quod pro dormitione ejus apud vos fiat oblatio, aut deprecatio aliqua nomine ejus in ecclesia frequentetur."—*St. Cyprian.* Epist. lxvi.

‡ "Meminisse sanctorum, sive in collectis solemnibus, sive pro eo ut ex recordatione eorum proficiamus aptum et conveniens videtur."—*Origen in Job*, vol. iv. p. 652. Ed. Benedict.

faith, as well in order to rejoice in their refreshment as to desire for themselves a pious consummation in the faith."*

St. Cyril of Jerusalem, in his full and laborious description of the order and rites of the Eucharist, thus gives an account of the act of sacerdotal intercession which immediately follows the canon or prayer of consecration:—

"We offer this sacrifice in memory of all those who are fallen asleep before us; first patriarchs, prophets, apostles, and martyrs, that God by their prayers and intercessions may receive our supplications; and then we pray for our holy fathers and bishops, and all who are fallen asleep before us, believing it to be a considerable advantage to their souls to be prayed for, while the holy and tremendous sacrifice lies upon the altar." †

St. Epiphanius, in replying to the Aerians, a sect which denied both the advantage and benefit of praying for the dead, declared that the orthodox Christians had many good reasons for mentioning the

---

* "Et memorias sanctorum facimus, et parentum nostrorum, vel amicorum in fide morientium devote memoriam agimus, tam illorum refrigerio gaudentes, quam etiam nobis piam consummationem in fide postulantes."—*Origen in Job,* vol. ii. p. 902. Ed. Benedict.

† St. Cyril. Cat. Mystag. p. 297. Ed. Oxon., 1703. Ἵνα μνημονεύωμεν . . . . . θυσίας.

names of the departed: firstly, because such mention was an argument that they were still in existence, and living in the Lord; secondly, because it was of a certain advantage to sinners, though it did not altogether blot out their crimes; and thirdly, because it put a distinction between the perfection of Christ and the imperfection of all other men. Therefore he declared they rightly and properly prayed for just men, fathers, patriarchs, prophets, apostles, evangelists, martyrs, confessors, bishops, hermits, and all orders of men.*

Again: St. John Chrysostom expressly maintains that it was customary to offer the Christian sacrifice for the martyrs;† and in his Forty-first Homily, commenting on the 1st of Corinthians, writing against immoderate‡ sorrow for the death of sinners, he declares: "They are not so much to be sorrowed for as helped with prayers and supplications and alms and offerings; for these things were not planned in

---

* Epiphan. Hæres. lxxv. Ærian., n. iii. "Responsio Epiphanii," vol. i. p. 908. Ed. Colon., 1682. This passage is paraphrased, though with strict literalness, in the text above.

† See the passage beginning Τί οἴει τὸ ὑπὲρ μαρτύρων προσφέρεσθαι, κ. τ. λ., in St. Chrysostom's Twenty-first Homily on the Acts. "Opera Omnia," vol. ix. p. 176. Ed. Benedict., 1718.

‡ Vide Chrysost., Hom. iv. in Heb. Ed. Ben. 1718, vol. xii. p. 47; Hom. xxix. De Dormientibus, vol. i. p. 764; Hom. xli. in 1 Cor., p. 701; Hom. iii. in Phil., p. 1225; Hom. xxiv. in Ioan., p. 159; also Cassian. Collat., ii. c. v.

vain, neither is it without reason that we remember those who are departed in the Holy Mysteries, interceding on their behalf to the Lamb who is slain to take away the sins of the world, that some comfort may consequently accrue to them. Neither is it in vain that he who stands at the altar when the tremendous mysteries are celebrated cries, 'We offer unto Thee for all those who are asleep in Christ, and all who make commemorations for them;' for if there were no commemorations made for them these things would not be uttered. Therefore let us not grow weary in rendering them help, and in offering prayers on their behalf, for the common propitiation of the whole world is now before us. Consequently we now pray for the whole world, and mention them with martyrs, confessors, and priests; for we are all one body, though one member be more exultant than another. And we may obtain a general pardon for them by our prayers, alms, and the help of those who together are mentioned with them."*

Furthermore, the same saint, in his Third Homily on the Epistle to the Philippians, writes thus: "When at that time" (*i.e.*, the Christian Sacrifice) "all the

---

* Εἰ δὶ καὶ ἁμαρτωλὸς ἀπῆλθη, κ. τ. λ. (Hom. xli. in 1 Cor. vol. x. p. 392. Ed. Benedict, 1718.)

people stand with their hands extended towards heaven, and all the company of the priests with them, and the tremendous sacrifice lies upon the altar, how shall we not move God to mercy, when we call upon Him for those who are departed in the faith? I speak of those only; for the catechumens are not allowed this consolation, but are deprived of all help, save only the giving of alms on their behalf."*

In his treatise "On the Priesthood," the same saint declares that "a bishop is to be the intercessor for all the world, and to pray to God to be merciful to the transgressions of all men, not solely for the living, but also for the dead."†

Several writers point out that self-murderers— *Biothanati*, as they were termed—were not permitted to participate in the church's prayers, nor to have a part in her sacred oblations. Examples of such a

---

* "Ὅταν ιιστήκει λαὸς ὁλόκληρος χεῖρας ἀναντείνοντες, κ. τ. λ. Hom. iii. in Phil., vol. xi. p. 217. Ed. Benedict., 1718.

St. Chrysostom discusses this question elsewhere; *e. g.*, Hom. xxiv. in Ioan., "Opera Omnia," vol. viii. p. 147.) Vide also "Labbe," vol. v. Conc. ii. c. xvi.—xvii. p. 841:—

"Placuit, ut hi, sibi ipsis aut per ferrum, aut per venenum, aut per praecipitium, aut suspendium, vel quolibet modo violentam inferunt mortem, nulla pro illis in oblatione commemoratio fiat, neque cum psalmis ad sepulturem corum cadavera deducantur. Item placuit, ut catechumenis, sine redemptione baptismi defunctis, simili modo, neque oblationis commemoratio, neque psallendi impendatur officium."

† Chrysostom de Sacerdot., lib. vi. c. iv. Ed. Benedict., vol. i. p. 424. Vide also Hom. xxii. in Matt., *in loco*.

judgment on the part of authority are on record. The Council of Braga, the decree of which is already given, recognises this decision, and declares that such sinners as the self-murderer, and the catechumens who in their lifetime had deliberately deferred baptism, are to receive neither Christian burial nor the much-valued petitions of the church on behalf of the faithful departed.

St. Ambrose* sets forth an idea which gradually grew up and expanded, founded upon an apostolic statement which had been previously reproduced by Tertullian† and others. St. Ambrose maintains that those whose transgressions have not been duly ex-

---

* On the general question, St. Ambrose, writing to one Faustinus, who grieved immoderately because of his sister's death, maintains the following duty: "I do not hold that your sister ought to excite your tears, but rather your prayers; nor that her soul is to be dishonoured by your weeping, but rather recommended to God by sacrifices." (Ep. xxxix. Opera, Ed. Ben. tom. ii. p. 944.) The same eminent saint, in his celebrated Funeral Oration upon the great Theodosius, asks that God Almighty would be pleased to bestow upon him that perfect rest which has been prepared for the saints (Opera, tom. ii. Ed. Ben. p. 1207): "I loved him," writes St. Ambrose, "therefore I follow him into the land of the living. Neither will I forsake him, until by prayers and tears I bring the man, whither his merits call him, into the Lord's holy mountain." See also his Funeral Sermon on Valentinian, tom. ii. p. 1193.

† Tertullian, De Anim., Opera, p. 689. "In summa, quum carcerem illum quod Evangelium demonstrat, inferos intelligimus; et novissimum quadrantem, modicum quoque delictum mora resurrectionis illic luendum interpretamur: nemo dubitabit, animam aliquid pensare penes inferos; salva resurrectionis plenitudine, per carnem quoque."

piated in their time of probation below,* will undergo the punishment of a purgatorial fire in the period elapsing between the first and the final resurrection; and maintains that the punishment of some will continue even beyond the final resurrection, if they have not then completed the entire length of their patient waiting during the intermediate period.†

St. Augustine appears to have maintained another opinion, which is not borne out as universally, nor even commonly received, from a consideration of the ancient Liturgies. He maintained that the martyrs were admitted to the immediate enjoyment of the glories and bliss of heaven, and consequently that they needed not the prayers of the faithful, and ought not to be prayed for."‡

---

* "Qui autem non veniunt ad primam resurrectionem, sed ad secundam reservantur: isti urentur, donec impleant tempora inter primam et secundam resurrectionem; aut, si non impleverint, diutius in supplicio permanebunt. Ideo ergo rogemus, ut in prima resurrectione partem habere mereamur."—*Ambros. Enarr. in Psalm* l., Opera, *in loco*.

† More than a century after the time of St. Ambrose, St. Gregory the Great alludes to the punishment so as by fire, in connection with the thirty days' prayer for the departed, as follows: "Diu est quod frater ille qui defunctus est, in igne cruciatur; debemus ei aliquid caritatis impendere, et eum inquantum possumus, ut eripiatur, adjuvare. Vade, itaque, et ab hodierna die diebus triginta continuis offere pro eo sacrificium stude, ut nullus omnino prætermittatur dies, quo, pro absolutione illius hostia salutaris non immoletur."— *Sti. Gregorii Dial.* (Paris, 1705), lib. iv. c. p. 468.

‡ Opera Augustini. Ed. Benedict., 1703, vol. v. p. 533.; Serm. xvii. De Verbis Apostoli.

On the main question under consideration, he is very lucid and definite: "Beyond all doubt the dead are assisted by the prayers of Holy Church, and by the salutary sacrifice, and by the alms which are bestowed for the repose of their souls; so that the Lord may deal with them more mercifully than their sins deserve: for this has been handed down by the Fathers, and is observed throughout the whole church. Such exercises most assuredly benefit the departed, but then those persons alone are profited who have so lived before death that these deeds may be beneficial to them after their departure."*

Nothing could be more distinct and dogmatic than this statement, the principle laid down † in which is supported by the avowed practice of the saint himself. St. Augustine both prayed in private for his departed mother Monica, and alludes to the public prayers of

---

* "Orationibus vero sanctæ Ecclesiæ, et sacrificio salutari, et eleemosynis. . . . . ut possint eis hæc utilia esse post mortem."—*Opera*, vol. x. Serm. xxxii. p. 138.

† "Nor is it to be denied that the souls of the departed are relieved by the piety of their living friends, when the sacrifice of the Mediator is offered for them, or alms are distributed in the church. But these things are profitable to those who whilst they lived deserved that they might avail them. There is a life so good as not to need them: there is another so wicked that after death it can receive no benefit from them. When therefore the sacrifices of the altar or alms are offered for all Christians: for the very good they are thanksgivings: for those not very sinful they are propitiatory. For the very wicked they are only some kind of comfort to the living."—*Enchiridion*, c. cx., and *De Curâ pro Mortuis*.

the church at the altar for her soul:—" I now pour out unto Thee, O God my Lord," he wrote, "another kind of tear for Thy handmaiden, flowing from a troubled spirit; and in consideration of the danger in which is every soul who dies in Adam. For although she was made alive in Christ, and lived so in the days of her flesh, as, by her faith and practice, to bring glory to Thy Name, yet I dare not maintain that from the time she was regenerated by baptism no word escaped her lips contrary to Thy command. And Thou hast told us by Him Who is truth itself that 'whosoever shall say to his brother, Thou fool, shall be in danger of hell fire.' Woe, then, to the most praiseworthy life of man if Thou without mercy shouldest sift and examine it. But because Thou art not extreme to mark what is done amiss, we have hope and confidence to find some place and room for indulgence with Thee. But whoever reckons up his true merits before Thee, what does he further than reckon up Thine own gifts? O that all men would know themselves, and they who glory would glory in the Lord! Therefore, O my Praise and my Life, the God of my heart, setting aside her good actions, for which I joyfully give Thee thanks, now make intercession for my mother's transgressions. Hear me through the medicine of His wounds who hung upon the tree, and now sitteth at Thy right hand to make intercession for us. . . . I ask that the lion and the dragon may not either by violence or subtlety interpose himself: for she would not answer that she was no debtor lest the crafty adversary should convict her, and lay hold of her; but she would reply that her sins were forgiven her by Him to whom no man can return what He gave to us without any obligation. Therefore, let her rest in peace with her husband, and do Thou, O my Lord God, inspire all those Thy servants who read this to remember at Thine altar Thy servant Monica with her husband Patricius."[*]

The faith concerning, and duty to, the departed, here so practically set forth, find a response in other writers of the early ages of the church, which can leave little doubt on the minds of the impartial as to the nature of primitive practices.

St. Ephrem the Syrian, in his last will and testament, earnestly entreats his surviving friends to offer for him, after his decease, the accustomed sacrifices,

---

[*] Aug. Confess., lib. ix. c. xii. vol. i. p. 123; Ibid., c. xiii. vol. i. p. 124. "Ego jam sanato corde ab illo vulnere . . . . . quibus et voce et corde, et litteris servio, ut quotquot hæc legerint, meminerint ad altare Tuum Monicæ famulæ tuæ, cum Patricio quondam ejus conjuge."

prayers, intercessions, and alms; more especially on the thirtieth day after his departure from earth.* St. Athanasius informs Constantius that he had earnestly prayed for the repose of the soul of that emperor's departed brother Constans. Eusebius puts on record the fact that Constantine the Great was most anxious to be interred within the porch of the Church of the Holy Apostles, in order that he might enjoy the communication of the holy prayers, the mystic sacrifice, and the sacred ceremonies therein celebrated. The same writer informs us that after Constantine's death numberless multitudes poured forth prayers to God with sighs and tears for the Emperor's soul, repaying a most grateful duty to their pious ruler. It is recorded of St. Paulinus that, upon his brother's decease, he wrote to his friends, earnestly recommending his soul to their prayers, that he might obtain refreshment and rest in the Lord. And so of other saints and holy men. What had been received from their Lord and master by the apostles, what had been embodied in the most ancient Liturgies was found to be taught likewise by the most renowned Fathers of the church. Certain mysterious doctrines were wisely shrouded from the rude gaze of the unbeliever and the biting

* "Opera Sti. Ephrem." Ed. Romæ, tom. ii. pp. 230-236.

sarcasm of the scoffer; but duties such as that of prayer for the dead in Christ—the duty of putting into actual practice a belief in the communion of saints—were neither forgotten nor obscured, but at the same time gave hope and joy to the bereaved, and comfort and consolation to the anxious souls of those waiting for perpetual light and eternal rest in the land beyond the grave.

CHAPTER VII.

THE PRACTICE OF THE ANGLO-SAXON CHURCH.

WHAT was received and taught as regards the subject under consideration by the ancient Fathers soon spread amongst nations won to the faith, and became as a matter of course generally received by the faithful everywhere. When St. Augustine, the Apostle of England, brought the Gospel hither, it appears certain that both the faith and practice of the Church Universal, as pertaining to the dead in Christ, were at once a part of the sacred deposit of Divine Truth taught by authority and generally accepted by Christians.*

That this was certainly the case with our Anglo-Saxon forefathers is capable of proof.† As has already been shown, what was termed by the Fathers the

---

* Bedæ Hist. Eccl., lib. iv. c. vii., xi., xix., xxii., and xxiii.; Ibid., lib. v. c. xii.; Thorpe's "Homilies of the Anglo-Saxon Church," vol. ii. p. 357; Wilkins's "Concilia," tom. 1, p. 171; Fabyan's "New Chronicles of England" (Ed. Ellis, London, 1811), p. 263.

† Homilia Bedæ apud Thesaur. Aneod. (Ed. Martene), tom. v. p. 326.

"salutary" or "life-giving sacrifice," was duly offered on the departure of any one of the Church's members.* The body,† with a cross of wood, jet, or metal on its breast, was taken into the church, with cross and tapers and chanted psalms, and then placed before the altar, at which the parish priest or monk solemnly remembered the dead person before Almighty God, and in the presence of sorrowing friends.‡ An offering of money under the term of "mortuary" or "soul-shot" was made for the benefit

---

* There are three modes, as has been commonly taught, in which, and by which, the quick may aid the departed. First and chiefly, by the sacrifice of the Eucharist; secondly, by the giving of alms; and, thirdly, by prayer. The first two are efficacious for this object by reason of that charity which binds together the living and the dead: the third by reason of its direction of the intention. 1. The Holy Eucharist in a most special manner belongs to charity, because it is the sacrament of ecclesiastical unity, containing Him in whom the whole church is united together and firmly consolidated, namely—our Blessed Lord. 2. A chief and leading result of the existence of charity is the giving of alms. 3. Prayer, from its very idea and nature, specially directs the intention towards its subject. These three works, therefore, are the chief modes of aid to the dead: but every good work, done from love, profits them.

† "De S. Birino Ep. Dorcest.," apud Surium., tom. vi. p. 688; "Proceedings of the Society of Antiquaries," 2nd series, vol. i. p. 399. Also, on the use of the cross in funerals and sepulture in general, see a treatise by the learned canon, John de Vita, "De Antiquitatibus Benoventanis" (Romæ, 1721), Dissert. xi. p. 291; also the "Origines Christianæ" of Mamachi, lib. 1, cap. iii. n. 6. Both these writers testify to its universality and antiquity.

‡ This may be gathered from a remarkable MS. known as "Leofric's Missal," in the Bodleian Library, press mark, No. 579. Also from a MS. of the eighth century, lettered "Passio Christi," in the British Museum, being No. 2966 of the Harleian MSS., and the "Anglo-Saxon Psalter," Vespasian, A 1, also in the British Museum.

of the church, in return for which the clergy attached thereto charitably continued their intercessions on behalf of the departed for certain stated periods. The relatives at the time of sepulture distributed gifts of food, clothing, and alms to the poor, whose prayers were solicited in return; and these donations were sometimes repeated at each anniversary either of death or burial.* Before the doles were given away they were formally blessed—an impressive ceremony in which the name of the departed was mentioned, with a special petition on his behalf for peace and light. Men of rank and position sometimes on their deathbed enjoined upon their representatives to give freedom to a certain number of serfs, in order that these latter might specially remember the soul of their master, period by period, in the future. Those who in their lifetime had conferred benefits, whether temporal or spiritual, on any particular town, church, or locality, were personally remembered in prayer year by year by those who had been favoured through the bestowal of such.† Under the head of the corpse

---

* Bedæ Hist. Eccl., lib. ii. c. iii. p. 105.

† Leland's "Itinerary," vol. ii p. 40; Ibid., vol. v. p. 58. The following occurs at p. 157 of the "Rituale Ecclesiæ Dunelmensis" (Ed. Stevenson): "Ascendant ad Te Domine, preces nostras [*sic*] intercedentibus omnibus sanctis agminibus angelorum ut animæ famulorum tuorum famularum tuarum quorum et quarum nomina hic sunt conscripta, gaudia

at burial was placed a stone, on which the pillow rested; upon which stone was engraved, both in Runic and Latin characters, a prayer for the person to whose head it was a support. Such stones have been found in recent times, with the pious inscriptions almost perfect.* Over the grave of the departed was placed a cross, with a simple inscription praying for God's mercy upon the dead man's soul.† Kings, nobles, and others gave lands for the endowment of religious houses and churches, on condition of being remembered constantly after their death in the prayers and oblations daily or weekly offered therein.‡ Frequently they enrolled themselves as brethren of a religious order or society, so as to obtain the privilege of reposing after death within the precincts of the church attached, and to be near those whose love and

---

eterna suscipiant, ut quos fecisti adoptionis participes, jubeas hereditatis tuæ esse consortes. Per Jesum." See also "Acts of the Synod of Chalkhythe," Wilkins's "Concilia," tom. i. p. 171.

* "Archæologia," vol. xxvi. p. 480, plate lii.

† "Archæological Journal," vol. iii. p. 73, and pp. 259—261. The Runic inscription remaining upon a curious memorial cross at Lancaster contains the following petition: "Pray for Cynibalde, son of Cuthbert." ("Archæological Journal," vol. iii. p. 72.)

‡ The following is the conclusion of the "Oratio" in the "Agenda Mortuorum" of Leofric's Missal: "Non eum tormentum mortis adtingat, non dolor horrendæ visionis officiat, non pœnalis timor excruciat, non reorum proxima catena constringat, sed concessa sibi delictorum omnium venia optata quietis consequatur gaudia repromissa."—Folio 251.

labour it was daily to remember the dead. As the anniversary came round, the Christian sacrifice was offered again, with dignified solemnity. Once more the poor crowded round the grave to join in the plaintive *Miserere* and *De Profundis*, or respond to the petitions which asked at God's hands mercy, light, and refreshment for the faithful departed. At the formal social gatherings of distinguished families, as well as on the duly-observed solemn anniversaries of religious houses, and likewise with the poor, when the body had been sustained and refreshed by food, the soul was not forgotten in the " Act of Thanksgiving after Meat." Nor were the souls of the faithful dead. They, too, were remembered. Again, at social gatherings, when the loving-cup went round, symbol of good-will and Christian charity, a similar prayer, uttered or breathed in all truthfulness and without affectation, was sent up to God; of the duty of doing which men were reminded by the pious inscription asking their prayers commonly found engraved on the cup's rim.

In truth, amongst our Anglo-Saxon forefathers the Christian doctrine of the Communion of Saints was a reality. They realized, as their deeds indicated, the momentous nature of death, and the practical duties of the living in regard to the departed. This was the case with all, from the highest to the lowest, with all classes and gradations, from the king to the hind. Earnestly desiring the prayers of the living after their own departure, they appear to have been regular and hearty in their petitions for those already called away.* Bede's well-known story of Imma and Tunna, the former a soldier, the latter a priest, sets forth as much. The former, who had been taken captive, tells the nobleman who kept him prisoner— "In my own province I have a brother who is a priest, and I know well that he, thinking me to be dead, constantly offers the holy sacrifice for me.

---

* The following beautiful prayers are from the "Missal of Leofric," in the Bodleian Library:—

"Oremus fratres karissimi Domini misericordiam pro fratribus ac sororibus nostris ab oriente usque ad occidentem, ut et illi orent pro nobis unusquisque in diversis locis per Xpm. Dominum nostrum.

"Oremus etiam pro unitate æcclesiarum, pro infirmis, pro debilibus, pro captivis, pro pœnitentibus, pro laborantibus, pro navigantibus, pro iter agentibus, pro elemosinas facientibus, pro defunctorum spiritibus, et pro his qui non communicant ut det illis Dominus dignam agere pœnitentiam per Xpm. Dnum. nrum.

"Oremus etiam Domini misericordiam pro spiritibus carorum nostrorum pausantium ill. ut eis Dominus placidum refrigerium tribuere dignetur, et in loco quietis ac refrigerii sanctorum suorum intercessione eos transferret per Ihm. Xpm. Dnm.

"Offerimus Tibi Dne. Ihu. Xpe. hanc orationem ab ortu solis usque ad occidentem, a dextera usque ad sinistram, in honorem et gloriam divinitatis Xpi. et humanitatis, in honorem et gloriam patriarcharum, apostolorum ac martyrum, pro omnibus virginibus, fidelibus, pœnitentibus, pro omnibus matrimoniis, pro bonis non valde, pro malis non valde, pro omnibus merentibus orationem et deprecationem nram."

Moreover, were I in the other life, my soul would be assisted because of his intercession." *

So, too, does the same writer's touching account of the death of Hilda, abbess of Whitby. Within the mynchery of Hackness in Yorkshire, some distance away, Begu, one of the religious, asleep in the sisters' dormitory, suddenly heard the well-known sound of the bell by which the community in general was summoned to prayer when any one of them had died, by the ringing of which she was miraculously informed of what had happened. Rising immediately, she repaired to Frigyth—that sister who had been set over the convent in place of an abbess—to announce the death of Hilda. All the members of the house were at once aroused, convinced of the loss they had sustained. They went immediately to the church, where the accustomed psalms and prayers were said. The remainder of the night was spent in similar holy offices. In the morning a messenger from Whitby duly came to announce the death which had occurred, and to console the religious in their loss.†

The decease of bishops, abbots, chiefs of religious houses and guilds, was announced formally; so that all connected with them by office or in other modes

* Bedæ Hist. Eccl., lib. iv. cap. xxii.
† Bedæ Hist. Eccl., lib. iv. cap. xxiii.

might be informed of the same. So likewise was it with kings, princes, and nobles. And this in order that those who knew them, or had been benefited by them in their lifetime, might not fail to remember them in their public and private prayers after death. All this,* enjoined by ecclesiastical authority, appears to have been duly and regularly performed in a true spirit of Christian faith and charity by every class.

We thus see how the principles relating to the departed in Christ, set forth both in the Liturgies and writings of the Fathers, brought hither by St. Augustine of Canterbury, at once took root amongst our Anglo-Saxon forefathers, and were adopted, becoming part and parcel of our common Christianity.†

---

* The following is part of a decree of the Council of Cloveshoo, A.D. 747: "Statuerunt ut deinceps per canonicas orationum horas non solum pro se ecclesiastici sive monasteriales, sed etiam pro regibus ac ducibus totiusque populi Christiani incolumitate, divinam incessanter exorarent clementiam . . . et ut pro viventibus divina precaretur clementia, et pro mortuis piæ placationis celebratio sæpius pro illarum requie animarum, per plurimorum officia sacerdotum Christi agerotur."—*Wilkins's* "Concilia," tom. i. p. 100.

† There is preserved in the Record Room of York Minster a MS. copy of the Holy Gospels, written in a plain bold Anglo-Saxon hand, with remarkable illuminations. At the end are recorded certain bequests of land, two short homilies in Anglo-Saxon, with Latin headings, together with a form for "Bidding the Beads," very similar to that given above. This MS., from internal evidence, appears to have originally belonged to Sherborne Minster.—See also, as regards the general subject, "Historia Ingulphi, in Rex. Angl. Scriptores," Ed. Gale, vol. i. p. 24; "Codex Diplom. Anglo-Sax.," vi. p. 177.

CHAPTER VIII.

THE FAITH AND PRACTICE OF THE MEDIÆVAL CHURCH.

IN the middle ages the faith and principles of the Church Universal of previous periods were reasonably expanded and developed. Some, from a human point of view, overlooking the Church's divine character, may question the wisdom of this policy, but none can deny the fact of its existence and energy. As regards the doctrines received and taught by the ancient Fathers in reference to Prayers for the Departed, though in the main they were precise, consistent, and identical, yet some amongst the early Christian writers are found to have been vaguer in their statements than others, and to have left scope for considerable ambiguity and speculation in the general belief of the faithful. As disputes and discussions arose, the received propositions of a previous age were fully and freely discussed, as well as the respected opinions of individuals; apparent contradictions were reconciled, and fresh light thrown upon that which was vague, misty, and undefined. Crude ideas were carefully examined, classified, and set forth anew; misconceptions and inconsistencies removed. The speculative, as well as Authority, co-operated in this work. Precision took the place of vagueness. The common opinion of the Western Church during the middle ages, fairly and faithfully stated, may be set down as follows:—

There are five receptacles of disembodied souls. First, Paradise for saints since the time of our Blessed Lord; secondly, the *Limbus Patrum*, for the saints before His advent in the flesh; thirdly, Purgatory for those who have not yet satisfied the justice of God, because of their sins during their time of probation below; fourthly, Hell, the abode of Satan and his angels, for the lost; and, fifthly, the *Limbus Infantium* for children dead in original sin.

Now, admitting the position to be possible that a person dies in original sin in conjunction with venial sin only, in which of the five receptacles of disembodied souls, it was asked, would his soul find a place? Such a question was frequently put. And it was answered thus:—(a) Not in Paradise, as wanting grace. (β) Not in the *Limbus Patrum*, for the same reason. (γ) In like manner, not in the *Limbus Infantium*, for in that abode there is no sensible pain, and sensible pain is due because of venial sin. (δ) Not in Purgatory, for in that state there is only temporal pain, while to such an one is due perpetual pain. (ε) Not in Hell, for he lacks actual mortal sin.

St. Thomas Aquinas, on this point, comes to a distinct and definite conclusion as follows, and in so doing appears to have accurately represented the judgment and belief of many of his contemporaries:—

"Admitting the position to be possible, which it is not," he writes, "such an one would be punished in hell, and eternally. For that venial sin is punished temporally, and in purgatory, takes place, because, being alone, such sin co-exists with grace. If it co-existed with mortal sin it would exist apart from grace, and so be punished eternally and in hell. Since, then, he who dies in original sin, in conjunction with venial sin, has venial sin without grace, it is not unmeet that he be punished eternally."*

On other details of this important question, the faith of the mediæval church was as follows:—

All the faithful, joined together by charity, are

* "De Incarnatione," quæst. 461.

members of the one body of Christ, that is, of the church. But one member is helped by another. So likewise one man may be assisted by the merits of another. Although, however, one man may ask for another that the latter may attain to everlasting life, yet it was plainly taught and believed that such could never take place except by the means and because of his own works. For life everlasting is not bestowed upon any one save because of his own just deeds. By the prayers of one man grace is showered down upon another man, by which grace that other merits eternal life. Furthermore, the work which is done for any particular person is effectual for him for whom it is done. Charity, the bond of union amongst members of the church, men believed extended itself not only to the living, but likewise to the departed. For charity is the life of the soul, even as the soul is the life of the body. "And charity," as St. Paul declared, "never faileth."[*] Neither does it forget. So then the dead live in the memories of the living. The intention of the living, therefore, can be directed towards them; and so, in two modes, the prayers of the living avail the departed even as they do the living: first, by reason of the union of

[*] 1 Cor. xiii. 8.

charity, and, secondly, by reason of intention directed towards them. The prayers of the living were not held to avail the dead in such a manner as to change their state from happiness to misery, or the reverse; but only so as to secure a diminution of punishment, or anything of a like kind which does not change the state of the dead. Furthermore, it was maintained that the departed require prayer to be made for them more than do the living: for the dead cannot help themselves as can those alive. Moreover, the condition of the living was regarded as better than that of the dead, for the former can be transferred from a state of mortal sin to a state of grace; whereas with the dead such a change is impossible. As the tree falls, so shall it lie.

Now this is that doctrinal system which in the main was sanctioned, adopted, and current in the middle ages. It sank deep into the public mind, colouring thought and action for many a generation. And, on the whole, it may be truly said to have taught men recollectedness, generosity, and love.

When put into practice it served but to develop those principles of action in regard to the departed which have been set forth in the previous chapter. And these, satisfying the aspirations of believers, grew with the growing years and widely expanded themselves.

In what manner these principles were set forth in act and deed has now to be considered. And first as to the Mass for the departed, called by our ancestors "Soul Mass," or "Mass of Requiem." This rite, where it differed from the ordinary mass, was noble and touching in its language, and eminently impressive; solemn, and full of teaching in its external aspect and ceremonial action. Its leading idea was that through the merits of Christ, and because of His sacrifice, the souls of the faithful dead obtained refreshment, light, and peace. The detailed rites of it were not idly and pointlessly magnificent, but feelingly beautiful and rife with instructive lessons for those who witnessed them. Charity spake in every act and utterance. In this service, to notice certain ritual characteristics, neither the "Gloria in excelsis" nor the "Alleluia" was said. After the "Gradual" *Requiem eternam*, came the Tract *Sicut cervus desiderat ad fontes aquarum*, etc., or *De profundis*. There was no Sequence. The use of the *Dies Iræ* is not found in the Salisbury rite. There was an offertory prayer relating specially to the departed, the response to which was the oft-repeated

Requiem æternam, etc. The *Agnus Dei* twice ended with "Dona eis requiem," the third time with "Dona eis requiem sempiternam." In this mass the use of the Pax was omitted. The celebrant neither received the kiss of peace himself, nor gave it to others. All these customs, more or less, had come down from very ancient times. Theodore, Archbishop of Canterbury, the sixth after St. Augustine, wrote as follows: "Missa pro mortuis in hoc differt a consueta missa, quod sine *Gloria,* et *Alleluia* et *Pacis osculo* cœlebratur."* The chant used throughout was solemn and plaintive, admirably adapted to the service, and remarkable for its simple grandeur. Prior to the Mass of Requiem were sometimes said two others at earlier hours, viz., the Mass of the Holy Trinity and the Mass of Our Lady. Still prior to this, however, over night the choir service for the dead, termed, according to the Salisbury use, "Vigilia Mortuorum," which corresponded with the Roman "Officium Defunctorum," had been recited. The Evensong for the dead was commonly called "Placebo," because such is the first word of the antiphon, or anthem which stands before the first psalm in that

---

* "Liber Pœnitentialis," cap. xlv. in Thorpe's "Ancient Laws," vol. ii. p. 51.

service; and this was always the preliminary part of the funeral solemnity. On the morrow, Mattins for the dead—commonly called "Dirige," or "Dirge," from the first Mattins' anthem—was chanted. Then followed Mass,* and in due course sepulture; hence the whole of this latter part of the service came to be known in ordinary language as "the Dirge." At the Offertory during the chief mass there was solemnly borne up to the altar, with state and solemnity, the "mass-penny"—a technical term for the offerings made on behalf of the deceased. These were sometimes of great value and richness.

Around the hearse,† or the bier ‡ if the former was not used, stood lighted tapers of unbleached wax. Smaller tapers were borne around an uplifted crucifix in the procession to the grave, and sometimes torches. Over the coffin, during the funeral ceremonies, was placed a pall, or hearse-cloth of black or purple velvet, charged with a cross. Sometimes hearses were of

---

* Vide "Manuale juxta usum Eccl. Sarisburiensis" (inter Annotationes), p. 278. Duaci, 1610. This book was twice printed at Douay, early in the seventeenth century, once in duodecimo and once in quarto. The first edition is rare; the latter may frequently be found in old Roman Catholic libraries.

† On the title-page of "The Crafte to lyve and to dye well," printed by Wynken De Worde, A.D. 1505, is a woodcut representing a burial hearse drawn by a horse.

‡ Wilkins's "Concilia," Concilia Examen., tom. ii. p. 139; Ibid., i. 671—714.

extraordinary magnificence, and very large sums were spent on funeral rites.* Occasionally the hearse was permanently erected over the tomb of the person departed, as in the case of the well-known Beauchamp monument at Warwick, and of the tomb of the Marmions, at Tanfield Church, near Ripon. These were hung with a hearse-cloth, charged with armorial bearings, and powdered with such scrolls as "Sancta Trinitas unus Deus miserere nobis," "Jesu, mercy," "Mary, help." Lamps or tapers were either kept constantly burning, or were lit on Sundays, certain holidays, and solemn anniversaries, from the commencement of the parish mass until the close of evensong. The actual rites of sepulture were almost similar to those set forth in the last chapter. After the mass, the priest, divesting himself of his chasuble,† went to the head of the body or bier, attended by his servers or assistants, and began the burial service. The corpse was censed and sprinkled with holy water, after which, while the clerks sang the psalm *In exitu Israel*, the bearers carried it forth

---

* See Nichol's edition of "Machyn's Diary," *in loco*, more especially pp. 44, 101, 106, 109, 110, 119, 167, 171; also "Vetusta Monumenta," vol. iv.; Blomfield's "Norfolk," vol. vi. p. 484; and Leland's "Collectanea," vol. v. p. 318.

† According to the York rite, the officiant was vested in a cope.

to the place of sepulture. While the grave was being dug, the psalm *Confitemini Domino* was chanted, then a collect, after which the priest blessed the grave, sprinkling it with holy water, and then the corpse was lowered into it, during which the psalm *Quemadmodum* was sung. Then followed a collect, asking on the dead person's behalf God's forgiveness for past sins, after which the officiant placed upon the breast of the corpse a scroll on which was written the absolution,* which he himself pronounced. Other psalms and prayers, in appointed order, were said. Earth was strewn upon the corpse in the form of a cross. Then followed prayers for the soul of the departed, with other psalms and collects, when the procession returned to the church chanting the seven penitential psalms. Every psalm, antiphon, lesson, versicle, and response told but one story—a perfect belief of the faithful in the distinctive doctrines of the Christian religion, and the presence of a charity that might be both envied and imitated. Doles were given to the poor in abundance, in order that they might gratefully pray for the deceased.

For three days after the funeral it was frequently the custom to repeat certain religious rites, including

---

* Dugdale's "History of St. Paul's Cathedral," p. 32.

"Placebo," "Dirige," and the Christian sacrifice. This was commonly the case upon the third day after the death or funeral, upon the seventh,* and upon the thirtieth, on each of which occasions doles were again distributed. The observances on the thirtieth day after the death were described by the term "Month's mind," those twelve months afterwards by the term "Year's mind," or "Obit." Notice of this latter was given some time previously by an inferior church officer or the parish bellman, in order that all who remembered, loved, or respected the departed

---

* In some instances the following rule was followed:—

"First, on the Sonday cause a masse to be song or said in the worship of the Trinitie. Let also iii candles burn before the Sacrament at the masse tyme. Fede also iii pore men, or gyve three almosses to the nedye.

"Secondly, on the Monday, cause a masse to be song or said in the worship of all Angels. Light also ix candles in the honoure of the ix Orders of Aungells. Fede ix pore men or give ix almosses.

"Thirdly, on the Tuesday, cause a masse to be song or said in the honor of Saint Spirite, and lighten vii candles in the worship of the vii gyftes which he gyveth. Fede also vii pore men or give vii almosses.

"Fourthlye, on the Wednisday cause a masse to be song or said in the worship of St. Jhon Baptiste, and of all the patriarches. Light foure candles and feede foure poore men, or geve four almosses.

"Fifthlye, on the Thursdaye cause a masse to be songe or said of St. Peter and of the xii apostles. Lighten xii candles and fede xii pore men, or geve xii almosses.

"Sixthly, on the Fryday cause a masse to be song or sayd in the worship of S. Crosse. Lighten v candles. Fede v poore men, or give v almosses.

"Seventhly, and finally, on the Saturday cause a masse to be song or sayde in the honor of our lady and all virgines. Lighten v candles. Fede v pore men or geve v almosses. Iesu mercy. Ladye helpe."—*Becon's* "Reliques of Rome," p. 206. A.D. 1563.

might attend. On the evening prior to the day of commemoration, and again at the dawn of the day itself, the church bells tolled a knell,* the grave was covered with a pall, and if within the walls of the church, the hearse was once more erected, with pall and pennon, tapers and armorial bearings. The kinsfolk of the deceased, the clergy of the parish, the religious of an adjoining monastery, and the poor attended these obits in numbers. After the mass, a dole of money,† raiment, and food were solemnly distributed to the poor, and a banquet commonly given to those friends and relations who had attended the ceremonies. Sometimes, amongst the rich and noble, an endowment was left for the support of one or more priests who should daily offer the holy sacrifice in a particular chapel, either already erected or to be built in due course over the tomb of the person departed; and to celebrate for ever the anniversaries of his death. This was known as a perpetual chantry. Others were endowed for a limited period, for two, ten, twenty, or fifty years after a person's decease.‡ To the perpetual chantries were frequently attached other and independent endowments for the

---

* Blomfield's "History of Norfolk," vol. viii. p. 536.

† Dugdale's "History of Warwickshire," vol. ii. p. 959; "Valor Ecclesiasticus," vol. i. p. 63.

‡ Vide MS. "Cotton. Claudius,"

support and clothing of a certain number of poor men and women, whose chief occupation and duty it was to attend divine service twice daily, and to pray constantly for the repose of their benefactor's soul.* They were called "beadsmen" or "beadswomen,"† because it was sometimes enjoined that they were to recite every day the Psalter of the Blessed Virgin or Rosary, and to take a formal part in the annual Year's mind.

Here, before this part of the subject is brought to a close, it should be noted that what riches enabled the wealthy to obtain for themselves and their relations, the church of our fathers anxiously and lovingly provided for the poorest and the most friendless‡ like-

---

A. viii. fol. 44, 45; Herbert's "Livery Companies," vol. ii. p. 605; "Wills of the Northern Counties," pp. 20, 47, 50, 52, 105, 111, 112; Dugdale's "History of St. Paul's Cathedral," pp. 19, 21, 335; "Antiquities of Durham," p. 21; Lupton's "History of Thame," p. 78, with regard to the Quartermayne Chantry.

* "Testamenta Vetusta" (Nicolas), vol. i. p. 428; Ibid., vol. ii. 508—610, 611; Stow's "History of London," vol. iii. p. 4; Swinden's "History of Great Yarmouth," p. 823.

† It may here be noted that so thoroughly was the idea ingrained into the mind of our pre-Reformation forefathers that it was a duty to pray for the departed, that when any inferior asked a favour of a superior, he very frequently signed himself, "Your poor beadsman," indicating that both during life and after death he would remember him in his prayers.

‡ The following, much older in substance than the date of the book from which it is taken, entitled, "A Praier to God for them that be departed, having none to praie for them," illustrates this point abundantly:—

"Have mercie, we beseche thee, Lord God, through the precious

wise. Anciently, as is commonly allowed, the bonds that bound together rich and poor were many, and strong and efficient. The marked and dangerous divisions between class and class which now exist were comparatively unknown. Neither rich nor poor were then so isolated as now. Whenever a mass was said for any particular person, therefore, whether noble or prelate, the celebrant prayed always for all the faithful. This was specially enjoined in the majestic rite of St. Osmund.* Every Sunday and high festival, on the return of All Souls' Day, when individual anniversaries came round, the faithful departed were borne in mind both generally and specially. The Church in her simplest manuals for the poor and for children taught that no one should ever pass through a churchyard without remembering the souls of those whose bodies had found a resting-place there, and beseeching for them Almighty God's infinite mercy and pity. The inscriptions on tombs

passion of thy only begotten sonne, Our Lorde Iesue Christa, have mercie on those soules that have no intercessors to thee to have them in remembrance. Delivor them from the torments of their paines, and bring them unto the companie of the celestial citizons, through thine exceedinge great mercies."—*The Primer in Latine and Englysh, after Salisburie Use.* Caley, 1556.

* "Portiforium seu Breviarium ad inignis Sarisburiensis Ecclesie usum," pars hyemalis (Parisiis, 1529), folio 6. "Hore Beatissime Virginis Marie ad legitimum Sarisburiensis Ecclesie ritum" (Parisiis, 1526), fol. cxliv.

and monuments likewise expressed this conviction, calling on the living to do their duty, in every form and shape.* In such legends the Blessed Trinity was asked to succour and defend the dead. Each Person of the same was implored to have mercy on those whose time of probation had for ever passed away. The saints, more especially the Blessed Mother of God, were invoked for their prayers. There were no vulgar and pompous inscriptions, as radically false in their laudatory statements as they are out of place in the house of God, such as now disfigure almost every cathedral and parish church of this land, but simple and humble prayers for mercy from the Almighty and most pitiful Creator, and for charity and succour from those left behind.

The faith on this subject which had been brought hither by St. Augustine certainly took root downward and bore fruit upward for many long centuries. "O Lord, be mindful of Thy servants who have gone before us with the sign of faith, and now rest in the sleep of peace," was the appointed daily utterance of the pastors of our beloved church, as they stood at God's earthly altar. And they fittingly closed

* See the introductory part to Appendix No. XI.

their solemn devotions day by day, and week by week, as did the faithful likewise, with the unbroken petition of undying charity—" May the souls of the faithful, through the mercy of God, rest in peace. Amen."

CHAPTER IX.

THE DOCTRINE OF PURGATORY.

HISTORY is abundantly clear that various conceptions of a purgatory or place of future cleansing were current amongst Christian writers and fathers of the early church. Some ideas were definite, others were vague. Occasionally the same writer broached different conceptions of the doctrine at various periods. Under what circumstances these conceptions obtained form, currency, and acceptance; whether certain of them had been taught by the Apostle St. Paul, and received as part of the faith from the earliest times of Christianity; how far they were accepted generally, or became the subject of dispute—are details on which much may be said on several sides.* Here, however,

---

* Vide "Canons and Decrees of the Council of Trent," sess. xxv.; "Creed of Pope Pius IV."; Bossuet's "Exposition," etc.; Dr. Deacon, the Nonjuror, "On Purgatory," *in loco*; "The Catechism of Montpellier," vol. ii. p. 342; "Tractatus De Purgat.," Mediolani, 1758; Fonta-

facts rather than speculation as to the rise and influence of different modes of thought will be dealt with.

The statement of St. Paul, on which the primitive opinions regarding purgatory,* or a mode or state of future cleansing by fire, appear to have been founded, is as follows: "For other foundation can no man lay than that is laid, which is Jesus Christ. Now if any man build upon this foundation gold, silver, precious stones, wood, hay, stubble; every man's work shall be made manifest: for the day shall declare it, because it shall be revealed by fire; and the fire shall try every man's work of what sort it is. If any man's

---

nini, "De Vindiciis Veterum Codicum," *in loco;* Gavantus "Comment. in Missal.," par. iv. p. 275; Bellarminus, "De Purgatorio," lib. i. c. 1; Archbishop Usher's "Treatise on Purgatory," *in loco;* Klee's "Dogmatik," vol. ii. pp. 428—435; "All for Jesus," by Very Rev. Father Faber, D.D.

* "It is a well-known historical fact," writes the Bishop of Brechin, in the ablest comment on the Thirty-nine Articles which the English Church possesses, "that it was the shameless traffic in indulgences which burst the barrier which had long pent up the dissatisfaction which prevailed on account of the scandals and corruptions in the church. The reforming councils had no power to stem the increasing corruption; and the expensive tastes of the Roman Curia demanding more and more money, *a doctrine which had its root in primitive antiquity,* was preached in a way to destroy all Christian morality. To the Dominican and Franciscan Orders, now fallen from their first purity, much of the blame is due, though it is fair to state that they were not the only guilty persons."—*An Explanation of the Thirty-nine Articles,* by A. P. Forbes, D.C.L., Bishop of Brechin, vol. ii. p. 352. London, 1868.

work abide which he hath built thereupon, he shall receive a reward. If any man's work shall be burned, he shall suffer loss: but he himself shall be saved; yet so as by fire." *

Now on this remarkable passage were founded several conceptions of purgatory, of which the following may be instanced as those accepted by great authorities :—

1. That the final conflagration of the world, when Christ comes to judge both the quick and the dead, will be an ordeal through which all men will pass, even the blessed Virgin Mary herself; but that she will pass it unscathed. That others will suffer loss under the ordeal which some writers believed will be prolonged, but that none will fail during the fiery trial who are built upon the right foundation.

2. That for all mankind, those sins which have not been duly and adequately punished in this life, there will be a purgatorial punishment by fire at, or immediately preparatory to, the last great day.

3. A third doctrine was maintained by the Greeks at the Council of Florence, who held that there is a cleansing after death, but it is a *pœna damni*, not a *pœna sensûs*—not a positive sensible infliction, still

* 1 Cor. iii. 11—15.

less a purgatorial fire,* but chiefly the withdrawal and absence of the presence of God.†

4. Fourthly, it has been maintained—and here it should be noted that this doctrinal aspect of the subject is not contrarient to the last—that the work of cleansing the soul between the day of death and the day of the general judgment, is a cleansing by a pro-

---

* Klee, a modern and very distinguished German Roman Catholic writer on dogma, puts on record the following opinion: "Nothing has been decided, as a matter of doctrine, about any or even about the place of purification after death. So likewise nothing as to the manner. Concerning the latter, the Fathers have expressed themselves only problematically and hypothetically, and Doctors and believers *have only assumed a fire as matter of opinion*, in which only Ignorance or Malice, so as to make room for Sarcasm, can find occasion to think of our ordinary fire. Purification, as the act of sloughing-off the imperfection ingrown, as it were, with the soul; her straining to be free from all earthliness upon her; a longing for the sight of God, from which the imperfections still clinging to her render her unworthy; a struggle towards the full overcoming of the results of the evil within her, and towards the full life of good desired—this upstirring of her deepest and inmost sense implies fire, that is, fiery suffering sufficient."—*Klee's* "Dogmatik," vol. ii. pp. 429, 430.

† This opinion appears to be still held by the Orientals. The well-known Russian Catechism "On the Duty of Parish Priests," which is an universal text-book in that empire, is entirely silent regarding purgatory, but under its sixteenth section, "Concerning Prayer," contains the following: "The injunctions and examples hitherto set forth regard prayers and supplications for the living, but the priest, as steward of the mysteries of God, ought beside this to pray likewise for the departed, in the hope and faith of the resurrection of those who sleep. Of this we have certain assurance, both from Scripture, and also from Christ's Holy Church in apostolical and primitive times." In many parts of the Eastern Church it has been customary to offer the holy sacrifice on behalf of the faithful departed every Saturday.

gressive sanctification, and there is no pain in the process.

These being the four leading current opinions, it will now be well to refer to certain specific statements of distinguished early Christians.

St. Clement of Alexandria thus writes: "We hold that fire purifies not flesh but sinful souls; speaking not of that all-devouring and common fire, but of that discriminating fire which penetrates the soul passing through the fire."*

Origen declares, less generally, and with a distinct reference to St. Paul's statement:—"Sin in its nature is like to that matter which fire consumes, and which the apostle declares to be built up by sinners, who upon the foundation of Christ build wood, hay, and stubble, which words plainly show that there are some sins so light as to be compared to stubble, in which when fire is placed it remaineth not long; that there are others like hay, which the fire easily consumes, but more easily than it does stubble; and others resemble wood, in which, according to the degree of sinfulness, the fire finds an abundant substance on which to feed. Thus each crime in pro-

---

* St. Clem. Alex. Strom., vii. 6, p. 851.

portion to its nature experiences a just degree of punishment."*

Again: "If, after the forgiveness of sins and the dispensation of the washing of regeneration, we sin, as most of us do, who are not, like the apostles, perfected; and after, or at the time of this sinning, do such things as befit us, what then awaits us? If, after the foundation, Christ Jesus, thou hast gold, much or little, precious stone, but also wood, hay, stubble, what wouldest thou shouldest happen to thyself after thy departure? Would you enter into the holies with thy wood, hay, and stubble, to defile the kingdom of God? Or again, abide in the fire for the hay, wood, and stubble, and receive nothing for the gold, silver, and precious stone? This were neither equitable. What then follows? To receive first for the wood? Clearly that the fire consumeth the wood, hay, stubble. For God, a consuming fire, consumed not His own image and likeness, but the wood, hay, and stubble superbuilded. It is manifest that in the first place the fire destroyeth the wood of our transgressions, and then returns to us the reward of our good works."†

* Homil. xiv. in Levit., tom. ii. p. 259.
† Homil. xvi. in Jerem., tom iii. pp. 211, 232.

Furthermore: "All must be proved to us as by fire, even as many as desire to return to Paradise, for it is not put on record without a purpose that when Adam and Eve were expelled therefrom, God placed at the gates a fiery sword which turned each way. All must pass through the flame, whether he be St. John the Evangelist, whom the Lord so loved as to declare of him to Peter, 'If I will that he tarry, what is that to thee? follow thou Me.' Some have doubted of his death; of his passage through the fire we cannot doubt, for he is in paradise not departed from Christ. . . . . He who possesseth here the fire of love will have no reason to fear the fiery sword there. But he shall be tried as silver: I as lead. I shall burn until the lead melteth away. Alas for me if in me no silver be found! I shall be cast down into the lowest pit, and consume away entirely as the stubble. Should any gold or silver be found in me, not for my works, but through the mercy and grace of Christ, by the ministry of the priesthood, I shall declare, peradventure, 'They that hope in Thee shall not be ashamed.' The fiery sword, therefore, shall destroy iniquity, which is placed in the leaden scale."*

St. Hilary, in the following passage, plainly sup-

---

* Sermon xx. in Psalm cxviii., tom. i. p. 1225.

ports the idea set forth in the first of the four conceptions of purgatory already noticed:—

"Since we are to give an account for every idle word, shall we desire the judgment day, in which we must pass the ordeal of that unspent fire, and those heavy penalties for expiating the soul from its sins? The sword will pass through the soul of Blessed Mary, that the thoughts of many hearts may be revealed. If that virgin who could contain God shall come into the severity of the judgment, who shall dare desire to be judged of God?"*

St. Gregory Nazianzen, likewise following St. Paul's statement, declares of those who rejected the penitent: "Let these, if they will, go my way and Christ's; if not, their own. Perchance then they may be baptized with the last baptism, the baptism of fire, the more painful and longer, which devours what is coarse, like hay, and consumes the lightness of all sin."

Both St. Ephrem the Syrian and St. Jerome clearly had before their minds St. Paul's statement, when they commented as follows:—

St. Ephrem maintains that "both the just and the unjust shall pass through the fire which is to try them, and they shall be proved by it. The righteous

* In Psalm cxviii.

pass, and the flame is still. But it burneth the wicked, and snatcheth him away."*

And St. Jerome: "If he whose work was burned and perished shall in truth lose the reward of his labour, but himself be saved, yet not without the trial of fire, then he whose work abides, which he built upon the foundation, will be saved without the trial of fire, and so there will be some difference between the salvation of each."†

St. Augustine hands down the same traditional teaching, pointing out the distinction between the fire of temporary punishment and the fire of hell: "Cleanse me, O Lord, in this life, so that I may not require to pass through that purification designed for those who shall be saved yet so as by fire. And why, but, as the apostle declared, they have built upon the foundation wood, hay, and stubble? If they had built gold and silver and precious stones, they would be safe from both fires, not only from that in which the wicked shall be punished for ever, but likewise from that fire which shall purify those who shall be saved as by fire."

---

* "Opera Sti. Ephremi," vol. vi. p. 298.

† St. Jerom. adv. Jovin. Opera, tom. ii. p. 360.

‡ Enarrat. in Psalm xxxvii., Opera, tom. iv. p. 295. Vide also Serm. xxxii., Opera, tom. x. p. 138; and De Octo Dulcit., quæs. tom iv., p. 250.

In his later works he appears to differ in his explanation of the passage in question. For example, in his treatise "On Faith and Works," which the Benedictine editors of his works place about the year of our Lord 413, he does not follow his previous interpretation.* So likewise in his latest treatise, "On the City of God," he writes from a different point of view: "After the day of this body until the arrival of that last day of condemnation and reward after the resurrection of the bodies, should it be said that in this interval the spirits of the departed endure such a fire as they do not feel who had not habits and likings in the life of this body, which require their wood, hay, and stubble to be burned up: but those feel who have carried with them the like worldly tabernacles, whether there only, or here and there, or not there because here, though they experience the fire of a transitory tribulation, rescuing venial offences from damnation by consuming them, I do not condemn because perchance true." †

St. Paulinus of Nola continues the catena of authorities: "*Our God is a consuming fire.* The Lord grant unto me here that both in me and for me

---

* August. De Fide et Oper., c. xv.; Opera, vol. iv. pp. 28, 29.
† De Civitate Dei, xxi. 26.

He be a consuming fire. May my heart burn for me with this fire to life everlasting, lest my soul should burn with it to eternal punishment. For in this fire shall the day of the Lord be revealed, and *the fire shall try every man's work, of what sort it is.* If we dwell in the City of God by those works whereby we become fit for the citizenship of the saints, our work shall not be burned; and when we pass through the ordeal, that sagacious fire will enclose us with no severe heat of punishment; but as if we were commended to its care it will play around us with a kind caress, so that we may in truth declare, *We have gone through fire and water, and Thou hast brought us into a place of rest."*

St. Cyprian appears very plainly to have held the existence of a place of purgation, and to have used arguments founded on the same, both in his doctrinal and practical teaching.† He expresses his belief in the fact that sinners will have to undergo punishment

---

* Epistolæ xxviii. (ad Sever.), vol. i. p. 176. Paris. 1685.

† St. Jerome, St. Chrysologus, St. Paulinus, and St. Gregory of Nyssa, agree, more or less, with St. Cyprian, as to his general opinion, but differ in details. The first-mentioned refers to a prison, in which the very smallest sins will have to be atoned for; the last-mentioned, St. Gregory of Nyssa, appears to dwell rather on the work of the general than on the particular judgment, as determining the doom of each individual soul, which he declares must suffer sharp punishment before entering into joy.

in the world to come, and as by fire, contrasting such suffering hereafter with the pangs of the martyrs on earth whose sorrows and pains have, as he maintains, sufficed to purge away the stain of their sins. For those whose sins in their time of probation have not been duly atoned and suffered for, he holds "there is a prison-house, and none shall go forth from it until the uttermost farthing has been paid."* Elsewhere the same father speaks of waiting until the day of judgment in a state of suspense; and in another place of a sharp and severe punishment to be endured at or immediately before that great day.

The above are some few out of many passages in the Fathers in which Purgatory is mentioned or considered. They will be seen, when compared with later official statements of the Western Church, to be less definite, but not at all inconsistent with the generally-received and carefully-defined faith of Latin Christians.

What this amounted to in the floating opinion and common belief of people during the middle ages † may be summed up in the following propositions :—

---

* Epist. lv. ad Anton.'
† With regard to certain details of the faith of Roman Catholics concerning Purgatory, they have been notoriously founded upon special revelations to the saints and their visions. These, taken with conciliar decisions and universally-received traditions,

THE DOCTRINE OF PURGATORY.

1. It is alien to the faith of Catholics to deny that there is a Purgatory, for the cleansing and purifying

of course, are of due value and importance. But great authorities have ever urged such to be considered and received with circumspection and care. The cautious statements of the Tridentine Fathers are a sufficient evidence of this. The following remarkable statement from the "History of the Venerable Bede"—to take one well-known specimen—was very popular during the middle ages in England, and did much to give definiteness to the ordinary conception of Purgatory. Bellarmine, in his book, "De Gemitu Columbæ," quotes it at length, in conjunction with others of a similar character, but even more remarkable, and declares his firm belief that it has pleased God sometimes to raise his servants from the dead, and to send them to announce to the living what they have really beheld. The narrative is thus recorded: "A pious father of a family in Northumberland died after a long illness in the early part of a certain night; but, to the great terror of those who watched by his corpse, came to life again at the dawn of the following day. All but his faithful and affectionate wife fled at the sight of him, and to her he communicated, in the most soothing terms, the peculiar circumstances of his case—that he had indeed been dead, but was permitted to live again upon earth, though by no means in the same manner as before. In short he sold all his property, divided the produce equally between his wife, his children, and the poor, and then retired to the monastery of Melrose. He there lived in such a state of unexampled mortification, as made it quite evident that he had seen sights, whatever were their nature, which no one else had been permitted to behold. He declared that one whose aspect was as of light, and his garment glistering, conducted him to a valley of great depth and width, but of immeasurable length, one side of which was dreadful beyond expression because of its burning heat, the other as horrible and unendurable for its no less intolerable cold. Both were filled with the souls of men which seemed to be tossed, as by the fury of a tempest, from one side to the other; for being quite unable to endure the heat on the right hand, the miserable wretches kept throwing themselves to the opposite side into the equal torment of cold, and thence back again into the raging flames. He thought reasonably enough that this must have been hell, but his guide answered to his thought that it was not so. This valley, declared the guide, is the place of torment for the souls of those who, delaying to confess and expiate their sins, have at length in the article of death had recourse to penance, and so have died. These, at the day of judgment, will all be

of the souls of the faithful who depart hence in a state of grace.

2. Holy Scripture has nowhere expressly determined anything as to the locality of Purgatory. However, the probable opinion is that the place is twofold: one in close proximity to where the lost are punished, in which, in ordinary cases, the just are purged, and with the same fire as that by which the wicked suffer; another by dispensation in divers places, some here and some there, and not according to the ordinary rule.

3. In Purgatory there is a twofold pain *—one of

admitted into the kingdom of heaven, by reason of their confession and penance, late as they were. But, in the meanwhile, many of them may be assisted and liberated before that day by the prayers, alms, and fastings of those living, particularly by the holy sacrifice of the mass."

This vision, or subjects founded upon it, was frequently depicted on the walls of our old churches. There is scarcely a county in England— thanks to the efficient labours of the various local Architectural and Archæological Societies, by way of preservation of such records—in which ancient memorials of the religion and piety of our Catholic forefathers do not exist.

* "It is true," we read in a recently published book, issued by high Roman Catholic authority in England, "that the overflowing love of God bestows upon the souls in purgatory a happiness beyond expression great: but then this happiness does not in the least degree diminish the pain, rather the pain is constituted by this love finding itself impeded: the more perfect the love of which God makes the soul capable, the greater the pain. In this manner the souls in purgatory at the same time experience the greatest happiness and the most excessive pain, and one does not prevent the other."—*Treatise on Purgatory*, by St. Catherine of Genoa, edited by Archbishop Manning, chapter xiv. A similar idea is expressed in the following extract from the Oxford Prize Poem of 1854:—

loss, inasmuch as the Divine Vision is delayed; and one of sense, inasmuch as the souls are punished with corporeal fire.

4. Venial sin, that is, all sin that can co-exist with grace in the soul, is expiated by the pains of Purgatory, not simply as to its punishment, but also as to its guilt.

5. The purgatorial fire frees from the liability to that punishment under which sin lays the sinner. A person is loosed from a debt who pays it.

6. One venial sin receives, as it requires, a longer purgation and punishment than another, as being a greater drawing to the creature than that other. This difference in the value and punishment of venial sins has been set forth by St. Paul in his threefold distinction of (α) wood, (β) hay, and (γ) stubble. Of these the wood remains longest in the fire before it is consumed, the others being burnt more quickly.

"Then slumbering souls, methought,
   in weird repose,
Within the flowery groves of Paradise,
Hearing the ripples of the Stream of Life,
And distant harpings round the Eternal Throne,
Seeing bright gleams that flashed
   through golden bars,
Outcried in tones of *sweetest agony*—
'Lord, good and merciful, how long? how long?'"
—*Martyrs of Vienne and Lyons.* third edition (London, 1866), p. 16.

7. Severity of punishment in Purgatory corresponds to the greatness of the sin; length of purification corresponds to the hold which the sin has upon the subject of it.

So much for the general faith of the Western Churches during the middle ages.

The present doctrine of the Greek Church regarding the departed and their state appears to be in perfect consonance with that which the ancient Greek fathers taught, and, in many important particulars, not essentially diverse from that received in the West. It is set forth in their ordinary manuals of prayer, in catechisms and guides for the priesthood, and is embodied in the current practices, all more or less similar, of the Oriental communions. The following extract is taken from the *Synodus Bethlehemitica*, published in Paris in the latter part of the seventeenth century. It forms chapter xviii. of the authorized and most important Oriental Confession of Faith of the last three hundred years:—

"We believe that the souls of the deceased are either in rest or in torment, because immediately they have left their bodies they are borne to the place of joy or of sorrow and lamentation; although they do not yet receive the completion of their happiness or misery. At the general resurrection, however, when the soul shall again be united to its own body, in which it had behaved itself well or ill, then every one shall receive the completion of happiness or misery. But such as have not despaired on account of their deadly sins with which they have defiled themselves, and have begun their repentance for them in this life, but have not here brought forth works meet for repentance, that is to say, poured out tears of sorrow for sin, watched and prayed upon their knees, afflicted themselves, relieved the poor, showed forth their love to God and to their neighbour by their works, which the Catholic Church from the beginning has rightly called satisfaction; these and such souls as these, we believe, are carried to Hades, and there sustain the just punishment due to their sins, but know that by the goodness of God they shall be delivered from them by the prayers of the priests and the alms of each of their relations; and to this nothing contributes more than the unbloody sacrifice, which each person particularly offers for his relations, and which the Catholic Church daily offers for all. But we know not the time of this deliverance, only we know and believe that they shall be freed from their pains before the general resurrection and universal judgment, but when that shall be we know not."

A statement of considerable authority, somewhat later in date, drawn up by Chrysanthus, Patriarch of Jerusalem, A.D. 1718, in conjunction with Jeremiah, Patriarch of Constantinople, and Samuel, Patriarch of Alexandria, contains a more distinct set of negations than the decree of the Synod of Bethlehem. It stands thus:—

"As for the purgatorial fire, invented by the Papists to command the purse of the ignorant, we will by no means hear of it. For it is a fiction and a doting fable, invented for lucre and to deceive the simple; and in a word has no existence but in the imagination. There is no appearance nor mention of it in the Sacred Scriptures or Holy Fathers, whatsoever the authors or abettors of it may clamour to the contrary. But we say that the benefactions and holy sacrifices, the alms and prayers of the church and her priests for the dead, are the things that greatly profit them, and not the purgatorial fire, which does not by any means anywhere exist. For these relieve the pains which the souls endure in ᾅδης, as is plain from the centurion whose son our Lord healed at the centurion's petition, and from the paralytic whom He recovered by a double cure for the faith of those that brought him to Him, and might be proved by a thousand other instances as clear as the sun."—*Answer to the Proposals of the Nonjurors*, by Chrysanthus, Patriarch of Jerusalem, April 12, 1718.

But to return to the action and utterances of the Western Church. What was done and decreed regarding Purgatory at the Council of Trent now demands consideration. In the ninth and last session under Pope Pius IV., which began on the 3rd and ended on the 4th day of December, 1563,* there passed a "Decree touching Purgatory," remarkable for its extreme moderation.

It stands as follows: "Whereas the Catholic Church, instructed by the Holy Spirit, has from the sacred writings and ancient traditions of the Fathers, taught in sacred councils, and very recently in this

---

* It should here be especially noted that the Forty-two Articles of Cranmer were set forth A.D. 1553. They do not appear ever to have received the sanction of Convocation, nor were they largely signed by the clergy. Archbishop Parker revised them in 1562, and, thus revised, in their Latin form, they were subscribed by both Houses of Convocation in that year. They were printed in Latin and English in the spring of the year following—some time prior to the passing of the Tridentine Decree quoted above. It is absolutely certain, therefore, that the statements in Article xxii. of the Thirty-nine Articles could not have been directed against that decree, but only against popular and erroneous notions of Purgatory then current in England.

œcumenical synod, that there is a Purgatory, and that the souls there detained are relieved by the suffrages of the faithful, but chiefly by the acceptable sacrifice of the altar; the holy synod enjoins on bishops that they diligently strive that the sound doctrine concerning Purgatory, delivered by the Holy Fathers and Sacred Councils be believed, held, taught, and everywhere proclaimed by the faithful in Christ. But let the more difficult and subtle questions, and those which tend not to edification, and from which for the most part there is no increase of piety, be excluded from popular discourses before the uneducated multitude. In like manner such things as are uncertain,* or which labour under an appearance of error, let

---

* Some modern teaching amongst Roman Catholics, more especially certain opinions put forth in England, are judged both by authority and the learned, to be out of harmony with the wise suggestion of the text above. Private explanations, additions, and hypotheses with regard to Purgatory, set forth as a portion of the deposit of faith, are a stumbling-block to many on the Roman Catholic side of the wall of separation, and become a hindrance to reunion. This has been well pointed out by the late Dr. Lingard, Mr. Edward Price, of the Sardinian Chapel, Lincoln's Inn Fields, and by others. The following hymn from the pen of the late Rev. F. W. Faber, D.D., Superior of the London Oratory, contains several propositions and statements, some of which are not of faith, and yet have been put forth as if they were, without either caution or explanation:—

I.

"O turn to Jesus, Mother! turn,
 And call Him by His tenderest names;
Pray for the holy souls that burn
 This hour amid the cleansing flames. ["Ah!

them not allow either to be made public or discussed. But those things which tend to a certain kind of

II.

"Ah! they have fought a gallant fight;
　In death's cold arms they persevered;
And after life's uncheering night
　The harbour of their rest is neared.

III.

"In pains beyond all earthly pains,
　Favourites of Jesus! there they lie,
Letting the fire wear out their stains,
　And worshipping God's purity.

IV.

"Spouses of Christ they are, for He
　Was wedded to them by His blood;
The faithful cross their trysting-tree,
　Their marriage-bed its hallowed wood.

V.

"They are the children of thy tears
　Then hasten, Mother! to their aid;
In pity think each hour appears
　An age while glory is delayed.

VI.

"See, how they bound amid their fires,
　While pain and love their spirits fill;
Then with self-crucified desires
　Utter sweet murmurs, and lie still.

VII.

"Ah me! the love of Jesus yearns
　O'er that abyss of sacred pain,
And as He looks His bosom burns
　With Calvary's dear thirst again.

VIII.

"O Mary! let thy Son no more
　His lingering spouses thus expect;
God's children to their God restore,
　And to the Spirit His elect.

["Pray

curiosity or superstition, or which savour of filthy lucre, let them prohibit as scandals and stumbling-blocks of the faithful. And let the bishops take care that the suffrages of the faithful who are living, to wit, the sacrifices of masses, prayers, almsgivings, and other works of piety which have been wont to be

IX.

"Pray, then, as thou hast ever prayed;
Angels and souls, all look to thee:
God waits thy prayers, for He hath made
Those prayers His law of charity.

X.

"O turn to Jesus, Mother! turn,
And call Him by His tenderest names;
Pray for the holy souls that burn
This hour amid the cleansing flames."

"The writer here," remarks an acute and learned Anglican critic, the late Dr. Neale, "in a book intended for what he considers a missionary country, and where therefore the truth should be stated with all the caution possible, and that which is matter of opinion carefully distinguished from that which is matter of faith—intrudes two uncertain points, uncertain I mean according to the teaching of his own school. The first is that the pains of Purgatory are necessarily and certainly great beyond all earthly pains. This is an open question amongst Roman theologians. St. Bonaventura, for instance, teaches that though there are pains in that place greater than any earthly agonies, yet there also are pains less than any earthly affliction. Again, the Oratorian assumes that there is real and true fire in Purgatory. Yet this was strictly denied by the Greeks at Florence, and, in consequence of their sentiments, left an open question there and also at Trent. Again, the duration of Purgatory is a perfectly open question in the Roman Church. Some have believed it, in many instances, to extend to the end of the world. Others, as Dominic Soto, have held that in general it did not last more than ten or twenty years. Yet a precise, dogmatic, matter-of-faith belief is now thrust by Rome on her converts, in almost all these particulars."—*Neale's* "Lectures on Church Difficulties," pp. 194, 195, London, 1852.

performed by the faithful for the other faithful departed, be piously and devoutly performed, according to the institutes of the church, and that what things soever are due on their behalf from the endowments of testators, or in other way, be discharged not in a negligent manner, but diligently and accurately by the priests and ministers of the church, and others who are bound to render this service."

In the sixth session of the same council, at which the doctrine of justification had been under the consideration of the fathers assembled, the thirtieth canon, formally accepted and passed, stands thus:—

"If any one shall declare that after the grace of justification received, unto every penitent sinner the guilt is so remitted, and the penalty of eternal punishment so blotted out, that there remains not any penalty of temporal punishment to be discharged either in this world or in the next in Purgatory, before the entrance of the kingdom of heaven can be laid open, let him be anathema."

In the twenty-second session, held on September 17th, 1562, touching the Sacrifice of the Holy Eucharist, the following was set forth with regard to the mass being propitiatory as well for the dead as for the living:—

"Inasmuch as in this divine sacrifice, which is performed in the mass, that same Christ is contained and immolated in a bloodless manner, who once offered himself in a bloody manner on the altar of the cross; the holy synod teaches that this sacrifice is truly propitiatory, and that by means thereof this is effected—that we obtain mercy and find grace in convenient aid, if we draw nigh unto God, contrite and penitent, with a true heart and upright faith, with fear and reverence. For the Lord, appeased by the oblation thereof, and granting the grace and gift of penitence, forgives our heinous crimes and sins. For the victim is one and the same, the same now offering by the ministry of priests, who there offered Himself on the cross, the manner of offering alone being different. The fruits, indeed, of which oblation, of that bloody one to wit, are most plentifully received through this bloodless one; so far is this latter derogatory in any manner from that former. Wherefore, not only for the sins, punishments, satisfactions, and other necessities of the faithful who are alive, but also for those who are departed in Christ, and who are not as yet fully purified, it is rightly offered, agreeably to the tradition of the apostles."

Here, then, are those carefully drawn up and

authoritative statements of the Roman Church which set forth all that is to be received by her members *as of faith* regarding the doctrine of Purgatory.* The

---

* The following is the opinion of Cardinal Fisher, Bishop of Rochester:—

"No orthodox person now doubts whether there be a Purgatory, of which, however, among the ancients, there was no mention, or the very rarest. Nay, to this day the Greeks do not believe in Purgatory. Let who will read the commentaries of the ancient Greeks, and he will find no discourse, as I think, or the most infrequent, of Purgatory. Nor did the Latins all at once, but by degrees, conceive the truth of this matter. . . . Since, then, Purgatory was so late in being known and admitted by the Church Universal, can any man wonder that of a practice connected with the belief of it, there was no instance to be found in the early ages of the church?"— *Assert. Luther. Confut.*, art. xviii. 496.

And the following of Barnes, the celebrated Benedictine writer:—

"Punishment in Purgatory is a matter of human opinion, which cannot be satisfactorily deduced either from Scripture, the Fathers, or the Councils, nay (with deference to better judgments), the opposite opinion was more agreeable to them."— *Cath. Rom. Pacif.*, sec. 9, Paralip. c. p. 130.

Christopher Davenport, the Franciscan, thus writes in his "Problem," No. xxxvii.:—

"Concerning Purgatory, the older writers amongst them [members of the Church of England] allowed it, as is clear from Fox speaking of Latimer. Nor did Latimer absolutely deny it. I am not, however, engaged upon an inquiry into the opinions of individuals, having shown what is defined in the Anglican Confession; where, as I said, not the use of the church. but an abuse calumniously imputed to her, is condemned. On this point, we, on our side, shall have entire agreement with the Anglican Confession, if only men, as they ought to do, will weigh its statements in a spirit of zeal, not for party but for truth."—*Paraphrastica Expositio Articulorum Confessionis Anglicæ (in loco).*

As explaining the apparent divergence of opinion amongst ancient Christian writers, the following paragraph from Dr. Newman's celebrated "Essay on Development" may be put on record: "As time went on, the doctrine of Purgatory was opened upon the apprehension of the Church, as a portion or form of penance for sins committed after baptism."—Chap. viii. sec. i. p. 417.

The late "Cardinal Wiseman, when consulted by one who related

more attentively they are examined, the more evident will it appear that it is not against such as these that any protest was raised by our forefathers in the sixteenth century, when the *Doctrina Romanensium* was condemned; but through certain popular misconceptions or exaggerations of the doctrine,* which existed and wrought mischief, and certain of which are not altogether unknown in some places even at the present time.†

For when we pray, " Lord, Thy kingdom come," we may reasonably believe of the subjects of the New Creation that, as the apostle declares, at the Name of

---

the fact to me "—writes Dr. Pusey, in his " Eirenicon," p. 197 (London, 1865)—" after taking a day to reflect, stated that the belief that there would be suffering in the Day of Judgment would satisfy the [Roman Catholic] doctrine of Purgatory."

* See " Tracts for the Times," No. 90 (third edition), pp. 23—28. London, Rivingtons, 1841.

† In Ireland and in other countries societies have been founded during the present century for the relief of the souls in Purgatory, in which there has been that kind of traffic in masses and prayers condemned by the Council of Trent, and sometimes repudiated by authority. In the year 1806 a society existed at Dublin under the patronage of Mary and Joseph, in which, in return for certain sums of money paid to the directors of it, a kind of cheque was given, duly numbered and signed, with a representation of the " Eye of God " on the top, and a symbol of the Blessed Trinity below, assuring to the person holding it certain indulgences and benefits either for himself or his departed friends. It is but fair to add that Dr. Doyle, Roman Catholic Bishop of Kildare, stated before a committee of the House of Lords that this society was mainly originated by Dublin tradesmen, and was not authorized by the bishops of that communion. A Roman Catholic friend, exceedingly well-informed, however, asserts that many such societies still exist, and are tolerated, at all events in some of the dioceses of England, at the present day.

Jesus every knee shall bow, not only in heaven and in earth, so is it also with those under the earth—the dead in Christ in the hidden place of their abode. The latter will all adore Him as their Redeemer, for it is only because of His most precious bloodshedding that their purification surely continues, and is being duly completed. For the blood of Jesus Christ cleanses us from all sin. When, therefore, St. Paul speaks of the work which has been commenced in the baptized being continued and carried on to the day of Christ, it is evident that its progress is not in the smallest degree stayed by death, but advances in due course after death, until "the great day of the Lord," which is, as we know, the day of the general judgment. So that it is impossible to avoid the inevitable conclusion that the work of cleansing and preparation continues, and is completed after the separation of soul and body. And this, of course, is in perfect accordance with the teaching of our Blessed Saviour Himself. "Whosoever speaketh a word against the Son of Man," He declared, "it shall be forgiven him: but whosoever speaketh against the Holy Ghost, it shall not be forgiven him, neither in this world, neither in the world to come."* And again, referring to the interval between death and judgment, our Lord spoke of a prison-house, whence men should not be released until of the debt due they had paid the uttermost farthing.† In the life beyond the grave, therefore, it is clear that there is progress and retrogression, forgiveness of past transgressions and its opposite. Surely numbers of ordinary Christians enter upon that life in a state which sorely needs pardon, cleansing, and due preparation for an eventual entry into heaven. For perfect remission of sins, and the blotting out of all their stains and consequences, involves a complete purification by God's favour, in God's time, and in God's mode.

Do the formal statements of the Council of Trent —taken literally, and independent of modern gloss, and the fantasies of fervent fanatics—involve or imply more than this? A ready negative will be the fair and faithful answer of not a few.

* St. Matthew xii. 32. † St. Matthew xviii. 23—35.

CHAPTER X.

THE PRACTICE OF PRAYING FOR THE DEPARTED OBSCURED IN THE SIXTEENTH CENTURY.

MANY of God's most precious and valuable gifts, whether temporal or spiritual, are not only liable to abuse, but are abused. Memory, free will, understanding, food, raiment, drink, the gift of speech, freedom, authority, power—each in its turn comes under this category. And so it is with divine graces and donations bestowed in the Church. All the baptized do not use these aright and duly. Some men grievously abuse them. And what men do, as individuals, that same corporations of men sometimes effect. Both history and experience have taught us as much, melancholy as it is to contemplate the lesson.

Now it is asserted, and commonly believed, that no practical evil existing in the Western Church during the latter part of the fifteenth and the early part of the sixteenth centuries, had greater influence in bringing about the irreligious divisions and separations which were effected later, and exist still, than the sale of indulgences.

John Tetzel, a Dominican monk, the son of a goldsmith at Leipsic, was appointed by Albert, Archbishop of Mentz, to farm the most liberal indulgences, which his Grace had been commissioned by Pope Leo X. to dispense and dispose of; and he did his work well. It was an unclerical office, but profitable; and the successful working of it would, from a temporal point of view, eminently benefit both Archbishop and Pope. Tetzel claimed to possess the power to absolve, not only from ecclesiastical censures, but likewise from all sins, enormities, and transgressions, however terrible in their character and numerous; and even from those of which the Pope alone—as was commonly taught—could take cognizance. He declared that by virtue of his office and delegated privileges he had full and absolute power to release from all the punishments of purgatory; altogether independent of the parish clergy, he gave permission to frequent the sacraments; he promised, in the Pope's name, to those who were liberal in the purchase of his indulgences, that the gates of hell should be for ever closed against them, and that the doors of everlasting happiness should be infallibly opened at their decease. His mission for a while was a success. But, opposed by Luther and others, in due course its very success brought disaster and schism upon the whole Western Church. A small spark kindled a great fire. This is not the occasion to trace a great result from a comparatively trifling cause; but as the result was most sensibly experienced in the Church of England as well as elsewhere, the immediate cause may not improperly be here put on record.

In our own country, from the early part of the fourteenth century, the same kind of indiscreet traffic had been openly and largely carried on, mainly by the spiritual sons of St. Dominick. Sometimes the interests of one religious order were cleverly played off against those of another. When the Dominicans lost favour at Rome, for any cause, reasonable or unreasonable, the Augustinians were appointed to carry on the work. When these latter failed or faltered in doing it efficiently, the religious of the white scapular were ready to supplant them. So that the indulgences were duly and regularly disposed of, and the Pontifical exchequer replenished, it was no great matter who were the actual instruments of their sale. It is but fair to remark, however, that, both at home and abroad, several influential and pious members of both orders had from time to time opened their eyes to the turpitude of this disgraceful traffic and done something to discountenance it. Hence the opinion of the more thoughtful and religious amongst the people in general came to be such as that the sale of indulgences was disparaged and discountenanced, if not condemned.*

No such extensive changes as were effected under Henry VIII. and his illegitimate daughter, Elizabeth, could have been carried out had not corruptions existed of a nature such as to have practically eaten out the religion of the main body of the people, who, with only a few exceptions, passively witnessed the steady progress of Change and the triumphant success of Robbery.† The monks of the Charterhouse in London and the Observants at Richmond

---

* The work of reformation which, in this and other particulars, the Council of Trent so ably and judiciously effected, ought not to be forgotten. And all the good work accomplished by the Fathers there was done apart from the dangerous principle of destruction, which with some of our modern Anglican apostles is just at present greatly in favour— *e.g.*, as regards disestablishment. Such a destructive remedy may possibly cure ten evils; but it would surely originate ninety.

† "No other name but that of 'robbery' can be given to the infamous acts of spoliation perpetrated by Henry VIII."—*A New View of an Old Subject.* Introduction, p. xii.

and Greenwich were the first to taste the bitter lot of confiscation. The greater monasteries in due course succeeded the lesser in their fall. Slander, Falsehood, and Spoliation wrought wonderful changes. Foul means as well as fair were thought appropriate for the work in hand. One of the main pleas for the suppression of chantries and the confiscation of religious houses was that purgatory was a "vague myth," and masses for the dead were useless "abominations." From this it followed that the founders of chantries, as well as the priests who ministered in them, laboured under a deep religious delusion. Of course it was the interest of Thomas Cromwell and his pliant tools to foster and spread this notion; for, by so doing, precious metals, jewels, vestments, religious houses and lands, could more readily be transferred from their rightful owners to those who so earnestly coveted them. Hence it was that the labours of Tetzel and his less notorious allies in England practically assisted in carrying out the dark designs of an unscrupulous and adulterous king. The hired preachers, sent through the country by Cromwell to prepare the way of the thieves who in due course, for very practical purposes, were to follow them, were enabled to make much capital out of the sale of indulgences. The subject was one which pious Sarcasm and holy Buffoonery would of course treat with ease and success. And so it turned out. What the English satellites of Cromwell could not effect of themselves, or could only compass in part, was completed to the satisfaction of their employers by the foreign intruders, with their new gospel, loose morals, and most convenient doctrines, from Germany. The chantries were suppressed and destroyed. The houses of God in this favoured land were thrown down with axes and hammers. With deliberation, God Almighty was robbed.* Those who had served the chantries were turned adrift, if pliable and passive, with a small pension; if the reverse, to beg, to rot, and to die. The proceeds of houses, lands, and possessions were swept up with unnatural greed by king and courtier, willing tool and mushroom baron. And the danger to the State which was thought by some

---

* "When anything is granted for God, it is deemed in law to be granted to God; and whatsoever is granted to His Church, for His honour and the maintenance of His religion and service, is granted for and to God."— *Statutes relating to the Ecclesiastical and Eleemosynary Institutions of England*, by Archibald J. Stephens, barrister at law. 2 vols. page 1, note 1.

"There is nothing that the united voice of all History proclaims so loud as the certain unfailing curse that has pursued and overtaken Sacrilege. Make a catalogue of all the prosperous sacrilegious persons that have been from the beginning of the world to this day, and I believe they will come within a very narrow compass, and be repeated much sooner than the alphabet."—*South's Sermons*, "On Places for Divine Worship."

to exist,* that all the landed property of the kingdom was in a fair way of being swallowed up by religious foundations, was thus efficiently removed. The statute of Mortmain, re-enacted and made more stringent in a future era, successfully prevented the resurrection of the danger.

The last of the Ten Articles—put forth in 1536, and subscribed by the two Houses of Convocation, when the two archbishops, sixteen bishops, forty abbots and priors, and fifty of the second order of the clergy, formally attached their signatures to them—contained the following statement regarding purgatory:—

"Forasmuch as due order of charity requireth, and the Book of Maccabees and divers ancient doctors plainly show, that it is a very good and charitable deed to pray for souls departed, and forasmuch also as such usage hath continued in the church so many years, even from the beginning, we will that all bishops and preachers shall instruct and teach our people committed by us unto their spiritual charge, that no man ought to be grieved with the continuance of the same, and that it standeth with the very due

---

* Sir Henry Spelman allows this, who was a fair and faithful writer. In the reign of Edward I. the whole lands of England amounted to 67,000 knights' fees—of which 28,000 were in ecclesiastical hands. ("History of Sacrilege," p. 200. London, 1853.)

order of charity for a Christian man to pray for souls departed, and to commit them in our prayers to God's mercy, and also to cause others to pray for them in masses and exequies, and to give alms to others to pray for them, whereby they may be relieved and holpen of some part of their pain: but forasmuch as the place where they be, the name thereof, and kind of pain there, also be to us uncertain by Scripture: therefore this with all other things we remit to Almighty God, unto whose mercy it is meet and convenient for us to commend them, trusting that God accepteth our prayers for them, referring the rest wholly to God, to whom is known their estate and condition; wherefore it is much necessary that such abuses be clearly put away, which under the name of purgatory hath been advanced, as to make men believe that through the Bishop of Rome's pardon souls might clearly be delivered out of purgatory, and all the pains of it, and that masses said at *Scala Cœli*, or otherwhere, in any place, or before any image, might likewise deliver them from all their pain, and send them straight to heaven; and other like abuses."

In the other official and authoritative documents put forth in the early part of the Reformation period, the same or almost identical teaching is found.

For instance, in "The Necessary Doctrine and Erudition for any Christian Man," a revised form of an earlier and similar work entitled "The Institution of a Christian Man," the following passage appears, in which the influence of the movement against indulgences such as those disposed of by Tetzel is apparent, together with certain theological assertions which are, perhaps, rather bold than accurate:—

"Here is specially to be noted, that it is not in the power or knowledge of any man to limit and dispense how much, and in what space of time or to what person particularly* the said masses, exequies, or suffrages to be done, should yet (though their intent be more for one than another) cause them also to be done for the universal congregation of Christian people, quick and dead; for that power and knowledge afore rehearsed pertaineth only unto God, which knoweth alone the measures and times of His own judgment and mercies."

The fifteen years which intervened between the issue of the first-named of the above tractates, and the

---

* Compare the explicit doctrine of the Oriental Church set forth in the previous chapter, p. 120, with the above unsatisfactory and pointless statement.

formal publication of "The Book of Common Prayer" in 1549, were years in which many momentous subjects were frequently ventilated with deep feeling, and not altogether without haste.

As regards the popular and current notions of purgatory, they underwent a considerable change. Legends and records of supernatural visions—though put on record by such an eminent saint as Bede—were laid aside, without any proper respect for their possible authenticity and probable truth. The writings of the new gospellers from Germany, translated into our mother tongue, were circulated far and wide—for the contagion for change spread steadily—and these were neither choice in language, nor select in argument. Yet they did their work. And this amongst a class—the lower—which had hitherto shown considerable distaste for divers of the reforming propositions.

In the service for "The Supper of the Lord and Holy Communion, commonly called The Mass," the following formed a part of the canon, occurring immediately before that portion by which the acts of consecration and oblation are effected:—

"And here we do give unto Thee most high praise and hearty thanks for the wonderful grace and virtue declared in all Thy saints from the beginning of the world: and chiefly in the glorious and most blessed Virgin Mary, mother of Thy Son Jesus Christ our Lord and God; and in the holy patriarchs, prophets, apostles, and martyrs, whose examples (O Lord) and steadfastness in Thy faith, and keeping Thy holy commandments, grant us to follow. We commend unto Thy mercy (O Lord) all other Thy servants which are departed hence from us with the sign of faith, and now do rest in the sleep of peace: grant unto them, we beseech Thee, Thy mercy and everlasting peace; and that, at the day of the general resurrection, we and all they which be of the mystical body of Thy Son, may altogether be set on His right hand, and hear that His most joyful voice, Come unto me, O ye that be blessed of my Father, and possess the kingdom which is prepared for you from the beginning of the world."

In this book, though the ancient service of the dead, which had been in use for generations, was mutilated, transposed, and abbreviated, "The Order for the Burial of the Dead" contained the following beautiful and touching suffrages :—

"We commend into Thy hands of mercy (most merciful Father) the soul of this our brother departed, N. And his body we commit to the earth: beseeching Thine infinite goodness to give us grace to live in Thy fear and love and die in Thy favour; that when the judgment shall come, which Thou hast committed to Thy well-beloved Son, both this our brother and we may be found acceptable in Thy sight."

And again :—

"Almighty God, we give Thee hearty thanks for this Thy

servant whom Thou hast delivered from the miseries of this wretched world, from the body of death and all temptation; and, as we trust, has brought his soul, which he committed into Thy holy hands, into sure consolation and rest. Grant, we beseech Thee, that at the day of judgment his soul, and all the souls of Thy elect, departed out of this life, may with us and we with them, fully receive Thy promises, and be made perfect altogether, through the glorious resurrection of Thy Son Jesus Christ our Lord."

Then follow three psalms, two of which had been used in the old service, three kyries, and the Lord's Prayer in English, with the following versicles and responses:—

"*Priest.*   Enter not (O Lord) into judgment with Thy servants.
Answer.   For in Thy sight no living creature shall be justified.
Priest.   From the gates of hell,
Answer.   Deliver their souls, O Lord.
Priest.   I believe to see the goodness of the Lord,
Answer.   In the land of the living.
Priest.   O Lord, graciously hear my prayer.
Answer.   And let my cry come unto Thee."

To this succeeds a prayer, with which the service concluded, as follows:—

"O Lord, with whom do live the spirits of them that be dead, and in whom the souls of them that be elected, after they be delivered from the burden of the flesh, be in joy and felicity; grant unto this Thy servant, that the sins which he committed in this world be not imputed unto him: but that he, escaping the gates of hell, and pains of eternal darkness may ever dwell in the region of light, with Abraham, Isaac, and Jacob, in the place where is no weeping, sorrow, nor heaviness; and when that dreadful day of the general resurrection shall come, make him also to rise with the just and righteous, and receive this body again to glory, then made pure and incorruptible. Set him on the right hand of Thy Son Jesus Christ, among Thy holy and elect, that then he may hear with them those most sweet and comfortable words, Come to me, ye blessed of my Father, possess the kingdom which hath been prepared for you from the beginning of the world. Grant this, we beseech Thee, O merciful Father, through Jesus Christ our Mediator and Redeemer."

In this book there were likewise a special Introit, Collect, Epistle, and Gospel for the Celebration of the Holy Communion. The Introit was psalm *Quemadmodum*, previously the Tract of the Mass when the body was present; the Collect contained a definite prayer that "at the general resurrection in the last day, both we, and this our brother departed, receiving again our bodies, and rising again in Thy most gracious favour, may, with all Thine elect saints, obtain Thine eternal joy;" and the Epistle and Gospel were those used of old—the former in the first mass of the Salisbury rite when the body was present, the latter in the mass for Tuesday.* Thus, notwithstanding changes and curtailments, and the

* Vide Appendices, Nos. I., II., and III.

substitution, under Calvin's evil influence, of the term "elect" for the "faithful," there was an evident desire that the article of the creed "I believe in the communion of saints" should still remain a reality; and that the living should continue, as had been the case from the very days of the apostles themselves, to pray for those departed this life in God's faith and fear, and to commend their souls to the care and pity of a loving and all-merciful God.

But the promoters of change and innovation—many of them sceptics in their principles—remained dissatisfied and restless. And these qualities were still further stirred up with eminent success, as well by certain unctuous and immoderate fanatics at home, as by the mischievous influence of Calvin's "Institutes" and the less learned writings and manifestoes of his followers abroad. Peter Martyr and Bucer, pedantic, gloomy, narrow-minded, and meddling, had been invited over to England to assist in the work of destruction, which many reasonable people held was progressing quite rapidly enough, under the influence of such persons as Cox, Dean of Westminster, afterwards Bishop of Ely, and Taylor, Dean of Lincoln, afterwards Bishop of that see. The result of this active co-operation of German Calvinists and Anglican fanatics can be seen in what is known as "The Second Prayer Book of Edward VI." The first, in comparison with the older service-books, was poor, bald, and insufficient to satisfy the reasonable needs of those accustomed to the stately dignity and soothing sweetness of our ancient rites. But the second, when compared with the first, was as coarse husks to good grain. As regards prayers for the dead—under the plea that old customs and rites had been abused and perverted—the practice, in certain services, was either eliminated, altogether, or so obscured and clouded by vague language, capable of more meanings than one, as to have become practically out of use for several generations. In the prayer "for the whole state of Christ's church militant here in earth," in this book all mention of the saints, or of the faithful departed, is carefully removed. Not a trace remains. The Lord's Prayer, however, was left untouched. The innovators did not presume to eliminate the comprehensive petition, " Thy kingdom come." In the "Prayer of Oblation," as it has been termed, a petition asking that through the merits and death of our Lord Jesus Christ, and through faith in His blood, "we *and all Thy whole church* may obtain remission of our sins and all other benefits of His passion" is retained; but this, on the face of it, lacks that distinctness which was a feature of the ancient prayers for the departed. In the service "At the Burial of the Dead," the same process had likewise taken place. A selfish, semi-pagan consideration of the living alone characterizes this office.* Even the unimportant restorations of later periods do not serve to alter its main features. It must, therefore, be confessed, that notwithstanding our present service contains explicit statements concerning the resurrection of the body, clothed in pious, lofty, and touching language, with appropriate hortatory passages relating to the day of judgment

---

* "In our burial service," writes Mr. Procter, in his valuable "History of the Book of Common Prayer," "the ancient custom is retained of conducting the corpse to the grave with holy hymns, *fitted to cheer the heart of the mourner*. The promises of *our resurrection are pronounced*, as the priest receives the corpse at the entrance of the churchyard, and leads it to its resting-place. In the three processional anthems *we are reminded of the three necessary graces to be exercised at a funeral;* namely, faith, patience, and thanksgiving: and these are placed in their proper order; *for by faith we gain patience*, and when patience hath her perfect work, it will produce thanksgiving. The Thirty-ninth Psalm, probably composed by David after the death of Absalom, *is of use in this place to check all loud unseemly complaints*, and to turn them into prayers and devout meditations. Psalm xc., composed by Moses while the children of Israel were dying in the wilderness, shows us what thoughts befit a funeral; that *we should consider our own lot*, and apply the instance of mortality before us *to the improvement of our own condition*. The lesson is called St. Paul's Gospel; it includes the fullest account of the resurrection that is to be found in Scripture, and hence is fitted to *allay sorrow for the departed, and to prepare us freely to follow when God calls*."—P. 425.

for the living, it is manifestly imperfect as regards man's duty to the departed, and vastly inferior to those forms which were used of old in this country. The psalms *Dixi custodiam* ("I said, I will take heed to my ways") and *Domine, refugium* ("Lord, Thou hast been our refuge") refer to the living. They concern the mourners, and those left behind on earth. Unlike the psalms *Quemadmodum* ("Like as the hart desireth the water-brooks") and *De profundis* ("Out of the deep have I called unto Thee"), they make no mention of the departed, who, though wept and sorrowed for—as far as the public office is concerned —get neither aid nor active sympathy from those whose day of grace is still upon them. The dead, in the words of holy Job, seem plaintively to cry out, "Have pity upon me, have pity upon me, O ye my friends; for the hand of God hath touched me;"[*] but they cry in vain. As the generations pass, no response cometh. There is "neither voice, nor any to answer, nor any that regardeth."[†] The vulgar, extravagant,

---

[*] Job xix. 21.

[†] "The prayers which conclude the service [*i.e.*, our existing form, practically the same as that which was mutilated in 1552] are mainly compositions of our Reformers, and differ from those in the mediæval offices most widely, in having respect only to the living, instead of the dead, whose doom is already certain."—*History of the Book of Common Prayer*, by Francis Procter, M.A., p. 426. Sixth edition. London, 1864.

and fulsome flattery graven on the mortuary tablets of men and women who died in the sixteenth and seventeenth centuries, was but a poor substitute for the undying charity of our English forefathers of previous ages;* who, day by day, and year by year, with faith and true devotion,† abided by the apostolic precept, and the custom of the Church Universal in every clime and age, when in substance they asked of the All-pitiful from on high in behalf of a departed friend, "The Lord grant unto him that he may find mercy of the Lord in that day."

Thus it is manifest in what manner, and to what extent, the practice of praying for the departed was obscured here in England during the sixteenth century.

---

* See the prefatory remarks to Appendix No. XI., containing list of monumental inscriptions from 1550 to 1870.

† "There did lye on the High Altar an excellent fine Booke, very richly covered with gold and silver, conteininge the names of all the benefactors from the first originall foundation thereof. The laying that booke on the altar did shew how highly they esteemed theire founders and benefactors, and the daily and quotidiane remembrance they had of them did argue not onely theire gratitude, but a most divine and charitable affection to the soules of theire benefactors."—*Rites of the Church of Durham*, p. 14.

CHAPTER XI.

POST-REFORMATION DOCTRINE AND PRACTICE.

IT needed no particular gift of far-sight on the part of the rulers of our National Church to have perceived that, unless the extravagance and fanaticism of the democratic gospellers * of Queen Elizabeth's reign were curbed with a vigorous and potent hand, all true religion would be in grave danger of being either corrupted or banished. Formal caricatures of ancient Christianity might have sprung up, and enjoyed either a mere mushroom existence, or have changed and developed with every passing decennary; but that Gospel which St. Augustine brought hither

---

* Luther, in his "Letter to the German Nobility," gave a strong impetus to revolutionary ideas by his false statement regarding church authority and holy orders, as follows: "All men are priests, and able to decide what is right or wrong in doctrine," therefore, "any body of men may set any one to preach who pleases him, and depose him again when they like."—*Luther's Works* (Ed. Walsh), vol. xix. p. 1320. See also a most able and truthful volume, "Essays on the Reformation," by S. R. Maitland, D.D., F.R.S., Librarian to the Archbishop of Canterbury. London, 1849.

towards the close of the seventh century would speedily have been altogether abolished, with the advice and under the direction of the agitators imported from abroad, had it not been for the most needful and judicious action of Authority. As it was, since the year 1536 nearly a hundred sects had sprung into existence, each claiming to be the only true and original "congregation of Christ," each teaching the only pure and unadulterated Gospel. But their life as a rule was not long. Born with the seeds of decay in their systems, irreligious abortions, always wrangling with their rivals, they soon sank into a blessed obscurity and then died. For certainly they were of the earth earthy.

With many of them the most carnal notions and material conceptions of religion obtained. Babbling in a multitude of words about "faith," this was the very theological virtue which they possessed in the least degree. Hence men were offered a cloud of obscure phrases, clothed in language in which the most common-place platitudes concerning religion were enunciated, as though they had been ew revelations—a practice not altogether unknown mongst some of their admirers of the present day. With regard to the departed, many of these new religionists reverted to systems less illuminated than the loftiest current sentiments of heathen philosophers. Bucer had been the great champion of innovation as regards a true belief concerning the dead in Christ, and his rusty weapons were ready to hand for those who came after. He had maintained, amongst other singular propositions, that because our Blessed Saviour promised to hearers of His word that they should not come into condemnation,* therefore Christians ought not, under any circumstances or at any time, to pray for the dead. Other texts were quoted, with the intention of enforcing, by Bible authority, the same uncharitable negation. Of these were the following: "Whatsoever thy hand findeth to do, do it with thy might; for there is no work, nor device, nor knowledge, nor wisdom, in the grave, whither thou goest;"† "The night cometh, when no man can work;"‡ and "To-day if ye will hear His voice, harden not your hearts."§ Of course, if praying for the departed implied that any change could be made in the state of those who died in mortal sin, these and such like texts would be of some pertinence. But such an idea has never been entertained. It

* St. John v. 24.
† Eccles. ix. 10.
‡ St. John ix. 4.
§ Heb. iii. 7.

was the "dead in Christ," not the "dead in sins," who were prayed for.

The influence of the innovators, however, which had made itself felt for sixty years, took some time to curtail and circumscribe. Lax conceptions of ancient dogma had been current and popular for at least two generations. Some controversies had worn themselves threadbare. Others lived a feeble life, for the amusement of idlers, or as appropriate subjects of speculation for Calvinistic preachers. The reaction against all this, and such as this, began in the early part of James I.'s reign. In a modified degree it was supported by Abbot, Archbishop of Canterbury, under the patronage of the king. As regards the true nature of the Church and the necessity of episcopacy, for instance, Hooker and Bilson, afterwards Sanderson, and in later times Pearson, conclusively settled the question, and this in harmony with the concurrent voice of Antiquity. Several other losses effected by change in the last century were gradually but effectively recovered now. A new race of divines, of which the first in order was Andrewes, sprang up, who were unanimous in representing the National communion as identical with the Church of St. Augustine, and who measured

POST-REFORMATION DOCTRINE. 155

accurately both her political and internal needs. But until Laud became Archbishop of Canterbury, in 1633, no great and efficient steps were taken to secure these. He, however, under Providence, became the saviour and restorer of the English Church. Without him, and the ecclesiastical school he formed, it would in all probability have become a mere Protestant sect. Since his day and death, and because of his labours, it has regained much that was precious which had been then laid aside or lost.

In regard to the immediate subject under consideration—mixed up as it is very intimately with a sound conception of the Christian sacrifice, and a true belief in the communion of saints—though the duty of directly praying for the departed* had certainly

---

* "Our rulers in the sixteenth century," as Mr. Maskell wrote, "acted wisely, and I doubt not, overruled by the Spirit of God, they took not away all remembrance of them [the departed] from the holy office, but they did not venture to speak so loudly or so plainly as men did in purer times [which many English clergymen now hold to be a great misfortune.—F. G. L.]: they left the expression of their hopes and wishes, couched, not in dubious, but in cautious language, in words which careless eyes, it may be, overlook, but whose meaning cannot be denied. Therefore, with gratitude, we declare that the Liturgy of the Church of England is not wanting in this particular: in it we still include and pray for those who are gone before: we still beseech our Heavenly Father mercifully to accept our sacrifice, and to grant that we and all His whole church may obtain remission of our sins, and all other benefits of His passion."—*The Ancient Liturgy of the Church of England*, by the Rev. W. Maskell, M.A. (second edition), pp. cxlvii., cxlviii. London, 1846.

been obscured in the public services of the church, and the faithful had lost the full and ripe teaching of the ancient offices,* yet there were never wanting those in high places who openly testified to the truth of the doctrine, and who, we may reasonably believe, enjoined a practice, from which they themselves found comfort and consolation, upon their flocks in general. Traces of this policy may be found by those who search for them.†

A few, representative in their character, and not those most ordinarily quoted and best known, shall here be supplied.

---

* See Appendices Nos. I., II., and V.

† "I spoke severally to two of the best bishops we have in England [Gilbert Sheldon, Archbishop of Canterbury, and Walter Blandford, Bishop of Worcester], who both told me there were many things in the Roman Church which it were very much to be wished we had kept, as confession, which was no doubt commanded by God. That praying for the dead was one of the ancient things in Christianity, that for their parts they did it daily."—*The Paper of the late Dutchess of York*. (Published in London without date, year, or printer's name. Authenticated by Burnet's references to it, and by the replies thereto of other writers.)

On prayers for the dead in general, as defended by distinguished writers, as also concerning the offering of the Holy Sacrifice for persons departed, see Bishop Beveridge's comments on the forty-fourth canon of the Council of Carthage, which enjoined fasting communion, and distinctly forbad the reception of the Blessed Sacrament late in the day or during masses for the dead: and upon St. Augustine's Thirty-second Sermon. "Pandec. Canon," vol. i. p. 567; vol. ii. p. 207; also L'Estrange's "Alliance of Divine Offices," pp. 303, 304; "Conc. Brit.," vol. i. p. 327 [apud Spelman]; "English Ecclesiastical Laws and Canons" (Johnson), vol. i. ad an. 816; "An Essay towards a Proposal for Catholick Communion," London, 1704.

POST-REFORMATION DOCTRINE. 157

The following is from an authorized bidding prayer, commonly used both in cathedral and parish churches for many generations:—

"Finally, let us praise God for all those that are departed out of this life in the faith of Christ, and pray unto God that . . . . this life ended, we may be made partakers with them of the glorious resurrection in life everlasting."*

Bishop Andrewes† not only defended the practice of praying for the dead in his theological treatises,‡ but embodied it in his largely-used "Devotions," thus:—

"Remember, O Lord our God, all spirits and all

---

* "Constitutions and Canons Ecclesiasticall," No. lv. A.D. 1603.

† Bishop Andrewes writes thus, in his "Devotions" for Sunday:—

"De vivis misericordiam et gratiam, Defunctis requiem et lucem perpetuam."

In the Greek version, thus:—

ἐάν τι ζῶμεν, ἐάν τι καὶ ἀποθνήσκωμεν Κύριος ἡμῶν σύ;
Ζῶντας καὶ θανόντας ἐλέησον ὦ Κύριε.

Vide also Answer to the Epistle of M. de la Millitiere; "Bramhall's Works," vol. i. p. 60, and vol. ii. p. 494 and p. 633; "Works of Archbishop Ussher," Answer to the Jesuit, chapter vii.; Hammond's Annotations, 2 Tim. i. 16; Hickes

"On the Intermediate State," in loco. In truth, from the time of Sancroft and the Nonjurors to the commencement of the Oxford movement in 1829, the duty of praying for the departed was commonly and very generally enjoined, both publicly and privately, by all (and they were not a few, thank God!) who had been influenced by that respect for the Catholic faith and practice which the Nonjurors did so much practically to restore and deepen.

‡ "The Eucharist ever was, and by us is, considered both as a sacrament and a sacrifice. A sacrifice is proper and appliable only to divine worship. The sacrifice of Christ's death did succeed to the sacrifices of

flesh, whom we have remembered, and whom we have not remembered."*

The following prayer, for use in the consecration of a church and churchyard, was drawn up in the latter part of the reign of King James :—

"Grant to such bodies as shall be here interred, that they with us and we with them may have our perfect consummation and bliss both in body and soul in Thine eternal kingdom. God the Father, God the Son, and God the Holy Ghost, accept, sanctify, and bless this place to that end whereunto, according to Thine own ordinance, we have ordained it, even to bestow the bodies of Thy servants in, till, the number of Thine elect being accomplished, they with us and we with them, and with all other departed in the faith of Thy Holy Name, shall have our consummation and bliss, both in body and soul, in Thy eternal and everlasting glory."†

The following records the judgment of Bishop

---

the Old Testament. The sacrifice of Christ's death is available for present, absent, living, dead, yea, for them that are yet unborn. When we say the dead, we mean it is available for the apostles, martyrs, and confessors, and all, because we are all members of one body; these no man will deny."—*Andrewes' Answer to Cardinal Perron,* "Minor Works," p. 19. Oxford.

* See also Bishop Andrewes' "Private Devotions," p. 326.

† MS. "Form of Consecration of a Church or Chapel." A.D. 1620. (Lambeth Library.)

Overall on certain prayers and petitions in our present burial service:—

"The Puritans think that here is prayer for the dead allowed and practised by the Church of England, and so think I; but we are not both of one mind for censuring the Church for so doing. They say it is Popish and superstitious; I, for my part, esteem it pious and Christian. The body lies dead in the grave, but by Christ's power and God's goodness shall men be raised up again: and the benefit is so great that surely it is worth praying for, because then we may pray for what we ourselves or our deceased brethren as yet have not, therefore doth the Church pray for the perfect consummation of bliss, both in body and soul, to be given to our brethren departed. We believe the resurrection, yet may we pray for it as we do for God's kingdom to come. Besides, prayer for the dead cannot be denied but to have been universally used of all Christians in the ancientest and purest times of the Church, and by the Greek Fathers, who never admitted any purgatory, no more than we do, and yet pray for the dead notwithstanding. What though their souls be in bliss already? They may have a greater degree of bliss by our prayers: and when their bodies come to be raised, and joined to their souls again, they shall be sure of a better state. Our prayers for them, then, will not be in vain, were it but for that alone." (A.D. 1618).*

Elsewhere † he discusses the same subject in the following terms :—

"This is a plain oblation of Christ's death once offered, and a representative sacrifice of it, for the sins and for the benefit of the whole world, of the whole church: that both those which are here on earth, and those that rest in the sleep of peace, being departed in the faith of Christ, may find the effect and virtue of it. And if the authority of the ancient church may prevail with us, as it ought to do, there is nothing more manifest than that it always taught as much."

The following, in harmony with what has been quoted from other contemporary sources, preached at the obsequies of a pious lay member of the church, is from the pen of Dr. Cosin, Bishop of Durham :—

"To these everlasting joys and pleasures, in houses

---

* "Notes on the Prayer Book," by John Overall, D.D. A.D. 1618. Quoted by J. Nichols in his "Commentary on the Prayer Book," pp. 64, 65.

† "Notes on the Communion Service," by John Overall, D.D., Bishop of Norwich. A.D. 1618.

not made with hands, but eternal in the heavens, for which we daily sigh and groan, God for His mercy vouchsafe to bring us, that we with this our sister and all others departed in the faith of Christ may have our perfect consummation there in body and soul. And He bring it to pass for us that by His death hath purchased life for us, Christ Jesus the righteous." (A.D. 1623.) *

And so is the following:—

"Though the souls of the faithful be in joy and felicity, yet because they are not in such a degree of that joy and felicity as that they can never receive no more than they have already, therefore in the latter part here of this our prayer, we beseech God to give them

* "Sermon at the Funeral of Mrs. Dorothy Holmes," June 17, 1623, by John Cosin, D.D., Lord Bishop of Durham.—" O Lord, with whom doe live the spirits of them that dye, and by whom the soules of thy servants after they be delivered from the burthen of this flesh, bee in perpetuall joy and felicitie: We most meekely beseech Thee for this thy servant, that having now received the absolution from all his sins which *hee* hath committed in this world *hee* may escape the gates of hell and the paines of eternall darknesse; that *hee* may for ever dwell with Abraham, Isaac, and Jacob in the Region of light, and thy blessed presence, where there is neither weeping nor heavinesse. And that when the dreadful day of the generall judgement shall come, *hee* may rise again with the just, his bodie being reunited to his soul, pure and incorruptible, and be received into thy glorious kingdom for the merits of thy deare Son Our Saviour Jesus Christ, Amen."—(From a copy of the edition published in 1627, of Bishop Cosin's "Collection of Private Devotions, or the Houres of Prayer," which belonged to the Right Hon. George, Earl of Lichfield, some time Chancellor of the University of Oxford.)

a full and perfect consummation of bliss both in body and soul, in His eternal kingdom of glory which is yet to come. And whatsoever the effect and fruit of this prayer will be, though it be uncertain, yet hereby we show that charity which we owe to all those that are fellow-servants with us to Christ: and in this regard our prayers cannot be condemned, being neither impious nor unfit for those that profess the Christian religion."*

Bishop Buckeridge, of Ely, on a similar occasion, in a funeral sermon, likewise writes:—

"And so I end, beseeching God to give to us all, as He gave to him, our parts in the first resurrection from sin to grace, and to grant to him and all the faithful and saints departed, and us all with him, a joyful resurrection to everlasting life and glory in Jesus Christ." (A.D. 1626.)†

The following, specially drawn up for the occasion, was used at the consecration of St. Peter's Chapel, Cambridge:—

"Utque desinentes Te vocare hic in terris, possimus cum reliquis servis Tuis, qui consimilia

---

* Bishop Cosin's "Notes on the Book of Common Prayer" (quoted by Dr. Nichols), p. 65.

† "Sermon at the Funeral of Lancelot, late Lord Bishop of Winchester," by John [Buckeridge] late Lord Bishop of Ely.

loca dedicaverunt Numini Tuo, cumque omnibus sanctis Tuis in æternum laudare Nomen Tuum in summis cœlis. . . . . . Concede corporibus hic sepultis, ut illa nobiscum ut nos cum illis et cum omnibus aliis vitâ defunctis in verâ fide et confessione Nominis Tui, consequamur perfectam beatitudinem." (A.D. 1632.) *

Antony de Dominis, some time Archbishop of Spalato, and subsequently Dean of Windsor, appears from the following passage, which is quoted by William Forbes, Bishop of Edinburgh, and later writers, to have expressed himself on the subject in question with eminent moderation:—

"Prayers and oblations of the holy mysteries for the dead ought not to be condemned: for though not found in Scripture, they are agreeable to a most ancient practice of the church, which the Holy Fathers refer to apostolical tradition. And though no purgatory, strictly speaking, can be collected thence, yet we may gather that there is a certain place assigned to the souls of the departed, in which they may obtain a mitigation of the penalties of sin through the prayers of the church."

* MS. "Form for the Consecration of the Chapel of St. Peter's College, Cambridge," preserved in the College archives.

Bishop Forbes himself, in his "Considerationes Modestæ," wrote as follows:—

"The universal church has believed this practice not only to be lawful, but likewise to be beneficial to the souls departed, and has always most religiously observed it, as delivered, if not from the apostles, at least from the primitive fathers, as is manifest from the many places in their writings. Let it be granted that this custom was always judged lawful and also profitable by pious antiquity, and most universally received at all times in the church."

And again, in the same work, on the same subject, but from a slightly different point of view, even with regard to the corporate reunion of the separated churches:—

"Let not the ancient practice of praying and making oblations for the dead, received throughout the universal church of Christ, almost from the very time of the apostles, be any more rejected by Protestants as unlawful or vain. Let them reverence the judgment of the primitive church, and admit a practice strengthened by the uninterrupted profession of so many ages; and let them, as well in public as private, observe this rite, although not absolutely necessary or commanded by the divine law, yet as lawful and likewise profitable, and as always approved by the universal church, that by this means at length a peace so earnestly desired by all learned and honest men may be restored to the Christian world."

Herbert Thorndike,* some time Prebendary of Westminster, a theologian and canonist of known ability and repute, sets forth his judgment in the following passage with remarkable lucidity and force :—

"The practice of comprehending in all states of Christ's church the faithful departed has been so general in the church, that no beginning of it can be assigned, no time, no part of the church where it was not used. . . . . What have we in the New Testament for it, or against it? St. Paul says: 'God grant mercy to the house of Onesiphorus, for he refreshed me many times, and was not ashamed of my chain; but being in Rome carefully sought and found me. The Lord grant him to find mercy of the Lord in that day. For how many things he furnished

---

* It is asserted by Dr. Brett, at p. 425 of the "Dissertations," appended to his "Collection of Liturgies," that Thorndike composed the following inscription to be placed upon his tombstone in Westminster Abbey, of which he was one of the prebendaries: "Hic jacet corpus Herberti Thorndike, Prebendarii hujus Ecclesiæ, qui vivus, veram reformandæ Ecclesiæ rationem ac modum precihusque, studiisque prosequebatur. Tu Lector, requiem ei et beatam in Christo resurrectionem, precare."

me at Ephesus thou better knowest.' Shall I say that Onesiphorus was alive at Rome when St. Paul wrote this, and that, therefore, he prayeth for himself apart, and his household apart? Let impartial reason judge whether St. Paul would have prayed for him that was alive with him at Rome, and not ashamed of his bonds, found him out and refreshed him? or whether he prays for him being dead, that he may find mercy in that day; for his family only that they may find mercy? But fall that how it may, he prays for that which could not befall him until the day of judgment, though dead. And therefore all those scriptures which make the reward of the world to come to depend upon the trial of the day of judgment, do prove that we are to pray for the issue of it, in behalf of all, so long as it is coming. St. Paul says: 'Who also shall confirm you unto the end, that you *may be blameless in the day of our Lord Jesus Christ.*' 'Repent ye, and be converted,' says another apostle, ' that your sins may be blotted out when the time of refreshing shall come from the presence of the Lord.' 'That I may rejoice in the day of Christ,' writes St. Paul, 'that I have not run in vain, nor laboured in vain.' ' For what is our hope or joy, or crown of rejoicing? Are not even ye in the presence of our Lord Jesus Christ at His coming?' 'Who are kept by the power of God,' says St. Peter, 'through faith unto salvation, ready to be revealed at the last time.' 'That the spirit may be saved,' says St. Paul, 'in the day of the Lord Jesus.' 'Henceforth there is laid up for me a crown of righteousness, which the Lord the righteous judge shall give me at that day.' 'Thou shalt be recompensed at the resurrection of the just,' says our Lord Himself. For all which there were no reason to be given, but the mention of the day of judgment would be utterly impertinent if the reward were declared at the hour of death, and that judgment which then passeth. For how can that be expected which is already enjoyed? Certain we are that the estate of those who die in God's grace admits a solicitous expectation of the day of judgment, though assured of the issue of it. That is it, which so many texts of Scripture alleged afore, signify nothing, if they signify it not."*

The following extract from a Form of Prayer, first drawn up in commemoration of the martyrdom

---

* "Of the Laws of the Church," Epilogue, book iii. chap. xxvii., by Herbert Thorndike, Prebendary of Westminster. See also the same writer's "Weights and Measures," ch. xvi. pp. 106, 107.

of King Charles I., said to be from the pen of his near friend and spiritual adviser, Bishop Juxon, likewise embodies the same practice :—

"But here, O Lord, we offer unto Thee all possible praise and thanks for all the glory of Thy grace that shineth forth in Thine anointed, our late Sovereign, and that Thou wert pleased to own him (this day especially) in the midst of his enemies and in the hour of death, and to endue him with such eminent patience, meekness, humility, charity, and all other Christian virtues, according to the example of Thine Own Son, suffering the fury of His and Thine enemies, for the preservation of Thy Church and people. And we beseech Thee to give us all grace to remember and provide for our latter end, by a careful, studious imitation of this Thy blessed saint and martyr, and all other Thy saints and martyrs that have gone before us, that we may be made worthy to receive benefit by their prayers, which they in communion with Thy Church Catholick offer up unto Thee, for that part of it here militant, and yet in fight with and danger from the flesh; but following the blessed steps of their holy lives, we may also show forth the light of a good example; for the glory of Thy name, the conversion of our enemies, and the improvement of those generations we shall shortly leave behind us, and then with all those that have born the heat and burden of the day (Thy servant particularly whose sufferings and labours we this day commemorate) receive the reward of our labours, the harvest of our hopes, even the salvation of our souls; and that for the merits and through the mediation of Thy Son Our Blessed Saviour Jesus Christ." (A.D. 1661).*

---

* "A Form of Common Prayer to be used upon the Thirtieth of January." Published by His Majesty's direction. London, printed by John Hill, 1661. (In the Bodleian Library.)

And this from the reputed author of the "Eikon Basilike:"—

"It is our bounden duty never to fail, so long as we are in this flesh, to remember them, once with us, now in the spirit, and awaiting the tender mercy of our Father in heaven, who themselves wait for the consummation of their imperfect joy. As the ancient Fathers, in the most purest times of our holy religion, were always wont to pray when the oblation was made, so we do ask God on the like occasion, and in common prayers, as we should also in private prayer, to have mercy in His great day upon all Christian souls."* (A.D. 1662.)

The following, relating to the argument from Scripture, is from the pen of Bishop Jeremy Taylor, whose devotional writings are so popular still:—

"We find by the history of the Maccabees that the Jews did pray and make offerings for the dead, which also appears by other testimonies, and by their forms of prayer still extant, which they used in the captivity. Now it is very considerable that, given our Blessed Saviour did reprove all the evil doctrines and traditions of the Scribes and Pharisees, and did

---

* "Sermon of the Right Rev. Father in God, John [Gauden] Lord Bishop of Worcester, at Worcester," 1662.

argue concerning the dead and the resurrection, against the Sadducees, yet He spake no word against this public practice, but left it as He found it; which He who came to declare to us all the will of the Father would not have done if it had not been innocent, pious, and full of charity."

And this from one of the same writer's controversial works:—

"Upon what accounts the Fathers did pray for saints departed, and, indeed, generally for all, it is not now seasonable to discourse; but to say this only, that such general prayers for the dead as those above reckoned, the Church of England did never condemn by any express article, but left it in the middle."*

Richard Montagu, Bishop of Chichester, in reply to the objection regarding the existence of a locality for preparation or cleansing, because there is no such place mentioned in God's written Word, answers the objection thus: "Though there be no third place mentioned in Scripture, yet it would not follow hence that there was no such place, because there are many things which are not expressed in Scripture." Then, as to the texts which seem to restrain the state of

---

* "Dissuasive," by Jeremy Taylor, part i. chapter i. s. 4; part. ii. book ii. s. 2.

departed souls either to hell or heaven, he declares: "This is to be understood of the final state of souls, after the day of judgment, when there will be no more than two conditions of souls everlasting, viz., heaven and hell."*

Thomas Ken, some time Bishop of Bath and Wells, put forth the following two years after his deprival:—

"O my God, let it be Thy good pleasure to put a period to sin and misery, to infirmity, sickness, and death; to complete the number of Thine elect, to gather both living and departed again together, to hasten Thy kingdom of glory, that I, and all who wait for Thy living breath, whether they be in the flesh or sleeping in Christ, may in the church triumphant eternally love, praise, and glorify Thee, Father, Son, and Holy Ghost, God blessed for evermore. Amen." †

After the Revolution, the influence of the Nonjuring school was very largely felt, and sensibly affected theological thought in the National Church. With scarcely an exception, all the writers of this section of learned and conscientious Christians pronounced most definitely in favour of prayers for the dead. In truth, no treatise on the Christian sacrifice issued by them was without systematic and laborious

* Appar., p. 135.
† Ken's "Devotions," p. 59. London, 1686.

defences of the principle, which even Burnet, Bishop of Salisbury, was compelled to admit had abundant authority from primitive antiquity, the ancient Fathers, and the English Book of Common Prayer.* Amongst the most notable writers of the Nonjurors were Hickes, Brett, Gadderer, Archibald Campbell, Rattray, and Collier the historian, all of whom maintain the practical importance of this most pious and charitable observance. The last-named thus thoughtfully writes :—

"That the ancient church believed the recommending the dead a serviceable office, we need not question; otherwise, to what purpose was it so generally practised? The custom seems to have gone upon this principle, that supreme happiness is not to be expected till the resurrection; and that the interval between death and the end of the world is a state of imperfect bliss. The church might, therefore, believe her prayers for good people departed

---

* "Besides, the usual forms of wishing the dead peace, light, and refreshment, together with mercy, shew a state or place of uneasiness. And even in our Litany, as the middle state is evident in the prayer for deliverance in the hour of death, and in the day of judgment: insomuch that between death and the day of judgment there must be some state out of which we pray to be delivered at that great and last day; so the afflictive part is plainly implied in the word deliver, which is always from something disagreeable to us."—*An Essay on Catholick Communion*, chapter vii. p. 111. London, 1704.

might improve their condition, and raise the satisfactions of this period." *

The influence of the Nonjurors lasted almost to the dawn of the Oxford Revival, and served to tincture most of the literature regarding ecclesiastical antiquity. During the eighteenth century this was certainly the case with Bingham, whose learned and painstaking treatise has not only become a standard work at home, but has been recognized as masterly and most valuable abroad.

He thus delivers himself on the subject, when commenting upon the prayer of St. Augustine of Hippo for his mother Monica:—

"This was not a prayer for persons in the pains of purgatory, but for such as rested in peace only without dependence upon their own merits. . . . Another like reason for these prayers is that which we have heard before out of Epiphanius [Epiphan. Hæres., lxxv. Aërian., n. iii. vol i. p. 908. Colon. 1682.]: 'That it was to put a distinction between the perfection of Christ and the imperfection of all other men, saints, martyrs, apostles, prophets, confessors, etc., He being the only person for whom prayer was

---

* "An Ecclesiastical History of Great Britain," by Jeremy Collier, M.A. (in nine volumes), vol. v. pp. 283—284. London, 1845.

not then made in the church.' They prayed for all Christians as a testimony both of their respect and love to the dead, and of their own belief of the soul's immortality; to show, as Epiphanius words it in the same place, that they believed that they who were deceased were yet alive, and not extinguished, but still in being, and living with the Lord. Whereas the soul is but in an imperfect state of happiness till the resurrection, when the whole man shall obtain a complete victory over death, and by the last judgment be established in an endless state of consummate happiness and glory, the church had a particular respect to this in her prayers for the righteous, that both the living and the dead might finally attain this blessed estate of a glorious resurrection."*

Wheatley, whose treatise on the Prayer Book is still almost universally recommended by English bishops to theological students, thus writes with regard to the opinion of the Fathers on the subject :—

"They all agreed in this, that the interval between death and the end of the world is a state of expectation and imperfect bliss, in which the souls of the

---

* "Origines Ecclesiasticæ," by the Rev. Joseph Bingham, M.A. (in nine volumes), vol. v. pp. 121, 122. London, 1844.

righteous wait for the completion and perfection of their happiness at the consummation of all things; and therefore, whilst they were praying for the Catholic Church, they thought it not improper to add a petition on behalf of that larger and better part of it which had gone before them, that they might all together attain a blessed and glorious resurrection, and be brought at last to a perfect fruition of happiness in heaven. By this means they testified their love and respect for the dead, declared their belief in the communion of saints, and kept up in themselves a lively sense of the soul's immortality."* (A.D. 1772.)

The opinions already set forth, covering more than two centuries, were shared from time to time by Archbishop Laud, who expressed them most definitely in his "Answer to Fisher, the Jesuit;" by Henry Hammond; Archbishop Usher; † Goodman, Bishop of Gloucester; William Beveridge, Bishop of St. Asaph; George Smallridge, Bishop of Bristol; by Peter

---

* "Rational Illustration of the Book of Common Prayer," by Charles Wheatley, M.A., p. 243. Oxford, 1846.—Wheatley, as is well known, prepared the following inscription for his tomb: "Reader, join for him in the ejaculation of St. Paul, 'The Lord grant unto him that he may find mercy of the Lord in that day.' Amen."

† Usher's "Works," vol. iii. pp. 201, 202; and his "Answer to the Challenge," *in loco*.

Gunning, Bishop of Ely, in his treatise "On the Fast of Lent;" by John Lake, Bishop of Bristol, in his devotional manuals; by Samuel Parker, Bishop of Oxford, in his controversies with Roman Catholics; by Simon Patrick, Bishop of Ely; and other prelates and clergy of the second order too numerous to mention. Wilson, Bishop of Sodor and Man, taught the practice with much boldness of language. The theological section of our National Church, known for several generations as the High Church school, have consistently and continuously enjoined this duty with more or less lucidity and plainness of speech. The Puritans, as well as the followers of Burnet and the disciples of Hoadley, on the other hand, have all in turn either ignored or rejected the doctrine of Prayers for the Dead with persistent determination. And yet we know that next to the direct worship of God there is nothing which more immediately arises from true religious feeling than reverence and love for the departed. The amount of national religion in ancient as well as in modern times may be accurately gauged from this. Closely following a belief in God stands a belief in a future state, and consequently an interest in the whereabouts and welfare of those who have passed away. To profess ignorance or indifference to their state is an unvarying note of the presence and influence of unbelief.

This being so, it is reasonable to find unbroken evidence of the existence of a true faith in this doctrine and duty within the Church of England amongst the valued records and memorials of the dead in the past.* It is true that we have lost our old services, so full of piety and charity; with many of the advantages which their public use bestowed. The unbridled fanaticism of the foreign gospellers did its work for awhile. Still the doctrine of the Communion of Saints, with a belief that the principal part of the Church Universal is that which exists in the regions beyond the grave, is ours—a blessed heritage from the Upper Room at Jerusalem.

The prayers relating to the departed, both in the Communion Service of our present Book of Common Prayer, as well as in the Service for the Burial of the Dead, together with the principle of divine charity involved in their use and practice (a use and practice never condemned by the Church of England), are not without their legitimate influence in moulding thought and stamping a catholic character on the children of our national communion, though these

* See Appendices Nos. VI., IX., X., and XI.

prayers are less definite than those which were used of yore. Still, the old and unchangeable sentiment and traditions of the Church Universal live on, and their roots lie deep down in regenerated human nature. Consequently in every age, since the changes of the sixteenth century took place, there have been those who have put into a practical form their interest in departed friends, and have constantly and charitably remembered them in prayer before the throne of God.* And this not with the clergy alone, but

---

* The following extracts from two MS. volumes of prayers of the latter part of the last century, by a clergyman of the Church of England, related to the author, are worthy of being here put on record, because of their intrinsic beauty and catholic sentiments:—

(α) "Have mercy, O Lord God, God of all spirits, upon the souls of my friends and relations who have departed this life, especially upon . . . . and . . . . . . Look with the eye of pity on all their misdeeds in the flesh, pardon their sins, assuage their pains, and dew them with Thy heavenly grace. Remember them, O Lord, in Thy mercy and goodness, and be to them a Saviour and a Friend. Take them from the region of darkness, if there they wait expecting Thee, to a place of refreshment and light. Call not to mind their moments of weakness and forgetfulness of Thee and of Thy divine gifts, but remember that they were redeemed by the precious blood of Thy dear Son, and give unto them Thy peace. This grant for the sake of Thine only-begotten Son, Christ Jesus Our Lord."

(β) "Remember, likewise, O Lord God, all the faithful, departed in Thy faith and fear. Blot out their transgressions, because of the bloodshedding upon the cross. And in due course bestow upon them the full fruition of Thy adorable presence, Father, Son, and Holy Ghost."

(γ) "Likewise, O merciful God, look with pity on all who sleep in the church and graveyard of this parish. Refresh them with the dews of Thy grace, who pant for Thee as the hart panteth for the waterbrooks; and prepare them for the rest and glory of Thine eternal and everlasting kingdom." [The

with the laity, and especially with the poor. Amongst the latter, until quite recently, many very pious devotions, traditionally handed down from past times, with restorations of practical duties concerning the dead, taught by the Wesleys, were still in constant use, and came quite natural to all who professed a belief in the Communion of Saints.* The Poet

The clergyman who is believed to have drawn up the above, likewise made use of the following, relating to the faithful dead, in the Bidding Prayer, which it was his custom to use before the sermon on the Sunday morning—the first in each month—when the Holy Sacrament was celebrated in the church of which for fifty years he was the vicar:—

"We commend also unto Thy mercy, O Lord, all other Thy servants who are departed hence with the sign of faith and now rest in the sleep of death. Grant unto them, we beseech Thee, Thy mercy, and everlasting peace, that at the general resurrection, we and all they of the mystical body of Thy Son, may together be set on His right hand, and hear that his most joyful voice, 'Come ye blessed of my Father, receive the kingdom prepared for you from the foundation of the world.'"

* See "Life of Dr. Samuel Johnson," under date 1782; Mrs. Delany's "Memoirs," in which several examples may be found; and the following from the pen of Bishop Reginald Heber:—

"Having been led attentively to consider the question, my own opinion is on the whole favourable to this practice, which indeed is so natural and so comfortable that this alone is a presumption, that it is neither unpleasing to the Almighty, nor unavailing with Him. . . . I have accordingly been myself in the habit for some years of recommending on some occasions—as after receiving the Sacrament, etc.—my lost friends by name to God's goodness and compassion through His Son, as what can do them no harm, and *may*, and I hope *will*, be of service to them. Only this condition I always endeavour to observe—that I beg His forgiveness at the same time for myself, if unknowingly I am too presumptuous, and His grace lest I who am thus solicitous for *others*, should neglect the appointed means of my own salvation."—(Bishop Heber's judgment on Prayers for the Dead, given in "Diaries of a Lady of Quality," p. 196.)

"All doctrines of purgatory do not appear to be condemned by our Articles, and that there were several

Laureate of this present age appropriately and

doctrines is manifest from history. There is the doctrine of Origen, the teaching of Augustine, the statement put forth at the Council of Florence, and the later doctrine of Trent. But even this latter is not condemned, because it was put forth after our Articles were promulged. Prayers for the dead are not anywhere condemned by authority, except where they imply the Roman doctrine concerning purgatory. *Requiescat in pace* does not appear to involve this." —*Dr. Shute Barrington*, Bishop of Durham. "MS. Letter with regard to inscriptions on monuments erected during his episcopate, to Dr. Routh, of Oxford."

"I never pass through a churchyard, known to me or strange, in which I do not breathe a prayer to Almighty God for his mercy upon the spirits of those who rest there."— *Address to Churchwardens*, by Edward Legge, D.D., Lord Bishop of Oxford. Oxford, 1818.

In still more recent times, Bishop Kaye, of Lincoln, is reported to have given the following judgment on the subject:—

"It has, I believe, been determined that prayers for the dead, if they are not connected with the doctrine of Purgatory, are not forbidden in our Church. Independently, however, of this, as the case to which your letter refers is the restoration of an ancient monument; the inscription ought to preserve consistency, to be suited to the religious opinions of the age in which the monument was originally constructed.

"(Signed) J. Lincoln.
"Riseholme, August 1, 1849."

And the Bishop of Winchester (Dr. Samuel Wilberforce), in reply to a remonstrance from some persons at Ryde against the use of the words—
" Eternal rest give unto him, O Lord, And let perpetual light shine upon him,"

on a gravestone in the cemetery of that town, thus wrote:—

"I have given my best attention to your communication, but nothing which you have urged affects my judgment that the Church of England has nowhere disallowed the words I have permitted to be employed, and that their disallowance would, therefore, have been a breach of charity." (A.D. 1871.)

Sir Charles L. Young writes to me as follows, and I acknowledge his kindness with gratitude:—

"There is a tablet in Bristol Cathedral, of the last century, containing a *Requiescat in Pace*. Of course you know the last-century windows in New College Chapel, desiring prayers for the soul of the Founder."

Other correspondents inform me of the existence of several monuments with prayers for the dead inscribed upon them at Hereford Cathedral, Worcester Cathedral, Lincoln Cathedral, St. Alban's Abbey, Dorchester Church, Oxon, Tunstead Church, Norfolk, Carisbrooke Churchyard, Isle of Wight, etc.

naturally closes one of his most touching poems,* written because of the office he holds, with a prayer for the dead, thus additionally testifying to our belief and practice from the sixteenth century to the present time.

> * "The man is gone, who seem'd so great,
> Gone, but nothing can bereave him
> Of the force he made his own
> Being here, and we believe him
> Something far advanced in state,
> And that he wears a truer crown '
> Than any wreaths that man can weave him.
> But speak no more of his renown,
> Lay your earthly fancies down,
> And in the vast cathedral leave him,
> God accept him, Christ receive him."

—*Ode on the Death of the Duke of Wellington*, by Alfred Tennyson. p. 16, London, 1852.

CHAPTER XII.

THE CHRISTIAN DUTY OF PRAYING FOR THE DEPARTED.

OF the general necessity of earnest, systematic, constant, and devout prayer to God, no Christian can doubt. Prayer has been concisely and clearly defined by St. Thomas Aquinas to be an act of the reasoning powers of man making manifest the desire of his will, in which he asks God either to remove some evil or to bestow some good.* Such prayer, then, is most needful for us all. It is the channel through which the rivers of divine grace flow into the soul of the believer. No Christian can become utterly vicious and callous to his eternal interests, nor fall absolutely into scepticism and unbelief, unless he first relinquishes the great duty of prayer. And no Christian is worthy of the name who does not, like David of old, pray at least three times a-day, who declared, "In the evening, and morning, and at

* In Sec. Secund. Quæst. lxxxiii. i.

noonday will I pray, and that instantly, and He shall hear my voice." Prayer to become efficacious, however, and to bring down the abiding blessings of the Most High, must be made with a firm faith and confidence in God, with humility of heart and purity of intention. The Apostle St. Paul sets forth what kind of prayers should be used in the following passage: "I exhort therefore, that, first of all, supplications, prayers, intercessions, and giving of thanks [εὐχαριστίας] be made for all men."* Bishop Hammond, in his "Practical Catechism," following the order of the Catechism of the Council of Trent, thus divides the subject-matter of prayer:—

(a) "Supplications." The acknowledging of sin and asking pardon; or the removal of temporal and spiritual evil.

(β) "Prayers." The asking for those things which are needful both for our souls and bodies, especially for the bestowal of such gifts as may ensure our growth in grace.

(γ) "Intercessions." The prayers or requests which are made for others, whether friends or enemies, for the averting of evil from them, or the bestowal of gifts.

* 1 Tim. ii. 1.

(δ) "The giving of thanks." Acknowledging both God's temporal and His spiritual mercies to ourselves as well as to others.

With the third of these divisions, "intercessions," are we now specially concerned.

Theologians teach that we are without any doubt bound to intercede for all men, but especially for those who are of the household of faith. All, therefore, are to be included in our general acts of intercession, without the exception either of enemy, nation, or religion. For every person, be he foe, alien, or unbeliever, is our neighbour, whom by God's express commands we are enjoined to love, and for whom consequently we should continually offer up our prayers—a primary duty of love. Of course in these intercessions those things which pertain to the salvation of the soul should occupy the first place; things temporal the second.

We should pray, then, for all who are set over us in the Lord, and for all who have in times past occupied that position, whether they be still in the flesh, or have passed away to the unseen world. We should intercede for those without the pale of the visible Church, that is, for the idolaters, unbelievers, Jews, Moslems, heretics, and schismatics, that faith may be given to infidels, that idolaters and worshippers of false gods may be freed from the error of impiety, that Mahometans may be converted, that Jews may receive the light of Christian truth, that heretics, returning to soundness of doctrine, may be built up in the true teaching of the Church Universal, and that schismatics, inflamed once again by divine and not by false charity, may be re-united to the One Church of God. And particularly we should constantly, earnestly, and devoutly intercede for the departed, for father, mother, brother, sister, friend, relative; for all the dead who may have wronged us, and for all whom we have wronged. We should do so, as has been already set forth, on the following and on other grounds:—

1. The dead need our prayers, because their eventual final state is not yet settled. They are still in the keeping of the Most High. "The souls of the righteous are in the hands of God," but not yet in His presence.

2. Even those who are saints will have an additional happiness bestowed upon them in the future, when all the ransomed in Christ are joined with them at the last; as St. Paul declares, "God having provided some better thing for us, that

they [the saints] without us should not be made perfect."*

3. We know that the souls of those who have died in the faith and fear of God must have every stain, even the smallest, removed before they are fitted for heaven. For "there shall in no wise enter into it [the city of God] anything that defileth."†

4. There are (a) punishments inflicted after death, and (β) forgiveness of sins bestowed in the world to come. This we know for certain, because our Blessed Saviour declared that the person delivered by the judge to the officer, and by the officer cast into prison, shall not come out thence till he has paid the uttermost farthing; ‡ and, as regards the second case, that "whosoever speaketh against the Holy Ghost, it shall not be forgiven him, neither in this world, nor in the world to come." §

5. Furthermore, there is a progress constantly going on amongst the departed in Christ in the region beyond the grave. The work begun during lifetime in the soul by Christ Jesus our Saviour shall be completed, or confirmed, as the apostle declares, in the day of the Lord.‖

---

* Heb. xi. '40. † Rev. xxi. 27. ‡ St. Matt. v. 25, 26.
§ St. Matt. xii. 32. ‖ Phil. i. 6; 1 Thess. v. 23.

6. Just as we should not be so uncharitable and heartless as to refuse our prayers on behalf of a dying man, because we were doubtful as to his spiritual state, so we should charitably pray for all such as depart in the faith of the Gospel, holding that even if the souls for which we pray are incapable of relief, yet such intercessions will not be thrown away before God, Who is the true and faithful rewarder of charity, though in pardonable ignorance it may have been misapplied.*

7. Finally, though we may know but little of the needs of the departed, though many details upon which men desire information are withheld for some good and sufficient purpose by God, yet such want of accurate knowledge on our part should not prevent the charitable work being undertaken of praying for our lost friends and relations. We never, for example, hesitate to pray for those temporarily absent from our sight and homes, because we do not accurately and precisely know their immediate actual needs; why then should we withhold our interces-

---

* In truth this teaching is founded on the express commands of our Saviour himself. For when the Apostles greeted any with the blessed salutation, 'Peace be to this house,' the greeting was not lost, even if there were no one of peace to receive it, for it returned, as their Master had promised, to those who made the prayer of peace for their neighbour, and they themselves were blessed because of their charity.

sions for those who, though they have passed the gate of death, still belong to us and to the One Family of Christ, and, it may be, still require our prayers?

On the general subject something more must here be added. With some in the Latin Church it is held that those who have passed to the region of the departed suffer keenly, as the Council of Florence declared, because not yet admitted to the presence of God.* On the other hand, as St. Catherine of Genoa asserted, she did not believe "it would be possible to find any joy comparable to that of a soul in purgatory, except the joy of the blessed in Paradise, a joy which goes on increasing day by day as God more and more flows in upon the soul, which He does abundantly, in proportion as every hindrance to His entrance is consumed away." † Of course no tongue can declare what exquisite pain it would be

---

* "If when the soul is parted from all earthly distractions, it comes to see that God is its only Good, and is yet withheld from His beatific sight, that it may learn to long for Him, this is at once what the schools have called the *pœna damni;* and this awakened, unsatisfied longing, with the sense that through its own fault it remains in this darkness as to God, may be intenser pain than any, or than all the pain which could be accumulated in one in this life. We know what pain separation from an object of deep human love occasions. What may it not be, of God?" —*An Explanation of the Thirty-nine Articles*, by A. P. Forbes, D.C.L., vol. ii. p. 334. London, 1868.

† "On Purgatory," by St. Catherine of Genoa, edited by Archbishop Manning, c. 5.

to a soul freed from the body, impetuously desiring the attainment of complete and intimate union with God, to be withheld from His presence. Such, in its want, then, the tender mercy of God recommends to the charity of the faithful. If it be an essential ingredient of a Christian spirit to pray for all under temporary sorrows and needs; if here on earth the cup of cold water given in the Name of Christ shall not lose its due reward; if, in fact, all works of mercy certainly draw down God's abundant gifts, and will be surely repaid by Him at the last day; then we may reasonably believe and confidently hope that our Prayers for the Dead, whom we have loved and lost, shall not be in vain in the Lord. For such a charity is wholesome and profitable both for them and us.* They are our fellow-citizens and companions, only that the head of the one on-going procession in which they and we, and thousands of others, either have taken, or are taking, an appointed place, has reached

---

* Gerson, the pious and learned Chancellor of Paris, represents the departed as thus crying out to those of their friends still in the flesh: "Pray for us because we are unable to help ourselves. You who can do it, lend us your assistance. You who have known us on earth, you who have loved us, will you now forget and neglect us? It is commonly remarked that a friend is tested in the day of necessity. What need can be greater than ours? Let it move your compassion. A hard heart shall fare ill at the last day. Be moved by your own advantage."—*Gerson's* "Works," vol. iii. p. 193.

the quiet land, a land of repose and beauty beyond the everlasting hills, unseen by us who are here still journeying over the flats and quagmires of earth.

Two other considerations, most ably stated in a thoughtful but too brief essay on the general subject, are fittingly reproduced here:—

"Another truth which underlies the doctrine of Prayers for the Dead I believe to be this: that the race of man, and pre-eminently the Christian portion of it, is one family, and that death does not and cannot destroy that network of mutual interests and sympathies which bind us together and make us necessary to each other on earth. The great evil of our nature, the cause of nearly all its woes, is selfishness—the repudiation of our family relations and responsibilities. How does God contrive to cure us of that selfishness? By making us necessary to each other. 'Every good gift and every perfect gift is from above, and cometh down from the Father of lights, with whom is no variableness, neither shadow of turning.'

"But hardly one of these good gifts is bestowed on man directly from on high. They all reach him through the ministry of his fellows. It is right that no unnecessary obstacles should intervene between the soul of man and its God. But has not Protestantism pushed that principle too far? Goethe thought so, and he was a true interpreter of humanity in that opinion. It is God's will to save men, not as isolated and unconnected units, but as members of a body, and common subjects of a holy kingdom; and to bring this great truth home to them He makes them necessary to each other at every turn. In this respect man is more helpless than the brutes that perish. No animal is less self-dependent than he. From the moment he issues from the womb till he is laid in the grave he needs the help of parents, of nurses, of teachers. On the right hand and on the left he has to lean on the arm of his fellow-man. Life would be impossible to him without the aid, and would soon become insupportable without the sympathy, of his kind. And lest the migrations of the race should induce men to forget their common origin and the home for which they are destined, the necessity of mutual fellowship pursues them over seas and continents. Each land has some gifts peculiar to itself which makes it the interest of all nations to be on terms of friendship with one another. And thus a loving Providence makes even our temporal wants subservient to higher purposes, teaching us the impiety of the first murderer's selfish exclamation, and compelling us to see that our true happiness lies in being each his 'brother's keeper.' This principle of mutual interdependence runs through the whole of man's natural life; and it is no less conspicuous in his moral and spiritual life. Nor is it bounded by this earthly scene. Death does not destroy the family relationship of our race. The dead are 'not lost, but gone before,' and constitute, with those still left behind, one family—'the whole family in heaven and in earth,' as St. Paul expresses it. Now what can be so well calculated to keep this truth alive in our minds as the doctrine and practice of praying for the dead? Condemn that doctrine, and then see whether death has indeed 'lost its sting' as you stand by the grave of your beloved!

"The third truth implied in praying for the dead, and the last one which I shall touch on here, may be stated briefly as follows: The heart of man instinctively refuses to believe in death, and to accept it as its natural and final destiny. The heart searches for its vanished kindred, and will not believe that they cease to be, or that its interest in them, or theirs in it, is broken. It is a universal sentiment of humanity; and the more civilized humanity is, the deeper is the sentiment. It is seen in an Old Mortality going up and down the country laboriously renewing the time-worn tombstones of the Covenanters, and in the great orator of Athens, who knew the spell that it contained when he promised victory to his degenerate countrymen by a passionate adjuration of 'the dead at Marathon.' It is also seen in those legends of many lands which represent some hero or national benefactor as enjoying an immunity from the last debt of humanity; our own Arthur still living in the vale of Avalon, or the great German Kaiser sleeping in his mystic cave till his country shall again need his trusty sword. The fact is, we all pray for the dead—at least all loving hearts do. When our beloved pass away from us, we follow them with our longing thoughts, we speculate on their condition in the world unseen, we wish them well. And what is a wish but an unexpressed prayer? 'Every good and holy desire,' says Hooker, 'though it lack the form, hath notwithstanding in itself the substance and with Him the force of a prayer, who regardeth the very moanings and sighs of the heart of man.'" *

Therefore, to be practical in these closing lines of

* "Prayers for the Dead," by the Rev. Malcolm MacColl, in the *Contemporary Review* for January, 1871, pp. 277—279.

this treatise, day by day let us remember the departed. In the morning, when we rise refreshed anew for the day's labours; at noontide, when, by God's grace, we snatch a few moments of quiet from our worldly occupations to lift up our hearts with recollectedness to God; at our evening devotions, when the shadows gather and night draws on, let us remember those whose labours we have lost. Again, when we come together for our bodily sustenance, as did our forefathers of old, so in faith and love, having been ourselves sustained in the body, let us then ask refreshment for the souls of the dead in Christ. More particularly at the offering of the Sacred Oblation, Sunday by Sunday, and time by time, let us pray for all who have gone before us in the faith of Christ, and now rest in the sleep of peace, pleading His adorable Sacrifice for all their necessities. For those who most need our prayers pray we; for such as have few or none to pray for them; for all souls who are waiting for a full fruition of the Light of God's presence. Thus shall the shadow of the cross fall upon a lustrous pathway day by day in our onward journey. For in this particular we shall be living in charity. Bear we specially in mind, likewise, those whom we have known and loved. We should not, as is so commonly the case, be too much engrossed in self-contemplation and selfishness, but should extend our vision and expand our charity. As the writer has recently taught from the pulpit:* "Let us ever remember the departed. With some, their memories soon fade and are forgotten; with others they remain green and fresh through the summer and autumn of a long life, even into the chill and loneliness of its winter-time and close. So be it with all gathered here. Though others may forget and mention not their names, let no return of their anniversary remain unused and unhonoured by us. As the hart desires the waterbrooks, so do the souls of those departed in Christ long for Almighty God. To Him they cry out of the deep. As we turn over the sacred books they used in their lifetime, as we linger in the homes dearer to us because they were *their* homes too, when we go to visit the graves where their bodies rest, away from the dust and turmoil of this vast city, in a

---

* "Our Duty to the Departed," a Sermon on the Death of the Rev. J. A. Johnston, by the Rev. F. G. Lee, D.C.L., pp. 9, 10. London, 1871. The edition of this sermon, from which the above quotation is made, having been exhausted in a few days —a fact testifying to the respect in which the late Vicar of St. John's was so deservedly held—the author, at the request of several friends, has consented to re-produce it in its integrity at the end of this volume. It may be found, consequently, under Appendix No. XIII.

sleeping-place where the grass grows green and the sunshine falls; or when in dull November, year by year, All Souls' Day comes round again, with its hallowed associations and loving duties, let us always remember the departed and pray, 'Lord, Thy kingdom come.' . . . A little while, and this separation shall be ended. And when it is ended there shall be a break and a parting nevermore, for God shall be all in all."

Ad majorem Dei gloriam.

APPENDIX I.

INHUMATIO DEFUNCTI.

(Secundum Usum Sarum.)

Post Missam accedat Sacerdos ad caput defuncti, alba indutus, absque cappa serica: et duo Clerici de secunda forma ad caput defuncti stantes, incipiunt tribus vicibus Antiphonam sequentem, quam Chorus singulis vicibus totam prosequatur usque in finem.

Ant. Circumdederunt me gemitus mortis: dolores inferni circumdederunt me.

Deinde post tertiam repetitionem sequatur:

Kyrie eleyson.
Christe eleyson.
Kyrie eleyson.

Non dicatur Pater noster, *nec* Dominus vobiscum, *neque* Oremus: *sed tantum Oratio, Sacerdote dicente modesta voce, videlicet sine nota:*

Non intres in judicium cum servo tuo [*vel* servula tua] Domine, quoniam nullus apud te justificabitur homo, nisi per te omnium peccatorum tribuatur remissio: non ergo eum [*vel* eam] tua quæsumus judicialis sententia premat, quem [*vel* quam] tibi vera supplicatio fidei Christianæ commendat; sed gratia tua illi succurrente mereatur evadere judicium ultionis, qui [*vel* quæ] dum viveret insignitus [*vel* insignita] est signaculo Sanctæ Trinitatis. In qua vivis et regnas, etc.

Eodem modo dicuntur omnes Orationes sequentes.

Deinde incipiat Cantor:

R. Qui Lazarum resuscitasti a monumento fœtidum: Tu eis Domine dona requiem et locum indulgentiæ.

V. Qui venturus es judicare vivos, et mortuos, et sæculum per ignem.

Tu eis.

Et percantetur a choro cum suo versu, et interim Sacerdos cum thuribulo circumeundo corpus, illud incenset. Similiter fiat in Responsoriis sequentibus.

Deinde dicitur:

Kyrie eleyson.
Christe eleyson.
Kyrie eleyson.

Sine Pater noster, *et sine* Dominus vobiscum. *Sed tantum cum* Oremus.

Oratio. Deus cui omnia vivunt, cui non pereunt moriendo corpora nostra, sed mutantur in melius, te supplices deprecamur, ut quicquid famulus [*vel* famula] tuus [*vel* tua] vitiorum tuæ voluntati contrarium, fallente diabolo, et propria iniquitate atque fragilitate contraxit, tu pius et misericors abluas indulgendo, ejusque animam suscipi jubeas, per manus sanctorum angelorum tuorum deducendam in Sinum patriarcharum tuorum Abrahæ scilicet amici tui, et Isaac electi tui, atque Jacob dilecti tui, quo aufugit dolor et tristitia, atque suspirium, fidelium quoque animæ felici jocunditate lætantur, et in novissimo magni judicii die inter sanctos et electos tuos eam facias perpetuæ gloriæ tuæ percipere portionem, quam oculus non vidit, nec auris audivit, et in cor hominis non ascendit quam præparasti diligentibus te. Per Christum Dominum nostrum. R. Amen.

R. Heu mihi, Domine, quia peccavi in vita mea: quid faciam

APPENDIX I.

miser? ubi fugiam, nisi ad Te Deus meus? Miserere mei. Dum veneris in novissimo die.

V. Anima mea turbata est valde, sed Tu, Domine, succere ei. Dum veneris.

Et percantetur a choro cum suo versu, et interim incensetur corpus ut supra.

Deinde sequatur:

Kyrie eleyson.
Christe eleyson.
Kyrie eleyson.

Sine Pater noster, *et sine* Dominus vobiscum, *sed tantum cum* Oremus.

Fac quæsumus, Domine, hanc cum servulo tuo defuncto [*vel* servula tua defuncta] misericordiam, ut factorum suorum in pœnis non recipiat vicem, qui [*vel* quæ] tuam in votis tenuit voluntatem: et quia hic illum [*vel* illam] vera fides junxit fidelium turmis, illic eum [*vel* eam] tua miseratio societ angelicis choris. Per Christum Dominum nostrum.

Deinde incipiat Cantor:

R. Libera me, Domine, de morte æterna in die illa tremenda, quando cœli movendi sunt et terra. Dum veneris judicare sæculum per ignem.

V. Dies illa, dies iræ, calamitatis et miseriæ: dies magna et amara valde.

Et percantetur a choro cum uno versu tantum, scilicet Dies illa ut supra, et interim incensetur corpus a Sacerdote semel circumeundo, et postea aspergatur aqua benedicta.

Deinde sequatur:

Kyrie eleyson.
Christe eleyson.
Kyrie eleyson.

PRAYERS FOR THE DEPARTED.

Deinde roget Sacerdos circumstantes orare pro anima defuncti dicens:

Pro anima N. et pro animabus omnium fidelium defunctorum.
Pater noster.

V. Et ne nos inducas.
R. Sed libera nos a malo.
V. Non intres in judicium cum servo tuo [*vel* servula tua] Domine.
R. Quia non justificabitur in conspectu tuo omnis vivens.
V. A porta inferi.
R. Erue Domine animas eorum.
V. Credo videre bona Domini.
R. In terra viventium.
V. Domine exaudi, etc.
R. Et clamor, etc.
V. Dominus vobiscum.
R. Et cum, etc.

Oremus.

Inclina, Domine, aurem tuam ad preces nostras, quibus misericordiam tuam supplices deprecamur, ut animam famuli tui [*vel* famulæ tuæ], quam de hoc sæculo migrare jussisti, in pacis ac lucis regione constituas, et sanctorum tuorum jubeas esse consortem. Per Christum Dominum nostrum.

Hic deportetur corpus ad sepulchrum, Cantore incipiente:
Ant. In Paradisum. E. u. o. u. a. e.
Psalmus. In exitu Israel de Ægypto.

Alius psalmus si tantum restat iter, scilicet:
Ad te Domine levavi animam meam.

Finito psalmo vel psalmis, dicatur iste versus:
Requiem æternam dona eis, Domine: et lux perpetua luceat eis.

APPENDIX I.

Deinde repetatur Antiphona:

In Paradisum deducunt te angeli, in suum conventum suscipiant te martyres, et perducant te in civitatem sanctam Hierusalem.

Quibus dictis, dicat Sacerdos sine Dominus vobiscum, *sed tantum cum* Oremus, *humili voce:*

Piæ recordationis affectu, fratres carissimi, commemorationem faciamus cari nostri [*vel* caræ nostræ] quem [*vel* quam] Dominus noster de tentationibus hujus sæculi assumpsit. Obsecremus misericordiam Dei nostri, ut ipse ei tribuere dignetur placitam et quietam mansionem, et remittat ei omnes lubricæ temeritatis offensas, ut concessa sibi venia plenæ indulgentiæ quicquid in hoc sæculo proprio vel alieno reatu deliquit, totum ineffabili pietate ac benignitate sua deleat, et abstergat. Per Christum.

Alia Oratio cum Oremus. *Oratio.* Te Domine Sancte, Pater omnipotens, æterne Deus, suppliciter deprecamur pro spiritu fratris nostri [*vel* sororis nostræ,] quem [*vel* quam] a voraginibus hujus sæculi accersiri jussisti, ut digneris, Domine, dare ei lucidum locum refrigerii et quietis. Liceat ei transire portas inferorum et pœnas tenebrarum, maneatque in mansionibus sanctorum, et in luce sancta quam olim Abrahæ promisisti et semini ejus. Nullam læsionem sentiat spiritus ejus, sed cum magnus ille dies resurrectionis advenerit cum resuscitare eum [*vel* eam] digneris una cum sanctis et electis tuis, deleasque ejus omnia delicta atque peccata usque ad novissimum quadrantem, tecumque immortalitatis tuæ vitam et regnum consequatur æternum. Per Christum Dominum nostrum. *R.* Amen.

Finitis orationibus aperiatur sepulchrum: Cantore incipiente Antiphonam:

Aperite. E. u. o. u. a. e.

Psalmus. Confitemini Domino quoniam bonus.

Finito psalmo, tota dicatur Antiphona:

Aperite mihi portas justitiæ, et ingressus in eas confitebor Domino: hæc porta Domini, justi intrabunt in eam.

Qua dicta dicat Sacerdos. Oremus.

Oratio. Obsecramus misericordiam tuam, omnipotens æterne Deus, qui hominem ad imaginem tuam creare dignatus es, ut animam famuli tui [*vel* famulæ tuæ] N. quam hodierna die rebus humanis eximi, et ad te accersiri jussisti, blande et misericorditer suscipias. Non ei dominentur umbræ mortis, nec tegat eum [*vel* eam] chaos et caligo tenebrarum, sed exutus [*vel* exuta] omnium criminum labe in sinu Abrahæ collocatus [*vel* collocata] locum refrigerii se adeptum [*vel* adeptam] esse gaudeat: ut cum dies judicii advenerit, cum sanctis et electis tuis eum [*vel* eam] resuscitari jubeas. Per Christum Dominum nostrum. R. Amen.

Alia Oratio cum Oremus.

Deus qui justis supplicationibus semper præsto es, qui pia vota dignaris intueri, da famulo tuo [*vel* famulæ tuæ] N. cujus depositioni hodie officia humanitatis exhibemus, cum sanctis atque fidelibus tuis beati muneris portionem. Per Christum Dominum nostrum. R. Amen.

Deinde dicatur Benedictio Sepulchri, *sine* Oremus, *hoc modo:* Rogamus te, Domine sancte, Pater omnipotens, æterne Deus, ut bene✠dicere et sanctificare digneris hoc sepulchrum, et corpus in eo collocandum; ut sit remedium salutare in eo quiescenti et redemptio animæ ejus atque tutela et munimen contra sæva jacula inimici. Per Christum Dominum nostrum. R. Amen.

Alia Benedictio Tumuli:

Adjutorium nostrum in Nomine Domini.

Qui fecit cœlum et terram.

Benedic Domine locum sepulchri hujus, sicut benedixisti sepulchra Abrahæ, Isaac, et Jacob.

APPENDIX I.

V. Ostende nobis Domine misericordiam tuam.

R. Et salutare tuum da nobis.

Oratio. Deus qui fundasti terram et formasti cœlos, qui omnia sideribus instituta fixisti, qui captum laqueis mortis hominem lavacri ablutione reparas, qui sepultos Abraham, Isaac, et Jacob in spelunca duplici, in libro vitæ ac totius gloriæ principes annotasti benedicendos: ita bene+dicere digneris hunc famulum tuum [*vel* ancillam tuam], ut eum [*vel* eam] requiescere facias, et in sinu Abrahæ collocare digneris: qui Dominum nostrum Jesum Christum Filium tuum, devictis laqueis inferorum resurgere, et in se credentium suorum membra resuscitare jussisti. Qui venturus est judicare vivos et mortuos et sæculum per ignem.

Oratio. Respice Domine super hanc fabricam sepulturæ, et descendat in eam Spiritus tuus, ut te jubente sit ei in hoc loco quieta dormitio, et tempore judicii cum omnibus Sanctis sit vera resurrectio. Te prestante Domino nostro, qui in Trinitate perfecta vivis et regnas per cuncta sæcula sæculorum. *R.* Amen.

Hic aspergatur aqua benedicta super sepulchrum, et incensetur sepulchrum.

Finitis orationibus, ponatur corpus in sepulchro, Cantore incipiente:

Ant. Ingrediar. E. u. o. u. a. e.

Psalmus. Quemadmodum desiderat cervus.

Dicto psalmo, repetatur Antiphona: Ingrediar in locum tabernaculi admirabilis usque ad domum Dei.

Qua dicta dicat Sacerdos Orationem hoc modo:

Oremus, fratres carissimi, pro spiritu cari nostri [*vel* caræ nostræ] N. quem Dominus de laqueo hujus sæculi liberare dignatus est, cujus corpusculum hodie sepulturæ traditur, ut eum [*vel* eam] pietas Domini in sinu Abrahæ collocare dignetur, ut cum magni judicii dies advenerit, inter sanctos et electos suos eum [*vel* eam] in parte dextera collocandum [*vel* collocandam] resuscitari faciat. Qui vivit et regnat Deus. Per omnia sæcula sæculorum. R. Amen.

Alia Oratio cum Oremus:

Oratio. Deus qui humanarum animarum æternus amator es, animam famuli tui [*vel* famulæ tuæ] N. quam vera dum in corpore maneret tenuit fides, ab omni cruciatu inferorum redde extorrem, ut segregata ab infernalibus claustris sanctorum tuorum mereatur adunari consortiis. Per Christum.

Finitis orationibus, claudatur sepulchrum, ponente prius Sacerdote absolutionem super pectus defuncti, sic dicendo:

Dominus Jesus Christus qui beato Petro apostolo suo, cæterisque discipulis suis licentiam dedit ligandi atque solvendi, ipse te N. absolvat ab omni vinculo delictorum, et in quantum meæ fragilitati permittitur, precor sis absolutus [*vel* absoluta] ante tribunal ejusdem Domini nostri Jesu Christi, habeasque vitam æternam et vivas in sæcula sæculorum. R. Amen.

Hic aspergatur tumulus aqua benedicta et incensetur, Cantore incipiente Antiphonam:

Hæc requies mea. E. u. o. u. a. e.

Psalmus. Memento Domine David, et omnis mansuetudinis ejus.

Finito psalmo, sequatur Antiphona:

Hæc requies mea in sæculum sæculi: hic habitabo quoniam elegi eam.

Qua dicta, dicat Sacerdos Orationem, cum Oremus:

Oratio. Deus, apud quem spiritus mortuorum vivunt, et in quo electorum animæ, deposito carnis onere, plena felicitate lætantur, præsta supplicantibus nobis, ut anima famuli tui [*vel* famulæ tuæ] N. quæ temporali per corpus visionis hujus luminis caruit visu, æternæ illius lucis solatio potiatur. Non eam tormentum mortis attingat, nec dolor horrendæ visionis afficiat. Non

APPENDIX I.

pœnalis timor excruciet, non reorum pessima catena constringat, sed concessa sibi venia omnium delictorum, optatæ quietis consequatur gaudia repromissa. Per Christum Dominum nostrum. *R.* Amen.

Alia Oratio cum Oremus:

Oratio. Tu Domine Deus omnipotens, precibus nostris aurem tuæ pietatis accommodare digneris, tu miseris opem feras et misericordiam largiaris, et spiritum famuli tui [*vel* famulæ tuæ] N. vinculis corporalibus liberatum in pacem sanctorum tuorum recipias, ut locum pœnalem et Gehennæ ignem in regionem viventium translatus evadat. Per Christum.

Finitis orationibus, executor officii terram super corpus ad modum crucis ponat, et corpus thurificet et aqua benedicta aspergat: et dum sequens Psalmus canitur, corpus omnino cooperiatur, Cantore incipiente Antiphonam:

De terra plasmasti me. E. u. o. u. a. e.

Psalmus. Domine probasti me et cognovisti me.

Finito psalmo, tota dicatur Antiphona:

De terra plasmasti me, et carnem induisti me, redemptor meus Domine: resuscita me in novissimo die.

Qua dicta, dicat Sacerdos sine Dominus vobiscum, *et sine* Oremus:

Commendo animam tuam Deo Patri omnipotenti, terram terræ, cinerem cineri, pulverum pulveri, in nomine Patris, et Filii et Spiritus Sancti.

Deinde dicat Sacerdos hanc Orationem, sine Oremus:

Oratio. Temeritatis quidem est, Domine, ut homo hominem, mortalis mortalem, cinis cinerem tibi Domino Deo nostro audeat commendare: sed quia terra suscipit terram et pulvis convertitur in pulverem, donec omnis caro in suam redigatur originem, inde tuam Deus piisime Pater lachrymabiliter quæsumus pietatem, ut hujus famuli tui [*vel* famulæ tuæ] N. animam quam creasti de hujus mundi voragine cœnolenta ad patriam ducas, Abrahæ amici tui sinu recipias, et refrigerii rore perfundas. Sit ab æstuantis Gehennæ truci incendio segregata, et beatæ requiei, te donante, conjuncta. Et si quæ illi sunt, Domine, dignæ cruciatibus culpæ, tu eas gratia tuæ mitissimæ lenitatis indulge, ne peccati vicem sed indulgentiæ tuæ piam sentiat bonitatem. Cumque finito mundi termino supernum cunctis illuxerit regnum, novus homo sanctorum omnium cœtibus aggregatus [*vel* aggregata] cum electis tuis resurgat in parte dextera coronandus [*vel* coronanda]. Per Christum Dominum nostrum. R. Amen.

Alia Oratio Oremus :

Oratio. Deus vitæ dator, et humanorum corporum reparator, qui te a peccatoribus exorari voluisti, exaudi preces quas speciali devotione pro anima famuli tui [*vel* famulæ tuæ] N. tibi lachrymalibiliter fundimus : ut liberare eam ab inferorum cruciatibus et collocare eam inter agmina sanctorum tuorum digneris, veste quoque cœlesti et stola immortalilitatis indui, et Paradisi amœnitate confoveri jubeas. Per Christum Dominum nostrum. R. Amen.

Finita oratione, incipiat Cantor Antiphonam:

Omnis spiritus. E. u. o. u. a. e.

Psalmus. Laudate Dominum in cœlis.

Psalmus. Cantate Domino canticum novum.

Psalmus. Laudate Dominum in sanctis ejus.

Finito psalmo, tota dicatur Antiphona, scilicet :

Omnis spiritus laudet Dominum.

Qua dicta, dicat Sacerdos sine Dominus vobiscum, *et sine* Oremus.

Oratio. Debitum humani corporis sepeliendi officium fidelium more complentes, Deum cui omnia vivunt fideliter deprecemur, ut hoc corpus cari nostri [*vel* caræ nostræ] N. a nobis infirmitate sepultum, in ordine sanctorum suorum resuscitet, et ejus spiritum

APPENDIX I.

sanctis ac fidelibus aggregari jubeat, cum quibus inenarrabili gloria et perenni felicitate perfrui mereatur. Per Dominum nostrum Jesum Christum Filium ejus, Qui cum eo vivit, etc.

Finita Oratione, incipiat Sacerdos Antiphonam. Et intonetur Psalmus Benedictus, *modo sequenti: totus Psalmus dicatur et cantetur hic solenniter sicut ad matutinum.*

Ant. Ego sum.

Benedictus Dominus Deus Israel: quia visitavit et fecit redemptionem plebis suæ.

Finito psalmo, tota dicatur Antiphona:

Ego sum resurrectio et vita, qui credit in me etiam si mortuus fuerit vivet, et omnis qui vivit et credit in me non morietur in æternum.

Qua dicta, sequatur hoc modo:

Kyrie eleyson.
Christe eleyson.
Kyrie eleyson.

Hic roget Sacerdos orare pro anima defuncti, ita dicens:

Pro anima N. et pro animabus omnium fidelium defunctorum.

Pater noster.

Deinde dicat Sacerdos:

V. Et ne nos inducas in tentationem.
R. Sed libera nos a malo.
V. Requiem æternam dona eis Domine.
R. Et lux perpetua luceat eis.
V. A porta inferi.
R. Erue Domine animas eorum.
V. Credo videre bona Domini.
R. In terra viventium.
V. Non intres in judicium cum servo tuo, Domine.

R. Quia non justificabitur in conspectu tuo omnis vivens.

V. Domine exaudi orationem meam.

R. Et clamor meus ad te veniat.

    Dominus vobiscum.

    Et cum spiritu tuo.

    Oremus.

Oratio. Deus origo pietatis, pater misericordiarum solamem tristium, indultor criminum, de cujus munere venit omne quod bonum est, et procedit, respice propitius supplicum preces. Et quamvis propria nos reputet indignos conscientia, te dignum nostris flecti petitionibus, pulsamus tamen quantulumcunque conceditur aures tuæ pietatis. Nam si omittimus in utroque veremur esse rei, quoniam et te præcipis a peccatoribus exorari, nostroque, etsi non merito, hoc agendum te præstante tribuitur ministerio. Ergo te, Domine Sancte, Pater omnipotens, æterne Deus, qui unicum Filium tuum Dominum nostrum Jesum Christum incarnari de Virgine constituisti, quo vetustum solveret proprio cruore peccatum, et vitam redderet mundo, ipso opitulante animam fratris nostri [*vel* sororis nostræ] N. ab ergastulo cœnolentæ materiæ exemptam ab omnibus piaculis quæsumus absolvas. Nullas patiatur insidias occursantium dæmonum, propter quam misisti ad terras unigenitum Filium tuum. Libera et absolve eam ab æstuantis Gehennæ truci incendio, collocans in Paradisi amœnitate. Non sentiat, piissime Pater, quod calet in flammis, quod stridet in pœnis, et quod horret in tenebris: sed munificentiæ tuæ munere præventa mereatur evadere judicium ultionis, et beatæ requiei ac lucis æternæ felicitate perfrui. Per Christum.

    Alia Oratio, cum Oremus:

Tibi, Domine, commendamus animam famuli tui [*vel* famulæ tuæ] N. ut defunctus [*vel* defuncta] sæculo tibi vivat, et quæ per fragilitatem mundanæ conversationis peccata admisit, tu venia misericordissimæ pietatis absterge. Per Christum.

APPENDIX I.

Hic dictis, dicatur psalmus Miserere, *cum Ant.* Requiem æternam.

Qua dicta, dicat Sacerdos in auditu omnium :

Pater noster: pro anima ejus N. et pro animabus quorum ossa in hoc cœmeterio vel in aliis requiescunt, et pro animabus omnium fidelium defunctorum.

Deinde dicat Sacerdos Pater noster :

Et ne nos, etc.

Sed libera, etc.

V. A porta inferi.

R. Erue Domine.

V. Ne tradas Domine bestiis animas confitentes tibi.

R. Et animas pauperum tuorum ne obliviscaris in finem.

Dominus vobiscum. Et cum.

Oremus.

Oratio. Deus, cujus miseratione animæ fidelium requiescunt, animabus famulorum famularumque tuarum hic et ubique in Christo quiescentium, da propitius suorum veniam peccatorum, ut a cunctis reatibus absoluti, tecum sine fine lætentur. Per Christum.

Postea revertentes Clerici de tumulo, dicant Septem Psalmos Pænitentiales, vel Psalmum De profundis, *cum Antiphona* Requiem æternam :

Sequatur—

Kyrie eleyson.

Christe eleyson.

Kyrie eleyson.

Pater noster.

Et ne nos, etc.

Sed libera, etc.

V. A porta inferi.

R. Erue Domine.

V. Anima ejus in bonis demoretur.
R. Et semen ejus hæreditet terram.
V. Credo videre bona Domini.
R. In terra viventium.
V. Non intres in judicium cum servo tuo, Domine.
R. Quia non justificabitur in conspectu tuo omnis vivens.

Dominus vobiscum. Et cum.

Oremus.

Oratio. Satisfaciat tibi Domine Deus noster pro anima famuli tui [*vel* famulæ tuæ] N. fratris nostri [*vel* sororis nostræ], sanctæ Dei genitricis semperque virginis Mariæ, et sanctissimi apostoli tui Petri, omniumque sanctorum tuorum oratio, et præsentis familiæ tuæ humilis et devota supplicatio, ut peccatorum omnium veniam precamur obtineat, nec eam patiaris cruciari gehennalibus pœnis, quam Filii tui Domini nostri Jesu Christi pretioso sanguine redemisti. Qui tecum, etc.

In fine omnium demissa voce dicatur sic.

Anima ejus, et animæ omnium fidelium defunctorum per Dei misericordiam requiescant in pace. *R.* Amen.

APPENDIX II.

MISSÆ PRO DEFUNCTIS.

Secundum Ritum Romanum.

IN COMMEMORATIONE OMNIUM FIDELIUM DEFUNCTORUM.

Introitus. Requiem æternam dona eis Domine; et lux perpetua luceat eis. *Ps.* lxiv. Te decet hymnus Deus in Sion; et tibi reddetur votum in Jerusalem: exaudi orationem meam; ad te omnis caro veniet.

Deinde absolute repetitur Requiem æternam *usque ad Psalmum.*

Oratio. Fidelium Deus omnium Conditor et Redemptor, animabus famulorum famularumque tuarum remissionem cunctorum tribue peccatorum: ut indulgentiam, quam semper optaverunt, piis supplicationibus consequantur. Qui vivis et regnas cum Deo Patre.

Lectio Epistolæ beati Pauli Apostoli ad Corinthios 1, c. xv. 51:

Fratres: Ecce mysterium vobis dico . . . . Deo autem gratias, qui dedit nobis victoriam per Dominum nostrum Jesum Christum.

Graduale. Requiem æternam dona eis Domine; et lux perpetua luceat eis.

V. *Ps.* cxii. 6, 7. In memoria æterna erit justus; ab auditione mala non timebit.

Tractatus. Absolve, Domine, animas omnium fidelium defunctorum ab omni vinculo delictorum.

V. Et gratia tua illis succurrente, mereantur evadere judicium ultionis.

V. Et lucis æternæ beatitudine perfrui.

Sequentia.

Dies iræ, dies illa
Solvet sæclum in favilla,
Teste David cum Sibylla.

Quantus tremor est futurus,
Quondo Judex est venturus,
Cuncta stricte discussurus!

Tuba mirum spargens sonum
Per sepulchra regionum,
Coget omnes ante thronum.

Mors stupebit, et natura,
Cum resurget creatura,
Judicanti responsura.

Liber scriptus proferetur,
In quo totum continetur,
Unde mundus judicetur.

Judex ergo cum sedebit,
Quidquid latet apparebit:
Nil inultum remanebit.

Quid sum miser tunc dicturus?
Quem patronum rogaturus,
Cum vix justus sit securus?

Rex tremendæ majestatis,
Qui salvandos salvas gratis,
Salve me, fons pietatis.

Recordare, Jesu pie,
Quod sum causa tuæ viæ,
Ne me perdas illa die.

Quærens me, sedisti lassus,
Redemisti, crucem passus:
Tantus labor non sit cassus.

Juste Judex ultionis,
Donum fac remissionis
Ante diem rationis.

Ingemisco tanquam reus,
Culpa rubet vultus meus,
Supplicanti parce Deus.

Qui Mariam absolvisti,
Et latronem exaudisti,
Mihi quoque spem dedisti.

Preces meæ non sunt dignæ:
Sed tu bonus fac benigne,
Ne perenni cremer igne.

Inter oves locum præsta,
Et hab hœdis me sequestra,
Statuens in parte dextra.

Confutatis maledictis,
Flammis acribus addictis,
Voca me cum benedictis.

Oro supplex et acclinis,
Cor contritum quasi cinis
Gere curam mei finis.

Lacrymosa dies illa,
Qua resurget ex favilla
Judicandus homo reus.

Huic ergo parce, Deus;
Pie Jesu Domine,
Dona eis requiem. Amen.

APPENDIX II.

Sequentia sancti Evangelii secundum Johannem, c. v. 25—29:

In illo tempore: Dixit Jesus . . . . in resurrectionem judicii.

Offertorium. Domine Jesu Christi, Rex gloriæ, libera animas omnium fidelium defunctorum de pœnis inferni, et de profundo lacu: libera eas de ore leonis, ne absorbeat eas tartarus, ne cadant in obscurum; sed signifer sanctus Michael repræsentet eas in lucem sanctam:* Quam olim Abrahæ promisisti, et semini ejus. *V.* Hostias et preces tibi Domine, laudis offerimus: tu suscipe pro animabus illis, quarum hodie memoriam facimus: fac eas Domine de morte transire ad vitam.* Quam olim Abrahæ promisisti, et semini ejus.

Secreta. Hostias, quæsumus Domine, quas tibi pro animabus famulorum famularumque tuarum offerimus, propitiatus intende: ut, quibus Fidei Christianæ meritum contulisti, dones et præmium. Per Dominum.

Communio. Lux æterna luceat eis, Domine,* Cum Sanctis tuis in æternum, quia pius es. *V.* Requiem æternam dona eis Domine: et lux perpetua luceat eis.* Cum Sanctis.

Postcommunio. Animabus, quæsumus Domine, famulorum famularumque tuarum, oratio proficiat supplicantium: ut eas et a peccatis omnibus exuas, et tuæ redemptionis facias esse participes. Qui vivis.

Dicto Dominus vobiscum, *dicitur* Requiescant in pace. *R.* Amen. *Et non datur Benedictio: sed dicto secreto* Placeat tibi, Sancta Trinitas, *et osculato altari, legitur Evangelium S. Joannis.* In principio erat Verbum, *ut moris est.*

IN DIE OBITUS, SEU DEPOSITIONIS DEFUNCTI.

Introitus. Requiem æternam dona eis, Domine; et lux perpetua luceat eis. *Ps.* Te decet hymnus Deus in Sion; et tibi reddetur votum in Jerusalem; exaudi orationem meam, ad te omnis caro veniet. Requiem.

Oratio. Deus, qui proprium est misereri semper et parcere, te supplices exoramus pro anima famuli tui N. quam hodie de hoc sæculo migrare jussisti: ut non tradas eam in manus inimici, neque obliviscaris in finem, sed jubeas eam a sanctis Angelis suscipi, et ad patriam Paradisi perduci; ut, quia in te speravit et credidit, non pœnis inferni sustineat, sed gaudia æterna possideat. Per Dominum nostrum.

Lectio Epistola beati Pauli Apostoli ad Thessalonicenses 1, c. iv. 13—18:

Fratres, Nolumus vos ignorare de dormientibus . . . . Itaque consolamini invicem in verbis istis.

Graduale. Requiem; *Tractus.* Absolve; *et Sequentia dicenda,* Dies iræ, *ut supra* (p. 212).

Sequentia sancti Evangelii secundum Joannem, c. xi. 21—27.

In illo tempore . . . . . . quia tu es Christus Filius Dei vivi, qui in hunc mundum venisti.

Offertorium. Domine Jesu Christe, *ut supra* (p. 213).

Secreta. Propitiare, quæsumus Domine animæ famuli tui N. pro qua hostiam laudis tibi immolamus, Majestatem tuam suppliciter deprecantes: ut per hæc piæ placationis officia, pervenire mereatur ad requiem sempiternam. Per Dominum.

Communio. Lux æterna, *ut supra* (p. 213).

Postcommunio. Præsta, quæsumus, omnipotens Deus: ut anima famuli tui N. quæ hodie de hoc sæculo migravit, his sacrificiis purgata, et a peccatis expedita, indulgentiam pariter et requiem capiat sempiternam. Per Dominum.

In die tertio, septimo, et trigesimo depositionis Defuncti, dicitur Missa ut supra exceptis Orationibus, quæ dicuntur ut infra:

Oratio. Quæsumus, Domine, ut animæ famuli tui N. cujus depositionis diem tertium (*vel* septimum) (*vel* trigesimum) commemoramus, Sanctorum atque electorum tuorum largiri digneris

APPENDIX II.

consortium: et rorem misericordiæ tuæ perennem infundas. Dominum nostrum.

Secreta. Munera, quæsumus Domine, quæ tibi pro anima famuli tui N. offerimus, placatus intende: ut remediis purgata cœlestibus, in tua pietate requiescat. Per Dominum.

Postcommunio. Suscipe, Domine, preces nostras pro anima famuli tui N. ut, si quæ ei maculæ de terrenis contagiis adhæserunt, remissionis tuæ misericordia deleantur. Per Dominum.

IN ANNIVERSARIO DEFUNCTORUM.

Introitus. Requiem æternam dona eis, Domine; et lux perpetua luceat eis. *Ps.* Te decet hymnus Deus in Sion, et tibi reddetur votum in Jerusalem; exaudi orationem meam, ad te omnis caro veniet. Requiem æternam.

Oratio. Deus, indulgentiarum Domine, da animabus famulorum famularumque tuarum, quorum aniversarium depositionis diem commemoramus refrigerii sedem, quietis beatitudinem, et luminis claritatem. Per Dominum.

Si pro uno fiat anniversarium, dicatur sequens:

Oratio. Deus, indulgentiarum Domine, da animæ famuli tui, (*vel* famulæ tuæ) cujus anniversarium depositionis diem commemoramus, refrigerii sedem, quietis beatitudinem, et luminis claritatem. Per Dominum.

Lectio libri Machabæorum 2, c. xii.:

In diebus illis. Vir fortissimus Judas . . . . . ut a peccatus, solvantur.

Graduale, Requiem, *Tractus,* Absolve, *et Sequentia,* Dies iræ ut supra (p. 212).

Sequentia sancta Evangelii secundum Joannem, c. vi. 37—40.

In illo tempore : Dixit Jesus . . . . . . et ego resuscitabo eum in novissimo die.

Offertorium. Domine Jesu Christe, *ut supra* (p. 218).

Secreta. Propitiare, Domine, supplicationibus nostris, pro animabus famularumque tuarum, quorum hodie annua dies agitur, pro quibus tibi offerimus sacrificium laudis: ut eas Sanctorum tuorum consortio sociare digneris. Per Dominum.

Si pro uno fiat, dicatur sequens :

Secreta. Propitiare, Domine, supplicationibus nostris, pro anima famuli tui, (*vel* famulæ tuæ) cujus hodie annua dies agitur, pro qua tibi offerimus sacrificium laudis: ut eam Sanctorum tuorum consortio sociare digneris. Per Dominum nostrum.

Communio. Lux æterna, *ut supra* (p. 218).

Postcommunio. Præsta, quæsumus Domine, ut animæ famulorum famularumque tuarum, quorum anniversarium depositionis diem commemoramus, his purgatæ sacrificiis, indulgentiam pariter et requiem capiant sempiternam. Per Dominum nostrum.

Si pro uno fiat, dicatur sequens Postcommunio :

Præsta, quæsumus Domine, ut anima famuli tui (*vel* famulæ tuæ) cujus anniversarium depositionis diem commemoramus, his purgata sacrificiis, indulgentiam pariter et requiem capiat sempiternam. Per Dominum.

IN MISSIS QUOTIDIANIS DEFUNCTORUM.

Introitus. Requiem æternam dona eis, Domine; et lux perpetua luceat eis. *Ps.* Te decet hymnus Deus in Sion, et tibi reddetur votum in Jerusalem; exaudi orationem meam, ad te omnis caro veniet. Requiem æternam.

APPENDIX II.

Pro defunctis Episcopis seu Sacerdotibus:

Oratio. Deus, qui inter apostolicos sacerdotes, famulos tuos pontificali, seu sacerdotali fecisti dignitati vigere: præsta, quæsumus, ut eorum quoque perpetuo aggregentur consortio. Per Dominum nostrum Jesum Christum Filium tuum. Qui tecum vivit.

Pro defunctis fratribus, propinquis, et benefactoribus:

Oratio. Deus, veniæ largitor et humanæ salutis amator, quæsumus clementiam tuam; ut nostræ congregationis fratres, propinquos, et benefactores, qui ex hoc sæculo transierunt, beata Maria semper Virgine intercedente cum omnibus Sanctis tuis, ad perpetuæ beatitudinis consortium pervenire concedas.

Pro omnibus fidelibus defunctis:

Oratio. Fidelium, Deus, omnium Conditor et Redemptor, animabus famulorum famularumque tuarum remissionem cunctorum tribue peccatorum: ut indulgentiam, quam semper optaverunt, piis supplicationibus consequantur. Qui vivis et regnas.

Lectio libri Apocalypsis beati Joannis Apostoli, c. xiv. 13.

In diebus illis: Audivi vocem de cœlo, dicentem mihi: Scribe: Beati mortui, qui in Domino moriuntur. Amodo jam dicit Spiritus, ut requiescant a laboribus suis; opera enim illorum sequantur illos.

Graduale. Requiem æternam dona eis, Domine: et lux perpetua luceat eis. *V.* In memoria æterna erit justus: ab auditione mala non timebit.

Tractus. Absolve, Domine, animas omnium fidelium defunctorum ab omni vinculo delictorum. *V.* Et gratia tua illis succurrente, mereantur evadere judicium ultionis. *V.* Et lucis æternæ beatitudine perfrui.

Sequentia dicenda ad libitum:

Dies iræ, *ut supra* (p. 212).

Sequentia Sancti Evangelii secundum Joannem, c. vi. 85—89.

In illo tempore: Dixit Jesum turbis Judæorum . . . . . et ego resuscitabo eum in novissimo die.

Offertorium. Domine Jesu Christe, Rex gloriæ, libera animas omnium fidelium defunctorum de pœnis inferni, et de profundo lacu: libera eas de ore leonis, ne absorbeat eas Tartarus, ne cadant in obscurum: sed signifer sanctus Michael repræsentet eas in lucem sanctam:* Quam olim Abrahæ promisisti, et semini ejus. *V.* Hostias et preces tibi, Domine, laudis offerimus: tu suscipe pro animabus illis, quarum hodie memoriam facimus: fac eas, Domine, de morte transire ad vitam.* Quam olim.

Pro defunctis Episcopis seu Sacerdotibus:

Secreta. Suscipe, Domine quæsumus, pro animabus famulorum tuorum Pontificum, seu sacerdotum, quas offerimus hostias: ut quibus in hoc sæculo pontificale, seu sacerdotale donasti meritum, in cœlesti regno Sanctorum tuorum jubeas jungi consortio. Per Dominum.

Pro defunctis fratribus, propinquis, et benefactoribus:

Secreta. Deus cujus misericordiæ non est numerus, suscipe propitius preces humilitatis nostræ: et animabus fratrum propinquorum, et benefactorum nostrorum, quibus tui nominis dedisti confessionem, per hæc Sacramenta salutis nostræ, cunctorum remissionem tribue peccatorum.

Pro omnibus fidelibus defunctis:

Secreta. Hostias, quæsumus Domine, quas tibi pro animabus famulorum famularumque tuarum offerimus, propitiatus intende: ut, quibus Fidei Christianæ meritum contulisti, dones et præmium. Per Dominum.

Communio. Lux æterna luceat eis, Domine,* Cum Sanctis tuis in æternum: quia pius es. *V.* Requiem æternam dona eis, Domine: et lux perpetua luceat eis.* Cum sanctis.

APPENDIX II.

Pro defunctis Episcopis seu Sacerdotibus:

Postcommunio. Prosit, quæsumus Domine, animabus famulorum tuorum Pontificum, seu sacerdotum, misericordiæ tuæ implorata clementia: ut ejus, in quo speraverunt et crediderunt, æternum capiant, te miserante, consortium. Per Dominum.

Pro defunctis fratribus, propinquis, et benefactoribus:

Postcommunio. Præsta, quæsumus omnipotens et misericors Deus: ut animæ fratrum, propinquorum, et benefactorum nostrorum, pro quibus hoc sacrificium laudis tuæ obtulimus Majestati: per hujus virtutem Sacramenti a peccatis omnibus expiatæ, lucis perpetuæ, te miserante, recipiant beatitudinem.

Pro omnibus fidelibus defunctis:

Postcommunio. Animabus, quæsumus Domine, famulorum famularumque tuarum oratio proficiat supplicantium: ut eas et a peccatis omnibus exuas, et tuæ redemptionis facias esse participes. Qui vivis et regnas.

¶ *Epistolæ et Evangelia, superius posita in una Missa pro Defunctis dici possunt etiam in alia Missa similiter pro Defunctis.*

*** The old English Masses for the Dead, being in certain particulars and details different from those now used throughout the whole of Latin Christendom, furnished in the text already given, some particulars of the former are here appended, which, when compared with the latter, serve to show—notwithstanding their want of identity—how completely the doctrine of the old Church of England, in its purest ages, before Schism, Dissent, and Scepticism had waxed rampant, is in accordance with the faith and practice of the Church Universal throughout the world.

The author is indebted to Mr. Albert H. Pearson's edition of the *Sarum Missal in English** (a most valuable contribution to our Liturgical treasures), for the following. Should his readers, however, desire to consult the original text, he recommends to them the "Missale ad usum Insignis et Præclaræ Ecclesiæ Sarum," most ably edited by the Rev. G. H. Forbes, Burntisland, 1861.

MASSES FOR THE DEAD.

Before the Day of Burial when the Corpse is Present.†

It is to be noted that a Mass is said daily in the Chapter-house through Advent (when the Choir is not ruled) till Christmas-eve, and from the Octave of the Epiphany to Wednesday in Holy Week, and from Trinity Monday to Advent, for the faithful departed, with Deacon and Sub-deacon in albs and amices only, unless a double Feast or Octave with Rulers occur the day before, or the corpse be present, or it be the Anniversary of a Bishop, for then the Mass is said at the special Altar, or at an Altar near which the body is buried. Also no Mass for the Dead is said in the Chapter-house in Easter-tide unless the body be present, or it be an Anniversary or Trental.

The Office.

Grant them, O Lord, eternal rest, and let light perpetual shine upon them.

Psalm lxv. Thou, O Lord, art praised in Sion : and unto thee shall the vow be performed in Jerusalem. Thou that hearest prayer, unto thee shall all flesh come.

At the Office *let the Deacon cense the corpse on either side, beginning at the head, but let him not go round it.*

---

* London, 1868.
† If the body be not present, all is said as in the Daily Mass.

APPENDIX II.

The Collect.

O God, whose property is always to have mercy and to forgive, we humbly pray thee in behalf of the soul of thy servant which thou hast this day commanded to depart out of this world: deliver it not into the hands of the enemy, nor forget it at the last, but command it to be received by the holy angels, and to be carried into the land of the living; and forasmuch as he hoped and believed in thee, let him be accounted worthy to rejoice in the communion of thy saints. Through.

Memorials are said of Bishops, Brethren, Parents, and all the Faithful Departed, if any person other than the King, Queen, or great Noble.

The Epistle. 1 Thess. iv. 13—18.

I would not have you be ignorant . . . . . comfort one another with these words.

The following Gradual is said for a Bishop only,* and that whether the body is present or not, by three Clerks of the second bench, standing at the head of the corpse. But if the body be not present, they stand at the step of the Quire.

Gradual. Psalm xxiii. Yea, though I walk through the valley of the shadow of death, I will fear no evil: for thou art with me, O Lord.

Vers. Thy rod and thy staff comfort me.

In all other Masses the following Gradual is sung by three Clerks of the second bench at the head of the corpse, if present; if it be not, it is said at the step of the Quire, the Choir sitting and chanting it.

Gradual. Grant them, O Lord, eternal rest, and let light perpetual shine upon them.

---

* This rubric is corrected according to the Defensorium Directorii, which states the one as it stands in the Missal to be wrong.

Vers. Psalm xxv. Their souls shall dwell at ease, and *their* seed shall inherit the land.

> *This is said by four Clerks of the highest bench, standing at the head of the corpse, if present; if not, at the step of the Quire, two singing each Versicle, but all four beginning and ending it together. In the meantime, after censing the Altar, let the Deacon cense the corpse.*

Tract. Psalm xlii. Like as the hart desireth the water-brooks, so longeth my soul after thee, O God.

Vers. My soul is athirst for God, yea, even for the living God: when shall I come to appear before the presence of *my* God?

Vers. My tears have been my meat day and night, while they daily say unto me, Where is now thy God?

The Gospel. John xi. 21—27.

At that time Martha said to Jesus . . . . . which should come into the world.

Offert. O Lord, Jesu Christ, King of Glory, deliver the souls of the faithful departed from the hand of hell, and from the deep pit: deliver them from the lion's mouth, that hell swallow them not up, that they fall not into the blackness of darkness; but let S. Michael the Standard-bearer bring them into the holy light which thou promisedst of old to Abraham and his seed.

> *Here again the Priest shall cense the corpse, and after washing his hands, shall say,* We offer to thee.

Secret. Accept, we beseech thee, O Lord, merciful Father, the oblation which we offer unto thee in behalf of the soul of thy servant N., which thou hast delivered this day from the corruption of the flesh; and grant that he may be restored and absolved from all the errors of this mortal state, and in eternal rest may await the day of resurrection. Through.

Comm. Grant unto those, O Lord, in memory of whom the Body of Christ is received, eternal rest.

Vers. And let light perpetual shine upon them. Grant unto those, O Lord, in memory of whom the Blood of Christ is received, eternal rest.

P. Comm. Grant, we beseech thee, Almighty God, that the soul of thy servant N. may be received by the angels of light, and carried to the habitations prepared for the blessed. Through.

MASS ON THE DAY OF BURIAL.

All as in the last Mass.

The Collect.

Almighty and everlasting God, we humbly entreat thy mercy that thou wouldst command that the soul of thy servant N., for whose body we perform the due Office of Burial, be laid in the bosom of thy Patriarch, Abraham; that when the day of thy recognition shall arrive, he may be raised up at thy bidding among the saints and thine elect. Through.

Secret. Receive, O Lord, in behalf of the soul of thy servant the Sacrifice which thou hast graciously offered unto God the Father for us; and because for the sake of men thou didst come down from heaven, when thou shalt come again let it be counted worthy to be united to the assembly of thy saints. Through thee, O Saviour of the world, Who.

P. Comm. Grant, we beseech thee, O Lord, that the soul of thy servant, for whose body we have this day performed the duty of man to man, may be cleansed by this Sacrifice, and give thanks unto thee for the perpetual gift of thy salvation. Through.

PRAYERS FOR THE DEPARTED.

Mass in Trentals and on the Thirtieth Day.

The Office.

As in the first Mass for the Dead.

The Collect.

O God, whose property is ever to have mercy and to forgive, be favourable unto the soul of thy servant, and forgive all *his* sins, that *he* being loosed from the chains of death may be found meet to pass unto life. Through.

The catafalque is not censed. If Mass is said for a body that is present, or an Anniversary occur during a Trental, then I. Collect *of* Anniversary *or* Burial, II. Trental, III. Bishops, IV. Brethren, V. All Faithful Departed.

The Lesson. 2 Macc. xii. 43—45.

In those days a mighty man of valour, Judas, made a gathering . . . . . that they might be delivered from sin.

In Trentals of Bishops the Epistle *is as in the first Mass for the Dead.*

Gradual. Grant them.

But it is sung by the whole Choir sitting, and only begun by the Clerks standing at the step of the Quire. If it is for a Bishop it is as in the first Mass, only the Clerks sing it at the step of the Quire.

Tract. If for a Bishop, as above; if not, as in the Daily Mass.

The rest as in the first Mass for the Dead; but the Gospel is one of those in the Daily Mass, if the Mass is not for a Bishop.

Secret. Look down, we beseech thee, Almighty God, and vouchsafe favourably to receive this Sacrifice which we offer unto thee in behalf of the soul of thy servant; and grant him perpetual peace and everlasting rest. Through.

P. Comm. We beseech thee, O Lord, let the celebration of the Divine Sacrament be profitable unto the soul of thy servant; that of thy mercy he may have eternal fellowship with him in whom he trusted and believed. Through.

Mass on Anniversaries.

The Office.
As above in the first Mass for the Dead.
The catafalque is censed if it be the Anniversary of a Bishop or Dean.

The Collect.

O Lord God of pardon, grant unto the soul of thy servant, the anniversary of whose burial we keep, a place of refreshing, a blessed rest, and the light of glory. Through.

The remaining Memorials *as above.*

The Epistle.

As in the Daily Mass, except it be for a Bishop, then as in the first Mass for the Dead.

Gradual and Tract. As in the Daily Mass, unless it be for a Bishop, then as in the first Mass for the Dead.

The Gospel.

One of those in the Daily Mass, unless it be for a Bishop, then as in the first Mass for the Dead.

The rest as in the first Mass for the Dead.

Secret. O Lord, we beseech thee, mercifully to hear our humble prayers in behalf of the soul of thy servant whom as on this day we yearly commemorate; in behalf of whom we offer unto thee the sacrifice of praise; that thou wouldst vouchsafe to admit him unto the fellowship of thy saints. Through.

P. Comm. Grant, we beseech thee, O Lord, that the soul of thy servant, the anniversary of whose burial we keep, may be cleansed by this Sacrifice, and alike obtain pardon and eternal rest. Through.

The Daily Mass for the Dead.*

The Office.
As above.

The Collects.
The first is for Bishops; *the second for* Brethren; *the third for* All the Faithful Departed.

At the Mass in the Chapter-house no incense is offered.

The Lesson. Rev. xiv. 13.
In those days I heard . . . . . their works do follow them.

The Epistle. 1 Cor. xv. 20—28.
Brethren, Christ is risen . . . . . every man in his own order.

This last Lesson *and* Epistle *are said alternately through the year.*

Gradual. As above, but it is sung by the whole Choir sitting, the Precentor beginning it.

Tract. Psalm cxxx. Out of the deep have I called unto thee, O Lord: Lord, hear my voice.

V. O let thine ears consider well: the voice of my complaint.

V. If thou, Lord, will be extreme to mark what is done amiss: O Lord, who may abide it?

V. For there is mercy with thee, therefore shalt thou be feared, O Lord.

* To be used at all times except on the above occasions.

APPENDIX II.

SUNDAY AND MONDAY.

The Gospel.

As in the first Mass for the Dead.

TUESDAY.

The Gospel. John vi. 37—40.

At that time Jesus said to His disciples and to the multitude of the Jews, All that the Father giveth me . . . . . at the last day.

WEDNESDAY.

The Gospel. John v. 24—29.

At that time Jesus said to His disciples and to the multitude of the Jews, Verily, verily . . . . . resurrection of damnation.

THURSDAY.

The Gospel. John v. 21—24.

At that time Jesus said to His disciples and to the multitude of the Jews, As the Father raiseth up the dead . . . . . from death unto life.

FRIDAY.

The Gospel. John vi. 51—54.

At that time Jesus said to His disciples and to the multitude of the Jews, I am the Living Bread . . . . . at the last day.

SATURDAY.

The Gospel. John vi. 53, 54.

At that time Jesus said to His disciples and to the multitude of the Jews, Verily, verily . . . . . at the last day.

We offer thee *is not said;* Offert. *as above.*

Comm. Let light eternal shine upon them, O Lord, together with thy saints, for ever, for thou art holy.

V. Grant them, O Lord, eternal rest; and let light perpetual shine upon them, together with thy saints, for ever, for thou art holy.

In the last service before Easter, the Comm. *is as in the first Mass for the Dead.*

APPENDIX III.

THE OFFICE FOR THE DEAD.
According to the Roman Rite.

[Translated into English.*]

When the whole Office is used, it is said in the manner of a Double, viz., the Vespers on the Eve, and the Invitatory, Matins, and Lauds, on the following morning, concluding with one or more appropriate prayers; but at Vespers the Psalm Lauda anima, *and at Lauds the Psalm* De profundis, *are omitted. On other occasions (when only one of the Nocturns and the Lauds are recited) there are but a few words of the Antiphon before each Psalm recited, and the whole Antiphon at the end thereof.*

AT VESPERS.

Antiphon. I will walk before the Lord.

PSALM CXVI. *Dilexi quoniam.*

I am well pleased : that the Lord hath heard the voice of my prayer;

---

* In this translation, made because no such complete English form of the whole service exists, the Prayer-Book version of the Psalms has been used; while other parts of the service have been so rendered into English as to make them consimilar to the ordinary phraseology of the Book of Common Prayer, in some few instances at the expense of a strict literalness. The Harleian MS., 3166, lettered "Officium Defunctorum," is a large vellum folio, in which the writing is bold and clear, with rubrics and red initial letters, of forty-four pages. It contains the First, Second, and Third Nocturns, and Lauds.

That he hath inclined his ear unto me: therefore will I call upon him as long as I live.

The snares of death compassed me round about: and the pains of hell gat hold upon me.

I shall find trouble and heaviness, and I will call upon the Name of the Lord: O Lord, I beseech thee, deliver my soul.

Gracious is the Lord, and righteous: yea, our God is merciful.

The Lord preserveth the simple: I was in misery, and he helped me.

Turn again then unto thy rest, O my soul: for the Lord hath rewarded thee.

And why? thou hast delivered my soul from death: mine eyes from tears, and my feet from falling.

I will walk before the Lord: in the land of the living.

V. Eternal rest give them, O Lord.
R. And let perpetual light shine upon them.
Ant. I will walk before the Lord in the Land of the living.

Ant. Woe is me.

Psalm CXX. *Ad Dominum.*

When I was in trouble I called upon the Lord: and he heard me.

Deliver my soul, O Lord, from lying lips: and from a deceitful tongue.

What reward shall be given or done unto thee, thou false tongue: even mighty and sharp arrows, with hot burning coals.

Woe is me, that I am constrained to dwell with Mesech: and to have my habitation among the tents of Kedar.

My soul hath long dwelt among them: that are enemies unto peace.

I labour for peace, but when I speak unto them thereof : they make them ready to battle.

V. Eternal rest give them, O Lord.

R. And let perpetual light shine upon them.

Ant. Woe is me, that I am constrained to dwell with Mesech.

Ant. The Lord.

Psalm CXXI. *Levavi oculos.*

I will lift up mine eyes unto the hills : from whence cometh my help.

My help cometh even from the Lord : who hath made heaven and earth.

He will not suffer thy foot to be moved : and he that keepeth thee will not sleep.

Behold he that keepeth Israel : shall neither slumber nor sleep.

The Lord himself is thy keeper : the Lord is thy defence upon thy right hand ;

So that the sun shall not burn thee by day : neither the moon by night.

The Lord shall preserve thee from all evil : yea, it is even he that shall keep thy soul.

The Lord shall preserve thy going out, and thy coming in : from this time forth for evermore.

V. Eternal rest give them, O Lord.

R. And let perpetual light shine upon them.

Ant. The Lord shall preserve thee from all evil, yea, it is even he that shall keep thy soul.

Ant. If thou, Lord, wilt be extreme.

Psalm CXXX. *De profundis.*

Out of the deep have I called unto thee, O Lord : Lord, hear my voice.

APPENDIX III.

O let thine ears consider well : the voice of my complaint.

If thou, Lord, wilt be extreme to mark what is done amiss : O Lord, who may abide it?

For there is mercy with thee : therefore shalt thou be feared.

I look for the Lord : my soul doth wait for him : in his word is my trust.

My soul fleeth unto the Lord : before the morning watch, I say, before the morning watch.

O Israel, trust in the Lord, for with the Lord there is mercy : and with him is plenteous redemption.

And he shall redeem Israel from all his sins.

V. Eternal rest give them, O Lord.

R. And let perpetual light shine upon them.

Ant. If thou, Lord, wilt be extreme to mark what is done amiss.

Ant. The works.

PSALM CXXXVIII. *Confitibor tibi.*

I will give thanks unto thee, O Lord, with my whole heart : even before the gods will I sing praise unto thee.

I will worship toward thy holy temple, and praise thy Name, because of thy loving-kindness and truth : for thou hast magnified thy Name, and thy Word, above all things.

When I called upon thee, thou heardest me : and enduedst my soul with much strength.

All the kings of the earth shall praise thee, O Lord ; for they have heard the words of thy mouth.

Yea, they shall sing in the ways of the Lord : that great is the glory of the Lord.

For though the Lord be high, yet hath he respect unto the lowly : as for the proud, he beholdeth them afar off.

Though I walk in the midst of trouble, yet shalt thou refresh me : thou shalt stretch forth thy hand upon the furiousness of mine enemies, and thy right hand shall save me.

The Lord shall make good his loving-kindness toward me : yea, thy mercy, O Lord, endureth for ever ; despise not then the works of thine own hands.

V. Eternal rest give them, O Lord.

R. And let perpetual light shine upon them.

Ant. Despise not them, O Lord, the works of thine own hands.

V. I heard a voice from heaven saying unto me,

R. Blessed are the dead that die in the Lord.

Ant. All that the Father.

Magnificat. St. Luke i.

My soul doth magnify the Lord : and my spirit hath rejoiced in God my Saviour.

For he hath regarded : the lowliness of his handmaiden.

For behold, from henceforth : all generations shall call me blessed.

For he that is mighty hath magnified me : and holy is his Name.

And his mercy is on them that fear him : throughout all generations.

He hath shewed strength with his arm : he hath scattered the proud in the imagination of their hearts.

He hath put down the mighty from their seat : and hath exalted the humble and meek.

He hath filled the hungry with good things : and the rich he hath sent empty away.

He remembering his mercy hath holpen his servant Israel : as he promised to our forefathers, Abraham and his seed, for ever.

V. Eternal rest, give them, O Lord.

R. And let perpetual light shine upon them.

Ant. All that the Father giveth me shall come to me ; and him that cometh to me I will in no wise cast out.

APPENDIX III.

The following prayers are said kneeling:—

Our Father, etc.

V. And lead us not into temptation,

R. But deliver us from evil. Amen.

The following Psalm is omitted on Nov. 2nd (All-Souls' Day), as also on the day of death and burial:—

PSALM CXLVI. *Lauda, anima mea.*

Praise the Lord, O my soul; while I live will I praise the Lord : yea, as long as I have any being, I will sing praises unto my God.

O put not your trust in princes, nor in any child of man : for there is no help in them.

For when the breath of man goeth forth he shall turn again to his earth : and then all his thoughts perish.

Blessed is he that hath the God of Jacob for his help : and whose hope is in the Lord his God :

Who made heaven and earth, the sea, and all that therein is : who keepeth his promise for ever;

Who helpeth them to right that suffer wrong : who feedeth the hungry.

The Lord looseth men out of prison : the Lord giveth sight to the blind.

The Lord helpeth them that are fallen : the Lord careth for the righteous.

The Lord careth for the strangers; he defendeth the fatherless and widow : as for the way of the ungodly, he turneth it upside down.

The Lord thy God, O Sion, shall be King for evermore : and throughout all generations.

V. Eternal rest give them, O Lord.

R. And let perpetual light shine upon them.

V. From the gates of hell
R. Deliver their souls, O Lord.
V. May they rest in peace.
R. Amen.
V. O Lord, hear my prayer;
R. And let my cry come unto thee.
V. The Lord be with you,
R. And with thy spirit.

Let us pray.

O God, by whose favour thy servants were raised to the dignity of bishops or priests, and so honoured with the apostolical functions; grant, we beseech thee, that they may be admitted to the everlasting fellowship of thine apostles in heaven. *R.* Amen.

O God, the giver of pardon, and the lover of human salvation, we beseech thy clemency, that the brethren, relations, and benefactors of our congregation, who are departed this life, may, by the intercession of the Blessed Mary, ever a Virgin, and of all thy Saints, attain to the fellowship of everlasting happiness. Through our Lord Jesus Christ. *R.* Amen.

O God, the Creator and Redeemer of all the faithful, grant to the souls of thy servants, men and women, the remission of all their sins; that by pious supplications they may obtain that pardon for which they have always hoped. Who livest and reignest world without end. *R.* Amen.

V. Eternal rest give them, O Lord.
R. And let perpetual light shine upon them.
V. May they rest in peace. *R.* Amen.

A PRAYER ON THE DAY OF DECEASE OF A MAN OR WOMAN.

Absolve, we beseech thee, O Lord, the soul of thy servant N., that being dead to the world, he [*or* she] may live to thee: and

APPENDIX III.

whatever he [*or* she] may have committed through human frailty, do thou of thy merciful goodness wipe away and pardon through our Lord Jesus Christ. *R.* Amen.

A PRAYER FOR A BISHOP OR PRIEST DEPARTED THIS LIFE.

O God, who amongst thine apostolic priests, hast bestowed on thy servant N. the pontifical [*or* priestly] dignity; grant, we beseech thee, that he may also be joined with them in perpetual communion: through our Lord Jesus Christ. *R.* Amen.

A PRAYER FOR A FATHER AND MOTHER DEPARTED THIS LIFE.

O God, who hast commanded us to honour our father and mother, mercifully have compassion on the souls of my father and mother, and forgive them their sins, and grant that we may meet in the joy of everlasting happiness: through Jesus Christ our Lord. *R.* Amen.

A PRAYER FOR A FATHER DEPARTED THIS LIFE.

O God, who hast commanded us to honour our father, have mercy, through thy goodness, on the soul of my father, and forgive him his sins, and grant that I may see him in the joy of eternal bliss: through Jesus Christ our Lord. *R.* Amen.

A PRAYER FOR A MOTHER DEPARTED THIS LIFE.

O God, who hast commanded us to honour our father and mother, have mercy, through thy goodness, on the soul of my mother, and forgive her her sins, and grant that I may see her in the joy of eternal bliss: through Jesus Christ our Lord. *R.* Amen.

A PRAYER FOR A MAN DEPARTED THIS LIFE.

Incline thine ears, O Lord, to these our prayers, in which we humbly beseech thy mercy; that thou wouldst place the soul of thy servant, which thou hast caused to depart out of this world in the land of peace and light; and unite it in the fellowship of thy Saints: through Jesus Christ our Lord. *R.* Amen.

A PRAYER FOR A WOMAN DEPARTED THIS LIFE.

We beseech thee, O Lord, for thy goodness, to have mercy upon the soul of thy servant; and, being freed from the corruptions of mortality, restore to her the portion of eternal salvation: through Jesus Christ our Lord. *R.* Amen.

AT MATINS.

The following Invitatory is recited on All-Souls' Day (Nov. 2), and as often as the three Nocturns are said, as before directed. At other times it is omitted, and the Office begins with the Antiphon of the Psalms of the Nocturns, when only one Nocturn is said with the Lauds in the following order, viz., on Monday *and* Thursday *the first Nocturn; on* Tuesday *and* Friday *the second Nocturn; on* Wednesday *and* Saturday *the third Nocturn.*

The Invitatory.

Come, let us adore the King, to whom all things live.

Come, let us adore the King, to whom all things live.

O come, let us sing unto the Lord: let us heartily rejoice in the strength of our salvation.

Let us come before his presence with thanksgiving: and shew ourselves glad in him with psalms.

Come, let us adore the King, to whom all things live.

For the Lord is a great God: and a great King above all gods.

In his hands are all the corners of the earth: and the strength of the hills is his also.

Come, let us adore the King, to whom all things live.

The sea is his, and he made it: and his hands prepared the dry land.

O come, let us worship and fall down : and kneel before the Lord our Maker.

For he is the Lord our God : and we are the people of his pasture, and the sheep of his hand.

Come, let us adore the King, to whom all things live.

To-day if ye will hear his voice, harden not your hearts : as in the provocation, and as in the day of temptation in the wilderness ;

When your fathers tempted me : proved me and saw my works.

Come, let us adore the King, to whom all things live.

Forty years long was I grieved with this generation, and said : It is a people that do err in their hearts, for they have not known my ways ;

Unto whom I sware in my wrath : that they should not enter into my rest.

Come, let us adore the King, to whom all things live.

V. Eternal rest give them, O Lord.

R. And let perpetual light shine upon them.

Come, let us adore. Come, let us adore the King, to whom all things live.

IN THE FIRST NOCTURN.

(To be said on Monday and Thursday).

Ant. O Lord my God, direct thou my steps in thy sight.

PSALM V. *Verba mea auribus.*

Ponder my words, O Lord : consider my meditation.

O hearken thou unto the voice of my calling, my King, and my God : for unto thee will I make my prayer.

My voice shalt thou hear betimes, O Lord : early in the morning will I direct my prayer unto thee, and will look up.

For thou art the God that hast no pleasure in wickedness : neither shall any evil dwell with thee.

Such as be foolish shall not stand in thy sight : for thou hatest all them that work vanity.

Thou shalt destroy them that speak leasing : the Lord will abhor both the blood-thirsty and deceitful man.

But as for me, I will come into thine house, even upon the multitude of thy mercy : and in thy fear will I worship toward thy holy temple.

Lead me, O Lord, in thy righteousness, because of mine enemies : make thy way plain before my face.

For there is no faithfulness in his mouth : their inward parts are very wickedness.

Their throat is an open sepulchre : they flatter with their tongue.

Destroy thou them, O God ; let them perish through their own imaginations : cast them out in the multitude of their ungodliness; for they have rebelled against thee.

And let all them that put their trust in thee rejoice : they shall ever be giving of thanks, because thou defendest them ; they that love thy Name shall be joyful in thee.

For thou, Lord, wilt give thy blessing unto the righteous : and with thy favourable kindness with thou defend him as with a shield.

V. Eternal rest give them, O Lord.

Ant. O Lord my God, direct thou my steps in thy sight.

Ant. Turn thee, O Lord.

PSALM VI. *Domine, ne in furore.*

O Lord, rebuke me not in thine indignation : neither chasten me in thy displeasure.

Have mercy upon me, O Lord, for I am weak : O Lord, heal me, for my bones are vexed.

My soul also is sore troubled : but, Lord, how long wilt thou punish me ?

Turn thee, O Lord, and deliver my soul : O save me for thy mercy's sake.

For in death no man remembereth thee : and who will give thee thanks in the pit?

I am weary of my groaning; every night wash I my bed : and water my couch with my tears.

My beauty is gone for very trouble : and worn away because of all mine enemies.

Away from me, all ye that work vanity : for the Lord hath heard the voice of my weeping.

The Lord hath heard my petition, the Lord will receive my prayer.

All mine enemies shall be confounded, and sore vexed : they shall be turned back, and put to shame suddenly.

V. Eternal rest give them, O Lord.

Ant. Turn thee, O Lord, and deliver my soul : for in death no man remembereth thee.

Ant. Lest he devour.

PSALM VII. *Domine, Deus meus.*

O Lord my God, in thee have I put my trust : save me from all them that persecute me, and deliver me.

Lest he devour my soul like a lion : and tear it in pieces while there is none to help.

O Lord my God, if I have done any such thing : or if there be any wickedness in my hands;

If I have rewarded evil unto him that dealt friendly with me : yea I have delivered him that without any cause is mine enemy;

Then let mine enemy persecute my soul, and take me : yea, let him tread my life down upon the earth, and lay mine honour in the dust.

PRAYERS FOR THE DEPARTED.

Stand up, O Lord, in thy wrath, and lift up thyself because of the indignation of mine enemies : arise up to me in the judgment that thou hast commanded.

And so shall the congregation of the people come about thee : for their sakes therefore lift up thyself again.

The Lord shall judge the people, give sentence with me, O Lord, according to my righteousness, and according to the innocence, that is in me.

O let the wickedness of the ungodly come to an end : but guide thou the just.

For the righteous God : trieth the very hearts and reins.

My help cometh of God : who preserveth them that are true of heart.

God is a righteous judge, strong and patient : and God is provoked every day.

If a man will not turn, he will whet his sword : he hath bent his bow, and made it ready.

He hath prepared for him the instruments of death : he ordaineth his arrows against the persecutors.

Behold, he travaileth with mischief : he hath conceived sorrow, and brought forth ungodliness.

He hath graven and digged up a pit : and is fallen himself into the destruction that he made for other.

For his travail shall come upon his own head : and his wickedness shall fall on his own pate.

I will give thanks unto the Lord, according to his righteousness : and I will praise the Name of the Lord most High.

V. Eternal rest give them, O Lord.

Ant. Lest he devour my soul like a lion and tear it in pieces while there is none to help.

V. From the gates of hell.

R. Deliver their soul, O Lord.

APPENDIX III.

First Lesson. Job vii.

Let me alone, for my days are vanity. What is man that thou shouldest magnify him? and that thou shouldest set thy heart upon him? And that thou shouldest visit him every morning, and try him every moment? How long wilt thou not depart from me, nor let me alone until I swallow down my spittle? I have sinned: what shall I do unto thee, O thou preserver of men? Why hast thou set me as a mark against thee, so that I am a burden to myself? And why dost thou not pardon my transgression and take away mine iniquity? For now shall I sleep in the dust; and thou shalt seek me in the morning, but I shall not be.

V. I know that my Redeemer liveth, and that he shall stand in the latter day upon the earth, and though after my skin, worms destroy this body, yet in my flesh shall I see God.

R. Whom I shall see for myself, and mine eyes shall behold and not another. In my flesh.

Second Lesson. Job x.

My soul is weary of my life; I will leave my complaint upon myself; I will speak in the bitterness of my soul. I will say unto God, Do not condemn me: shew me wherefore thou contendest with me. Is it good unto thee that thou shouldest oppress, that thou shouldest despise the work of thine hands, and shine upon the counsel of the wicked? Hast thou eyes of flesh, or seest thou as men seest? Are thy days as the days of man? Are thy years as man's days, that thou enquirest after mine iniquity and searchest after my sin? Thou knowest that I am not wicked; and there is none that can deliver out of thine hand.

V. Thou who didst raise Lazarus corrupt from the grave: Thou, O Lord, give them rest and a place of pardon.

R. Who art come to judge the quick and the dead, and the world by fire. Thou, O Lord.

Third Lesson. Job x.

Thine hands have made me and fashioned me together round about. Yet thou dost destroy me. Remember, I beseech thee, that thou hast made me as the clay, and wilt thou bring me into dust again? Hast thou not poured me out as milk, and curdled me like cheese? Thou hast clothed me with skin and flesh, and hast fenced me with bones and sinews. Thou hast granted me life and favour, and thy visitation hath preserved my spirit.

V. O Lord, where shall I hide myself from the countenance of thy wrath, when thou shalt come to judge the earth. Because in my lifetime I have sinned exceedingly.

R. I dread my misdeeds, and am ashamed before thee. Condemn me not when thou shalt come to judgment. Because in my lifetime I have sinned exceedingly.

V. Eternal rest give them, O Lord, and let perpetual light shine upon them. For I have sinned.

Here Lauds are said when the First Nocturn only is recited.

In the Second Nocturn.

Ant. He shall feed me in a green pasture.

Psalm XXIII. *Dominus regit me.*

The Lord is my shepherd : therefore can I lack nothing.

He shall feed me in a green pasture : and lead me forth beside the waters of comfort.

He shall convert my soul : and bring me forth in the paths of righteousness, for his Name's sake.

Yea, though I walk through the valley of the shadow of death, I will fear no evil : for thou art with me ; thy rod and thy staff comfort me.

Thou shalt prepare a table before me against them that trouble me : thou hast anointed my head with oil, and my cup shall be full.

But thy loving-kindness and mercy shall follow me all the days of my life : and I will dwell in the House of the Lord for ever.

V. Eternal rest give them, O Lord.

Ant. He shall feed me in a green pasture : and lead me forth beside the waters of comfort.

Ant. The sins and offences.

PSALM XXV. *Ad te, Domine, levavi.*

Unto thee, O Lord, will I lift up my soul ; my God, I have put my trust in thee : O let me not be confounded, neither let mine enemies triumph over me.

For all they that hope in thee shall not be ashamed : but such as transgress without a cause shall be put to confusion.

Shew me thy ways, O Lord : and teach me thy paths.

Lead me forth in thy truth, and learn me : for thou art the God of my salvation ; in thee hath been my hope all the day long.

Call to remembrance, O Lord, thy tender mercies : and thy loving kindnesses, which have been ever of old.

O remember not the sins and offences of my youth : but according to thy mercy think thou upon me, O Lord, for thy goodness.

Gracious and righteous is the Lord : therefore will he teach sinners in the way.

Them that are meek shall he guide in judgment : and such as are gentle, them shall he learn his way.

All the paths of the Lord are mercy and truth : unto such as keep his covenant, and his testimonies.

For thy Name's sake, O Lord : be merciful unto my sin, for it is great.

What man is he, that feareth the Lord : him shall he teach in the way that he shall choose.

His soul shall dwell at ease : and his seed shall inherit the land.

The secret of the Lord is among them that fear him : and he will shew them his covenant.

Mine eyes are ever looking unto the Lord : for he shall pluck my feet out of the net.

Turn thee unto me, and have mercy upon me : for I am desolate and in misery.

The sorrows of my heart are enlarged : O bring thou me out of my troubles.

Look upon my adversity and misery : and forgive me all my sins.

Consider mine enemies, how many they are : and they bear a tyrannous hate against me.

O keep my soul, and deliver me : let me not be confounded, for I have put my trust in thee.

Let perfectness and righteous dealing wait upon me : for my hope hath been in thee.

Deliver Israel, O God : out of all his troubles.

V. Eternal rest give them, O Lord.

Ant. The sins and offences of my youth, remember not, O Lord.

Ant. I believe verily to see.

PSALM XXVII. *Dominus illuminatio mea.*

The Lord is my light and my salvation; whom then shall I fear : the Lord is the strength of my life; of whom then shall I be afraid ?

When the wicked, even mine enemies and my foes, came upon me, to eat up my flesh : they stumbled and fell.

Though an host of men were laid against me, yet shall not my heart be afraid : and though there rose up war against me, yet will I put my trust in him.

One thing have I desired of the Lord, which I will require : even that I may dwell in the house of the Lord all the days of my life, to behold the fair beauty of the Lord, and to visit his temple.

For in the time of trouble he shall hide me in his tabernacle: yea, in the secret place of his dwelling shall he hide me, and set me up upon a rock of stone.

And now shall he lift up mine head: above mine enemies round about me.

Therefore will I offer in his dwelling an oblation with great gladness: I will sing, and speak praises unto the Lord.

Hearken unto my voice, O Lord, when I cry unto thee: have mercy upon me, and hear me.

My heart hath talked of thee, seek ye my face: thy face, Lord, will I seek.

O hide not thou thy face from me: nor cast thy servant away in displeasure.

Thou hast been my succour: leave me not, neither forsake me, O God of my salvation.

When my father and my mother forsake me: the Lord taketh me up.

Teach me thy way, O Lord: and lead me in the right way, because of mine enemies.

Deliver me not over into the will of mine adversaries: for there are false witnesses risen up against me, and such as speak wrong.

I should utterly have fainted: but that I believe verily to see the goodness of the Lord in the land of the living.

O tarry thou the Lord's leisure: be strong, and he shall comfort thine heart; and put thou thy trust in the Lord.

Ant. I believe verily to see the goodness of the Lord in the land of the living.

Vers. May the Lord place them with the princes.

Resp. Even with the princes of his people.

Our Father, *secretly.*

Fourth Lesson. Job xiii.

Answer thou me : how many are mine iniquities and sins? make me to know my transgression and my sin. Wherefore hidest thou thy face, and holdest me for thine enemy? Wilt thou break a leaf driven to and fro? and wilt thou pursue the dry stubble? For thou writest bitter things against me, and makest me to possess the iniquities of my youth. Thou puttest my feet also in the stocks, and lookest narrowly into all my paths: thou settest a print upon the heels of my feet. And he, as a rotten thing, consumeth, as a garment that is moth-eaten.

V. Remember me, O God, because my life is but a vapour : nor may the sight of men behold me.

R. Out of the deep have I called unto thee, O Lord : Lord, hear my voice. Nor may the sight.

Fifth Lesson. Job xiv.

Man that is born of a woman is of few days, and full of trouble. He cometh forth like a flower and is cut down : he fleeth also as a shadow and continueth not. And dost thou open thine eyes upon such an one, and bringest me into judgment with thee? Who can bring a clean thing out of an unclean? Not one. Seeing his days are determined, the number of his months are with thee, thou hast appointed his bounds that he cannot pass : turn from him that he may rest, till he shall accomplish, as an hireling, his day.

V. Woe is me, O Lord, because I have sinned exceedingly in my life. O miserable man, what shall I do, whither shall I flee but to thee, O God? Have mercy upon me when thou comest at the great day.

R. My soul is greatly troubled : Do thou, O Lord, succour it. Have mercy upon me.

APPENDIX III.

Sixth Lesson. Job xiv.

O that thou wouldest hide me in the grave, that thou wouldest keep me secret, until thy wrath be past, that thou wouldest appoint me a set time and remember me! If a man die, shall he live again? all the days of my appointed time will I wait, till my change come. Thou shalt call, and I will answer thee: thou wilt have a desire to the work of thine hands. For now thou numberest my steps: dost thou not watch over my sin?

V. Remember not my sins, O Lord, when thou shalt come to judge the world by fire.

R. Direct my way in thy sight, O Lord my God, when thou shalt come to judge the earth by fire.

V. Eternal rest give them, O Lord, and let perpetual light shine upon them, when thou shalt come.

Here the Lauds are recited when the Second Nocturn only is said.

In the Third Nocturn.

Ant. Let it be thy pleasure.

Psalm XL. *Expectans expectavi.*

I waited patiently for the Lord: and he inclined unto me, and heard my calling.

He brought me also out of the horrible pit, out of the mire and clay: and set my feet upon the rock, and ordered my goings.

And he hath put a new song in my mouth: even a thanksgiving unto our God.

Many shall see it, and fear: and shall put their trust in the Lord.

Blessed is the man that hath set his hope in the Lord: and turned not unto the proud, and to such as go about with lies

O Lord my God, great are the wondrous works which thou hast done, like as be also thy thoughts which are to us-ward: and yet there is no man that ordereth them unto thee.

If I should declare them, and speak of them: they should be more than I am able to express.

Sacrifice, and meat-offering, thou wouldest not: but mine ears hast thou opened.

Burnt-offerings, and sacrifice for sin, hast thou not required: then said I, Lo, I come,

In the volume of the book it is written of me, that I should fulfil thy will, O my God: I am content to do it; yea, thy law is within my heart.

I have declared thy righteousness in the great congregation: lo, I will not refrain my lips, O Lord, and that thou knowest.

I have not hid thy righteousness within my heart: my talk hath been of thy truth, and of thy salvation.

I have not kept back thy loving mercy and truth: from the great congregation.

Withdraw not thou thy mercy from me, O Lord: let thy loving-kindness and thy truth alway preserve me.

For innumerable troubles are come about me; my sins have taken such hold upon me that I am not able to look up: yea, they are more in number than the hairs of my head, and my heart hath failed me.

O Lord, let it be thy pleasure to deliver me: make haste, O Lord, to help me.

Let them be ashamed, and confounded together, that seek after my soul to destroy it: let them be driven backward, and put to rebuke, that wish me evil.

Let them be desolate, and rewarded with shame: that say unto me, Fie upon thee, fie upon thee.

Let all those that seek thee be joyful and glad in thee: and let such as love thy salvation say alway, The Lord be praised.

As for me, I am poor and needy: but the Lord careth for me.

Thou art my helper and redeemer : make no long tarrying, O my God.

V. Eternal rest give them, O Lord.

Ant. O Lord, let it be thy pleasure to deliver me : make haste, O Lord, to help me.

Ant. Heal my soul, O Lord.

Psalm XLI. *Beatus qui intelligit.*

Blessed is he that considereth the poor and needy : the Lord shall deliver him in the time of trouble.

The Lord preserve him and keep him alive, that he may be blessed upon earth : and deliver not thou him into the will of his enemies.

The Lord comfort him when he lieth sick upon his bed : make thou all his bed in his sickness.

I said, Lord, be merciful unto me : heal my soul, for I have sinned against thee.

Mine enemies speak evil of me : When shall he die, and his name perish?

And if he come to see me, he speaketh vanity : and his heart conceiveth falsehood within himself; and when he cometh forth, he telleth it.

All mine enemies whisper together against me : even against me do they imagine this evil.

Let the sentence of guiltiness proceed against him : and now that he lieth let him rise up no more.

Yea, even mine own familiar friend, whom I trusted : who id also eat of my bread, hath laid great wait for me.

But be thou merciful unto me, O Lord : raise thou me up again, and I shall reward them.

By this I know that thou favourest me : that mine enemy doth not triumph against me.

And when I am in my health, thou upholdest me : and shalt set me before thy face for ever.

Blessed be the Lord God of Israel : world without end. Amen.

V. Eternal rest give them, O Lord.

Ant. Heal my soul, O Lord, for I have sinned against thee.

Ant. My soul is athirst.

Psalm XLII. *Quemadmodum.*

Like as the hart desireth the water-brooks : so longeth my soul after thee, O God.

My soul is athirst for God, yea, even for the living God : when shall I come to appear before the presence of God ?

My tears have been my meat day and night : while they daily say unto me, Where is now thy God ?

Now when I think thereupon, I pour out my heart by myself : for I went with the multitude, and brought them forth into the house of God.

In the voice of praise and thanksgiving : among such as keep holy-day.

Why art thou so full of heaviness, O my soul : and why art thou so disquieted within me ?

Put thy trust in God : for I will yet give him thanks for the help of his countenance.

My God, my soul is vexed within me : therefore will I remember thee concerning the land of Jordan, and the little hill of Hermon.

One deep calleth another, because of the noise of the water-pipes : all thy waves and storms are gone over me.

The Lord hath granted his loving-kindness in the day-time : and in the night-season did I sing of him, and made my prayer unto the God of my life.

I will say unto the God of my strength, Why hast thou forgotten me: why go I thus heavily, while the enemy oppresseth me?

My bones are smitten asunder as with a sword: while mine enemies that trouble me cast me in the teeth;

Namely, while they say daily unto me: Where is now thy God?

Why art thou so vexed, O my soul: and why art thou so disquieted within me?

O put thy trust in God: for I will yet give him thanks, which is the help of my countenance and my God.

V. Eternal rest give them, O Lord.

Ant. My soul is athirst for God, yea, even for the living God: when shall I come to appear before the presence of God?

V. Deliver not to the beasts which perish, the spirits which praise thee.

R. And forget not the souls of the poor for ever.

Our Father, *secretly.*

SEVENTH LESSON. Job xvii.

My breath is corrupt, my days are extinct, the graves are ready for me. Are there not mockers with me? and doth not mine eye continue in their provocation? Lay down now, put me in a surety with thee; who is he that will strike hands with me? For thou hast hid their heart from understanding: therefore shalt thou not exalt them. My days are passed, my purposes are broken off, even the thoughts of my heart. They change the night into day: the light is short because of darkness. If I wait, the grave is my house: I have made my bed in the darkness. I have said to corruption, Thou art my father: to the worm, Thou art my mother and my sister. And where is now my hope? as for my hope, who shall see it?

V. The fear of death disquieteth me, sinning daily and not repenting : for in hell there is no redemption, have mercy upon me, O God, and save me.

R. O God, save me for thy Name's sake, and deliver me in thy strength. For in hell.

Eighth Lesson. Job xix.

My bone cleaveth to my skin and to my flesh, and I am escaped with the skin of my teeth. Have pity upon me, have pity upon me, O ye my friends; for the hand of God hath touched me. Why do ye persecute me as God, and are not satisfied with my flesh? Oh that my words were now written; oh that they were printed in a book! That they were graven with an iron pen and lead in the rock for ever! For I know that my Redeemer liveth, and that he shall stand at the latter day upon the earth: and though after my skin worms destroy this body, yet in my flesh shall I see God, whom I shall see for myself, and mine eyes shall behold, and not another: though my reins be consumed within me.

V. Judge me not, O Lord, according to my deeds : for I have done nothing worthy in thy sight : therefore I beseech thy Majesty, O God, to blot out all mine iniquity.

R. Wash me throughly from my wickedness: and cleanse me from my sin. Therefore I beseech thy Majesty, O God.

Ninth Lesson. Job x.

Wherefore then hast thou brought me forth out of the womb? Oh that I had given up the ghost, and that no eye had seen me! I should have been as though I had not been : I should have been carried from the womb to the grave. Are not my days few? cease then and let me alone that I may take comfort a little, before I go where I shall not return; even to the land of darkness and the shadow of death : a land of darkness as darkness itself ;

and of the shadow of death without any order, and where the light is as darkness.

V. Deliver me, O Lord, from the path of hell, who hast broken the gates of brass and hast visited Hades : and hast given light to them Who were in the pains of darkness that they might behold thee.

R. Crying out and saying, Thou art come, O Redeemer. Who were.

V. Eternal rest give them, O Lord, and let perpetual light shine upon them. Who were.

This is always said in the week-day office. But the following Responsory is only said on November 2, All-Souls' Day, and when the Three Nocturns are said together.

V. Deliver me, O Lord, from eternal death in that dreadful day when heaven and earth shall pass away : when thou shalt come to judge the world by fire.

R. I tremble and quake because of the examination that is to be, and because of the wrath to come : when heaven and earth is to be removed.

V. That day, that day of wrath, of calamity and misery, that great and bitter day, when thou shalt come to judge the world by fire.

R. Eternal rest give them, O Lord, and let perpetual light shine upon them.

V. Deliver me, O Lord, from eternal death in that dreadful day when heaven and earth shall pass away : when thou shalt come to judge the world by fire.

AT LAUDS.

Ant. May rejoice.

Psalm LI. *Miserere mei, Deus.*

Have mercy upon me, O God, after thy great goodness : according to the multitude of thy mercies do away mine offences.

Wash me throughly from my wickedness : and cleanse me from my sin.

For I acknowledge my faults : and my sin is ever before me.

Against thee only have I sinned, and done this evil in thy sight : that thou mightest be justified in thy saying, and clear when thou art judged.

Behold, I was shapen in wickedness : and in sin hath my mother conceived me.

But lo, thou requirest truth in the inward parts : and shalt make me to understand wisdom secretly.

Thou shalt purge me with hyssop, and I shall be clean : thou shalt wash me, and I shall be whiter than snow.

Thou shalt make me hear of joy and gladness : that the bones which thou hast broken may rejoice.

Turn thy face from my sins : and put out all my misdeeds.

Make me a clean heart, O God : and renew a right spirit within me.

Cast me not away from thy presence : and take not thy holy Spirit from me.

O give me the comfort of thy help again : and stablish me with thy free Spirit.

Then shall I teach thy ways unto the wicked : and sinners shall be converted unto thee.

Deliver me from blood-guiltiness, O God, thou that art the God of my health : and my tongue shall sing of thy righteousness.

Thou shalt open my lips, O Lord : and my mouth shall shew thy praise.

For thou desirest no sacrifice, else would I give it thee : but thou delightest not in burnt-offerings.

The sacrifice of God is a troubled spirit : a broken and contrite heart, O God, shalt thou not despise.

O be favourable and gracious unto Sion : build thou the walls of Jerusalem.

Then shalt thou be pleased with the sacrifice of righteousness, with the burnt-offerings and oblations : then shall they offer young bullocks upon thine altar.

V. Eternal rest give them, O Lord.

Ant. That the bones which thou hast broken may rejoice.

Ant. Thou that hearest.

Psalm LXV. *Te decet hymnus.*

Thou, O God, art praised in Sion : and unto thee shall the vow be performed in Jerusalem.

Thou that hearest the prayer : unto thee shall all flesh come.

My misdeeds prevail against me : O be thou merciful unto our sins.

Blessed is the man, whom thou choosest, and receivest unto thee : he shall dwell in thy court, and shall be satisfied with the pleasures of thy house, even of thy holy temple.

Thou shalt shew us wonderful things in thy righteousness, O God of our salvation : thou that art the hope of all the ends of the earth, and of them that remain in the broad sea.

Who in his strength setteth fast the mountains : and is girded about with power.

Who stilleth the raging of the sea : and the noise of his waves, and the madness of the people.

They also that dwell in the uttermost parts of the earth shall be afraid at thy tokens : thou that makest the outgoings of the morning and evening to praise thee.

Thou visitest the earth, and blessest it : thou makest it very plenteous.

The river of God is full of water : thou preparest their corn, for so thou providest for the earth.

Thou waterest her furrows, thou sendest rain into the little valleys thereof : thou makest it soft with the drops of rain, and blessest the increase of it.

Thou crownest the year with thy goodness : and thy clouds drop fatness.

They shall drop upon the dwellings of the wilderness : and the little hills shall rejoice on every side.

The folds shall be full of sheep : the valleys also shall stand so thick with corn, that they shall laugh and sing.

V. Eternal rest give them, O Lord.

Ant. Thou that hearest the prayer : unto thee shall all flesh come.

Ant. Thy right hand.

PSALM LXIII. *Deus, Deus meus.*

O God, thou art my God : early will I seek thee.

My soul thirsteth for thee, my flesh also longeth after thee : in a barren and dry land where no water is.

Thus have I looked for thee in holiness : that I might behold thy power and glory.

For thy loving-kindness is better than the life itself : my lips shall praise thee.

As long as I live will I magnify thee on this manner : and lift up my hands in thy Name.

My soul shall be satisfied, even as it were with marrow and fatness : when my mouth praiseth thee with joyful lips.

Have I not remembered thee in my bed : and thought upon thee when I was waking?

Because thou hast been my helper : therefore under the shadow of thy wings will I rejoice.

My soul hangeth upon thee : thy right hand hath upholden me.

These also that seek the hurt of my soul : they shall go under the earth.

Let them fall upon the edge of the sword : that they may be a portion for foxes.

But the king shall rejoice in God : all they also that swear by him shall be commended : for the mouth of them that speak lies shall be stopped.

Psalm LXVII. *Deus misereatur.*

God be merciful unto us, and bless us : and shew us the light of his countenance, and be merciful unto us;

That thy way may be known upon earth : thy saving health among all nations.

Let the people praise thee, O God : yea, let all the people praise thee.

O let the nations rejoice and be glad : for thou shalt judge the folk righteously, and govern the nations upon earth.

Let the people praise thee, O God : let all the people praise thee.

Then shall the earth bring forth her increase : and God, even our own God, shall give us his blessing.

God shall bless us : and all the ends of the world shall fear him.

Vers. Eternal rest give them, O Lord.

Ant. Thy right hand hath upholden me.

Ant. From the gate.

The Song of Hezekiah.

I said in the cutting off of my days, I shall go to the gates of the grave : I am deprived of the residue of my years.

I said, I shall not see the Lord, even the Lord in the land of the living: I shall behold man no more with the inhabitants of the world.

Mine age is departed and is removed from me as a shepherd's tent. I have cut off like a weaver my life: he will cut me off with pining sickness: from day even to night wilt thou make an end of me.

I reckoned till morning, that as a lion so will he break my bones: from day even to night wilt thou make an end of me.

Like a crane or a swallow, so did I chatter: I did mourn as a dove: mine eyes fail with looking upward: O Lord, I am oppressed; undertake for me.

What shall I say? he hath both spoken unto me, and himself hath done it. I shall go softly all my years in the bitterness of my soul.

O Lord, by these things we live, and in all these things is the life of my spirit: so wilt thou recover me and make me to live.

Behold, for peace I had great bitterness: but thou hast in love to my soul delivered it from the pit of corruption, for thou hast cast all my sins behind thy back.

For the grave cannot praise thee, death doth not celebrate thee: they that go down into the pit cannot hope for thy truth.

The living, the living he shall praise thee as I do this day: the father to the children shall make known thy truth.

The Lord was ready to save me: therefore we will sing my songs to the stringed instruments all the days of our life in the house of the Lord.

Vers. Eternal rest give them, O Lord.

Ant. From the gate of hell deliver my soul.

Ant. Let everything that hath breath.

PSALM CXLVIII. *Laudate Dominum.*

O praise the Lord of heaven : praise him in the height.

Praise him, all ye angels of his : praise him, all his host.

Praise him, sun and moon : praise him, all ye stars and light.

Praise him, all ye heavens : and ye waters that are above the heavens.

Let them praise the Name of the Lord : for he spake the word, and they were made ; he commanded, and they were created.

He hath made them fast for ever and ever : he hath given them a law which shall not be broken.

Praise the Lord upon earth : ye dragons, and all deeps ;

Fire and hail, snow and vapours : wind and storm, fulfilling his word ;

Mountains and all hills : fruitful trees and all cedars ;

Beasts and all cattle : worms and feathered fowls ;

Kings of the earth and all people : princes and all judges of the world ;

Young men and maidens, old men and children, praise the Name of the Lord : for his Name only is excellent, and his praise above heaven and earth.

He shall exalt the horn of his people ; all his saints shall praise him : even the children of Israel, even the people that serveth him.

PSALM CXLIX. *Cantate Domino.*

O sing unto the Lord a new song : let the congregation of saints praise him.

Let Israel rejoice in him that made him : and let the children of Sion be joyful in their King.

Let them praise his Name in the dance : let them sing praises unto him with tabret and harp.

For the Lord hath pleasure in his people : and helpeth the meek-hearted.

Let the saints be joyful with glory : let them rejoice in their beds.

Let the praises of God be in their mouth : and a two-edged sword in their hands ;

To be avenged of the heathen : and to rebuke the people ;

To bind their kings in chains : and their nobles with links of iron.

That they may be avenged of them, as it is written : Such honour have all his saints.

Psalm CL. *Laudate Dominum.*

O praise God in his holiness : praise him in the firmament of his power.

Praise him in his noble acts : praise him according to his excellent greatness.

Praise him in the sound of the trumpet : praise him upon the lute and harp.

Praise him in the cymbals and dances : praise him upon the strings and pipe.

Praise him upon the well-tuned cymbals : praise him upon the loud cymbals.

Let everything that hath breath : praise the Lord.

Vers. Eternal rest give them, O Lord.

Ant. Let everything that hath breath praise the Lord.

V. I heard a voice from heaven saying unto me :

R. Blessed are the dead that die in the Lord.

Ant. I am the resurrection.

Benedictus. St. Luke i. 68.

Blessed be the Lord God of Israel : for he hath visited, and redeemed his people ;

And hath raised up a mighty salvation for us : in the house of his servant David ;

As he spake by the mouth of his holy Prophets : which have been since the world began ;

That we should be saved from our enemies : and from the hands of all that hate us ;

To perform the mercy promised to our forefathers : and to remember his holy Covenant ;

To perform the oath which he sware to our forefather Abraham : that he would give us ;

That we being delivered out of the hand of our enemies : might serve him without fear ;

In holiness and righteousness before him : all the days of our life.

And thou, Child, shalt be called the Prophet of the Highest : for thou shalt go before the face of the Lord to prepare his ways ;

To give knowledge of salvation unto his people : for the remission of their sins,

Through the tender mercy of our God : whereby the day-spring from on high hath visited us.

To give light to them that sit in darkness, and in the shadow of death : and to guide our feet into the way of peace.

Vers. Eternal rest give them, O Lord.

Ant. I am the resurrection and the life : he that believeth in me though he were dead yet shall he live, and whosoever liveth and believeth in me shall never die.

Our Father, *secretly.*

V. And lead us not into temptation.

R. But deliver us from evil.

Here Psalm De Profundis * *is said with the following versicles,*

* See *Vespers for the Dead*, page 230.

PRAYERS FOR THE DEPARTED.

except on Nov. 2nd, All Souls' Day, and on the day of death and burial, when it is omitted.

Eternal rest give them, O Lord.
V. From the gates of hell.
R. Deliver their souls, O Lord.
V. May they rest in peace.
R. Amen.
V. Lord, hear my prayer.
R. And let my cry come unto thee.
V. The Lord be with you.
R. And with thy spirit.

Then certain prayers follow, according to the rank, degree, and sex of the deceased, set forth at the end of Vespers.

APPENDIX IV.

THE ORDER FOR THE BURIAL OF INFANTS.*

(According to the Roman Rite.)

The Priest meeting the corpse at the entrance of the burial-ground, sprinkles it with Holy Water, saying:—

Ant. Blessed be the Name of the Lord.

PSALM CXIII. *Laudate pueri.*

Praise the Lord, ye servants : O praise the Name of the Lord.

Blessed be the Name of the Lord : from this time forth for evermore.

The Lord's Name is praised : from the rising up of the sun unto the going down of the same.

The Lord is high above all heathen : and his glory above the heavens.

Who is like unto the Lord our God, that hath his dwelling so

---

* The first rubric stands as follows:—"Cum igitur infans, vel puer baptizatus defunctus fuerit ante usum rationis, induitur juxta ætatem, et imponitur ei corona de floribus, seu de herbis aromaticis et odoriferis, in lignum integritatis carnis et virginitatis; et parochus superpellicio et stola alba indutus et alii de Clero, si adsint, præcedente cruce, quæ sine hasta defertur, accedunt ad domum defuncti, cum Clerico aspersorium deferente. Sacerdos aspergit corpus."—*Rituale Romanum*, p. 276. Mechlin, 1856.

high: and yet humbleth himself to behold the things that are in heaven and earth.?

He taketh up the simple out of the dust : and lifteth the poor out of the mire ;

That he may set him with the princes : even with the princes of his people.

He maketh the barren woman to keep house : and to be a joyful mother of children.

Glory be to the Father, etc.

Ant. Blessed be the Name of the Lord : from this time forth for evermore.

While the corpse is being borne to the church, as much as may be needed of the following section of Psalm, Beati immaculati, *is said:—*

Ant. He shall receive.

Psalm CXIX. *Beati immaculati.*

Blessed are those that are undefiled in the way : and walk in the law of the Lord.

Blessed are they that keep his testimonies : and seek him with their whole heart.

For they who do no wickedness : walk in his ways.

Thou hast charged : that we shall diligently keep thy commandments.

O that my ways were made so direct : that I might keep thy statutes !

So shall I not be confounded : while I have respect unto all thy commandments.

I will thank thee with an unfeigned heart : when I shall have learned the judgments of thy righteousness.

I will keep thy ceremonies : O forsake me not utterly.

APPENDIX IV.

Wherewithal shall a young man cleanse his way : even by ruling himself after thy word.

With my whole heart have I sought thee : O let me not go wrong out of thy commandments.

Thy words have I hid within my heart : that I should not sin against thee.

Blessed art thou, O Lord : O teach me thy statutes.

With my lips have I been telling : of all the judgments of thy mouth.

I have had as great delight in the way of thy testimonies : as in all manner of riches.

I will talk of thy commandments : and have respect unto thy ways.

My delight shall be in thy statutes : and I will not forget thy word.

O do well unto thy servant : that I may live and keep thy word.

Open thou mine eyes : that I may see the wondrous things of thy law.

I am a stranger upon earth : O hide not thy commandments from me.

My soul breaketh out for the very fervent desire : that it hath alway unto thy judgments.

Thou hast rebuked the proud : and cursed are they that do err from thy commandments.

O turn from me shame and rebuke : for I have kept thy testimonies.

Princes also did sit and speak against me : but thy servant is occupied in thy statutes.

For thy testimonies are my delight : and my counsellors.

Glory be to the Father, etc.

Having come into the church, the following is said:—

Ant. He shall receive a blessing from the Lord, and righteousness from the God of his salvation : this is the generation of them that seek him, even of them that seek thy face.

PSALM XXIV. *Domini est terra.*

The earth is the Lord's and all that therein is : the compass of the world and they that dwell therein.

For he hath founded it upon the seas : and prepared it upon the floods.

Who shall ascend into the hill of the Lord : or who shall rise up in his holy place?

Even he that hath clean hands, and a pure heart : and that hath not lift up his mind unto vanity, nor sworn to deceive his neighbour.

He shall receive the blessing from the Lord : and righteousness from the God of his salvation.

This is the generation of them that seek him : even of them that seek thy face, O Jacob.

Lift up your heads, O ye gates, and be ye lift up, ye everlasting doors : and the King of glory shall come in.

Who is the King of glory : it is the Lord strong and mighty, even the Lord mighty in battle.

Lift up your heads, O ye gates, and be ye lift up, ye everlasting doors : and the King of glory shall come in.

Who is the King of glory : even the Lord of Hosts, he is the King of glory.

Glory be to the Father, etc.

Ant. He shall receive a blessing from the Lord, and righteousness from the God of his salvation : this is the generation of them that seek him, even of them that seek thy face.

Lord, have mercy upon us.

Christ, have mercy upon us.

Lord, have mercy upon us.
Our Father, etc., *secretly*.

Here the corpse is sprinkled with Holy Water.

V. And lead us not into temptation.
R. But deliver us from evil.
V. But because of mine innocence thou hast received me.
R. And hast confirmed me in thy sight for evermore.
V. The Lord be with you.
R. And with thy spirit.

Let us pray.

O almighty and most merciful God, who, without any merit on their part, vouchsafest to all baptized children departing out of this world eternal life, as we believe thou hast now bestowed upon the soul of this child; grant us, we beseech thee, O Lord, that by the intercession of the Blessed Mary, ever-virgin, and all saints, we may serve thee here with pure hearts and be united to thy blessed children hereafter in heaven, through Jesus Christ our Lord. *Resp.* Amen.

While the body is being borne to the grave, the following is said:—

Ant. Young men and maidens, old men and children : praise the Name of the Lord.

PSALM CXLVIII. *Laudate Dominum.*

[P. 259 of *The Office for the Dead*, with "Glory be to the Father," etc.]

Ant. Young men and maidens, old men and children : praise the Name of the Lord.

Lord, have mercy upon us.
Christ, have mercy upon us.
Lord, have mercy upon us.

Our Father, *secretly.*

V. And lead us not into temptation.

R. But deliver us from evil.
V. Suffer little children to come unto me.
R. For of such is the kingdom of heaven.
V. The Lord be with you.
R. And with thy spirit.

Let us pray.

O almighty and everlasting God, the lover of holy purity, who in thy mercy hast now called the soul of this child to thy kingdom in heaven: vouchsafe, we beseech thee, O Lord, to be also merciful to us, that through the merits of thy most sacred passion, and by the intercession of the Blessed Virgin Mary and all saints, we may rejoice together, with all thy saints and elect, in the same kingdom for ever. Who livest and reignest God world without end. *R.* Amen.

Here the body and the grave are sprinkled with Holy Water by the Priest and incensed, after which the corpse is buried.

In returning from the grave to the church is sung or said the Canticle Benedicite omnia Opera, *with the following* Antiphon, *which is doubled:*

Ant. O all ye elect of the Lord, bless ye the Lord, praise him and magnify him for ever.

Then the Priest and his assistant being before the altar, the following is said:

Vers. The Lord be with you.
Resp. And with thy spirit.

Let us pray.

O everlasting God, who hast ordained and constituted the services of angels and men in a wonderful order; mercifully grant, that as thy holy angels always do thee service in heaven, so by thy appointment they may succour and defend us on earth, through Jesus Christ our Lord. *R.* Amen.

APPENDIX V.

MISSA IN CEMETERIO.

[From Archbishop Ecgberht's Pontifical.]

Deus cujus miseratione animæ fidelium requiescunt animabus famulorum famularumque tuarum et omnibus in hoc cemeterio quiescentibus, da propitius veniam peccatorum ut a cunctus reatibus absolutæ sine fine laetentur. Per.

Omnipotens sempiterne Deus, animæ quaesumus precibus nostris ea quae poscimus et dona omnibus quorum hic corpora requiescunt, refrigerii sedem, quietis beatitudinem, luminis claritatem, ut qui peccatorum suorum pondere pregravantur eos supplicatio commendet Ecclesiæ. Per.

Secreta. Pro animabus famulorum famularumque tuarum et omnium hic dormientium hostiam Domine suscipe benignus oblatam, ut hoc sacrificio singulari vinculis horrendæ mortis exutæ vitam mereantur æternam. Per.

Postcommunionem. Deus fidelium lumen animarum adesto supplicationibus nostris, et da omnibus quorum corpora hic requiescunt refrigerii sedem, quietis beatitudinem, luminis claritatem. Per.—(*Pontificale Ecgberhti Archiep. Eburaci Civitatis.* MS. folio lxxiii. b. Paris, in the National Library.)

APPENDIX VI.

COMMUNION SERVICE.

[From the First Prayer-Book of King Edward VI.]

Canon. "And here we do give unto thee most high praise and hearty thanks, for the wonderful grace and virtue declared in all thy saints, from the beginning of the world; and chiefly in the glorious and most Blessed Virgin Mary, mother of thy Son Jesu Christ our Lord and God : and in the holy patriarchs, prophets, apostles, and martyrs, whose examples (O Lord), and steadfastness in thy faith, and keeping thy Holy Commandments, grant us to follow. We commend unto thy mercy (O Lord) all other thy servants, which are departed hence from us with the sign of faith, and now do rest in the sleep of peace : grant unto them, we beseech thee, thy mercy and everlasting peace; and that at the day of the general resurrection, we and all they which be of the mystical body of thy Son, may altogether be set on his right hand, and bear that his most joyful voice, Come unto me, O ye that be blessed of my Father, and possess the kingdom which is prepared for you from the beginning of the world."*

---

* It should be noted that in the above the distinction between the saints and the faithful in general, as in the ancient formularies, is most carefully preserved and distinguished.

APPENDIX VI.

CELEBRATION OF THE HOLY COMMUNION WHEN THERE IS A BURIAL OF THE DEAD.

[From the First Prayer-Book of King Edward VI.]

[*Introit*] *Quemadmodum.* PSALM XLII.

Collect. O merciful God, the Father of our Lord Jesus Christ, who is the resurrection of the life; in whom whosoever believeth shall live though he die; and whosoever liveth, and believeth in Him shall not die eternally; who also hath taught us (by his holy apostle Paul) not to be sorry as man without hope, for them that sleep in Him; we meekly beseech thee (O Father) to raise us from the death of sin unto the life of righteousness; that when we shall depart this life we may sleep in Him (as our hope is this our brother doth); and at the general resurrection in the last day, both we, and this our brother departed, receiving again our bodies, and rising again in thy most gracious favour, may, with all thine elect saints, obtain eternal joy. Grant this, O Lord God, by the means of our advocate Jesus Christ; which with thee and the Holy Ghost, liveth and reigneth one God for ever. Amen.

The Epistle. 1 Thess. iv.

I would not, brethren, that ye should be ignorant . . . . Wherefore comfort one another with these words.

The Gosp.l. John vi.

Jesus said to his disciples and to the Jews, All that the Father giveth me shall come to me. . . . . And I will raise him up again at the last day.

APPENDIX VII.

Celebratio Cœna Domini in Funeribus, si amici et vicini defuncti communicare velint.

Collecta. Misericors Deus, pater Domini nostri Jesu Christi, qui est Resurrectio et Vita, in quo qui credidit etiamsi mortuus fuerit, vivet; et in quo qui crediderit et vivit, non morietur in æternum : quique nos docuisti per sanctum apostolum tuum Paulum non debere mœrere pro dormientibus in Christo, sicut ii qui spem non habent resurrectionis : humiliter petimus, ut nos a morte peccati resuscites ad vitam justitiæ, ut cum exhac vita emigramus, dormiamus cum Christo, quemadmodun speramus hunc fratrem nostrum, et in generali resurrectione, extremo die, nos una cum hoc fratre nostro resuscitati, et receptis corporibus, regnemus una tecum in vitæ æterna. Per Dominum nostrum Jesum Christum. *R.* Amen.

Epistola. 1 Thess. iv.

Nolo vos ignorare, fratres, de his qui obdormierunt, ... Proinde consolemini vos mutus sermonibus his.

Evangelium. Ioan. vi.

Dixit Jesus discipulis suis et turbis Judæorum : Omne quod dat mihi Pater. . . . . habeas vitam æternam, et Ego suscitabo eum in novissimo die.

APPENDIX VII.

Vel hoc Evangelium.   Ioan. v.

Dixit Jesus discipulis suis et turbis Judæorum : Amen amen, dico vobis, qui sermonem meum audit . . . . qui vero mala egerunt, in resurrectionem condemnationis.

[Set forth in the year 1560.]

APPENDIX VIII.

VARIOUS FORMS OF BIDDING THE BEADS.

No. I.—From the Salisbury Processional.

Item conversus ad populum dicat Sacerdos in lingua materna.

Oremus pro animabus N. et N., *more solito.*

Et postea vertat se Sacerdos et dicat Psalmum De profundis, *supradicto modo.*

Gloria Patri, etc., cum Kyrie eleyson, Christe eleyson, Kyrie eleyson.

Pater Noster. Et ne nos. Sed libera.

Requiem æternam dona eis Domine.

Et lux perpetua luceat eis.

A porte inferi.

Erue Domine animas eorum.

Crede videre bona Domini.

In terra viventium.

Dominus vobiscum.

Et cum spiritu tuo.

Oremus. Absolve quæsumus, Domine, animas famulorum famularumque tuarum parentum parochianorum, amicorum benefactorum nostrorum, et animas omnium fidelium defunctorum ab omni vinculo delictorum, ut in resurrectionis gloria inter sanctos et electos resuscitati respirent. Per Christum Dominum nostrum. Requiescant in pace. Amen.

(*Processionale ad usum insignis Ecclesie Sarum*, folio 5, 6. Londini, A.D. 1535.*)

No. II.—From the "Liber Festivalis."
(Ed. Caxton, 1483.†)

Furthermore ye shall praye for al Kristen sowles, for all arch bysshoppis and bishoppis sowlis, and in especial for al them that have been bishoppis of this diocyse, and for al curatis, persones and vicaryes sowles, and in especial for them that have been curatis of this Chirche, and for the sowles that have servyd in this Chirche: Also ye shall pray for the sowles of alle cristen Kynges and Quenes, and in especial for the sowles of them that have been Kynges of this royame of Englond, and for al the sowles that to this Chirche have yeven boke, belle, chalys or vestement, or ony other thyng by whiche the servyce of God is better doon and holy Chirche worshipped: Ye shal also pray for your faders sowlis, for your moders sowlis, for your godfaders sowlis, for your godmoders sowlis, for your brethren and sisters sowlis, and for all the sowles that we ben bounde to pray for, and for the sowles that been in the paynes of purgatorye, there abyding the mercy of our Lord God, and in special for them that have most nede and leste helpe, that God for his endeless mercy lesse and mynysshe theyr paynes by the moyen of our prayers, and brynge them to his everlastyng blysse in heven: And also for the sowle of N. or of them, that on

---

* This form, though taken from one of the latest of the Sarum Books, is of great antiquity, being found in several MSS. of the fourteenth century, and was almost universally used in the Province of Canterbury.

† Vide also "Manuale Secundum unum Eboracensem," 1509; the Gough Missal, No. 54, Bodleian Library; the Douce MS., No. 246, folio 57; each of which contains prayers substantially similar to the above.

such a day this weke we shal have the annyversayre, and for all Cristen sowles ye shal devoutly say a Paternoster and an Ave, Psalmus, De Profundis, et cetera, with this colect.

Oremus. Absolve quæsumus, Domine, animas famulorum tuorum, pontificum, regum, sacerdotum, parentum, parochianorum, amicorum, benefactorum nostrorum et omnium fidelium defunctorum ab omni vinculo delictorum, ut in resurrectionis gloria inter sanctos et electos tuos resussitati respirent. Per Christum Dominum nostrum. Amen.

No. III.—CONCLUSION OF A BIDDING PRAYER[*] USED BY WILLIAM [Sancroft, some time] LORD ARCHBISHOP OF CANTERBURY.

Finally, let us laud Almighty God on behalf of those who have departed out of this transitorie life in the faith and feare of His Son Jesus Christ, rendering unto Him high and holy thanks for the same, and beseeching Him that it may please Him of His gracious goodness shortly to accomplish the number of his elect, and to hasten His Kingdom, that they with us, and we with them, may have our compleate and perfect consummation of blisse, both in body and soul, in His eternal and glorious kingdom, for ever and ever. Our Father, etc.

---

[*] From a MS. copy in the possession of the late Rev. Philip Bliss, D.D. It should here be noted that many, if not all, of the Post-Reformation Bidding Prayers contain only a most ambiguous clause in regard to the departed, in which no distinction is made between the saints and the ordinary faithful; and the prayer is mainly directed to obtain a benefit for the living, that they may follow the "good example" of the departed.

APPENDIX IX.

GRACES USED AT THE COLLEGES OF OXFORD AND CAMBRIDGE, AND ELSEWHERE, COMMEMORATING BENEFACTORS AND THE FAITHFUL DEPARTED.

No. I.—UNIVERSITY COLLEGE, OXFORD.

Vers. Benedictus sit Deus in donis suis,
Resp. Et sanctus in omnibus operibus suis.
Vers. Adjutorium nostrum in Nomine Domini,
Resp. Qui fecit cœlum et terras.
Vers. Sit Nomen Domini benedictum,
Resp. Ab hoc tempore usque in sæcula.
Oratio. Domine Deus, resurrectio et vita credentium, Qui semper es laudandus, tum in viventibus tum in defunctis; gratias tibi agimus pro omnibus Fundatoribus, cæterisque Benefactoribus nostris, quorum beneficiis hic ad pietatem, et ad studia literarum alimur; te rogantes ut nos, hisce tuis donis ad tuam gloriam recte utentes, una cum iis ad vitam immortalem perducamur, per Jesum Christum Dominum nostrum. *Resp.* Amen.

Deus det vivis gratiam, Ecclesiæ Catholicæ, Reginæ, Regnoque nostro, pacem et concordiam; et nobis peccatoribus vitam æternam.

No. II.—NEW COLLEGE, OXFORD.

Grace before Meat.

Benedicite.
Vers. Oculi omnium in te sperant Domine.

Resp. Et tu das iis escam in tempore opportuno.

Vers. Tu aperis manum et imples omne animal benedictione.

Gloria Patri, et Filio, et Spiritui Sancto. Sicut erat, etc.

Oratio. Benedic nobis, Domine Deus, et his donis quæ ex tua largitate sumus sumpturi, per Jesum Christum Dominum nostrum. *Resp.* Amen.

Mensæ cœlestis participes faciat nos Rex æternæ gloriæ. *Resp.* Amen.

Grace after Meat.

Deus pacis et dilectionis maneat nobiscum semper.

Tu autem, Domine, miserere nostri.

Deo gratias.

Laudate eum omnes gentes, laudate eum omnes populi ejus: quoniam confirmata est supra nos misericordia ejus, et veritas Domini manet in æternum.

Gloria Patri, et Filio, et Spiritui Sancto. Sicut, etc.

Vers. Dispersit, et dedit pauperibus;

Resp. Et justitia ejus manet in sæculum sæculi.

Vers. Benedicam Domino in omni tempore;

Resp. Et semper laus ejus erit in ore meo.

Vers. In Domino gloriabitur anima mea;

Resp. Audiant mansueti et lætentur.

Vers. Magnificate Dominum mecum;

Resp. Exaltemus Nomen Ejus et Ipsum.

Vers. Sit Nomen Domini benedictum;

Resp. Et hoc nunc usque in sæculum.

Oratio. Agimus tibi gratias, omnipotens Deus pro his et universis beneficiis tuis, quæ de tua largitate accepimus, qui vivis et regnas Deus in sæcula sæculorum. *Resp.* Amen.

Vers. In memoria æterna erit justus;

Resp. Ab auditione mala non timebit.

Vers. Justorum animæ in manu Dei sunt;

Resp. Neque tanget eos cruciatus.
Vers. Domine salvum fac Reginam nostram;
Resp. Et exaudi nos in die quocunque invocamus Te.
Vers. Domine exaudi orationem meam;
Resp. Et clamor meus ad Te veniat.
Oratio. Omnipotens et æterne Deus, qui semper tam es laudandus pro defunctis quam orandus pro viventibus, agimus tibi gratias pro Fundatore nostro *Gulielmo de Wykeham*, reliquisque quorum beneficiis hic ad pietatem et ad studia literarum alimur rogantes ut nos, his donis tuis ad Nominis Tui honorem recte utentes, ad resurrectionis Tuæ gloriam, preducamur immortalem, per Jesum Christum Dominum nostrum. *Resp.* Amen.

Ante Cœnam.

Benedicite.
Cœnam sanctificet qui nobis omnia præbet.
In Nomine Patris, et Filio et Spiritus Sancti.   Amen.

Post Cœnam.

Vers. Benedictus sit Deus in donis suis;
Resp. Et sanctus in omnibus operibus suis.
Vers. Adjutorium nostrum in Nomine Domini.
Resp. Qui fecit cœlum et terram.
Vers. Sit Nomen Domini benedictum;
Resp. Ex hoc nunc usque in sæculum.
Oratio. Agimus tibi gratias, etc. (*Ut post prandium.*)

Ante Prandium.

Benedic nobis Domine Deus atque his donis quæ de tua largitate sumus sumpturi per Jesum Christum Dominum nostrum. *Resp.* Amen.

Post Prandium.

Vers. Benedictus sit Deus in Donis suis,
Resp. Et sanctus in omnibus operibus Ejus,

Vers. Adjutorium nostrum in Nomine Domini.
Resp. Qui fecit cœlum et terram.
Vers. Sit Nomen Domini benedictum;
Resp. Ex hoc nunc usque in sæcula sæculorum. Amen.
Oratio. Agimus tibi gratias omnipotens Deus pro Fundatore nostro *Gulielmo de Wykeham*, reliquisque quorum beneficiis hic ad pietatim et ad studia literarum alimur, rogantes ut nos, his donis tuis ad Nominis tui honorem recte utentes, ad resurrectionis tuæ gloriam perducamur immortalem, per Jesum Christum Dominum nostrum. *Resp.* Amen.
Vers. Domine salvam fac Reginam *Victoriam*. *Resp.* Amen.
Vers. Da pacem in diebus nostris.
Resp. Et exaudi nos in die quocunque invocamus Te. Amen.

Ante Prandium.

Benedictus benedicat.

Post Prandium.

Benedicto benedicatur.

No. III.—Trinity College, Oxford.

Vers. Benedictus sit Deus in donis suis.
Resp. Qui sanctus est in omnibus operibus suis.
Vers. Adjutorium nostrum in Nomine Domini.
Resp. Qui fecit cœlum et terram.
Vers. Sit Nomen Domini benedictum.
Resp. Ut nunc est, sic in sæcula sæculorum.
Vers. Domine, salvam fac *Victoriam* Reginam nostram.
Resp. Et exaudi nos, cum invocamus Te.
Oremus. Domine Deus Resurrectio et Vita credentium, qui semper es laudandus cum in viventibus tum etiam in defunctis, agimus tibi gratias pro *Thoma Pope*, militi, Fundatore nostro et *Elizabetha* consorte ejus, defunctis, ceterisque Benefactoribus nostris, quorum beneficiis hic ad pietatem et ad studia literarum

APPENDIX IX.

alimur; rogantes ut nos his donis ad Tuam gloriam recte utentes, una cum illis ad resurrectionis gloriam immortalem preducamur, per Jesum Christum Dominum nostrum. *Resp.* Amen.

No. IV.—St. Mary Magdalen College, Oxford.

Deus pacis et caritatis digneris quæsumus habitare nobiscum, et Tu Domine miserere nostrum. *Resp.* Amen.

Laudant Te omnia opera tua, Domine : laudant Te omnes Sancti tui.

Laudate Dominum omnes gentes : Laudate cum omnes populi ejus.

Quoniam confirmata est supra nos misericordia ejus : et veritas Domini manet in æternum.

Vers. Gloria Patri et Filio et Spiritui Sancto.

Resp. Sicut erat in principio et nunc et semper et in sæcula sæculorum. Amen.

Vers. Dispersit et dedit pauperibus.

Resp. Et justitia ejus manet in sæculum sæculi, et cornu ejus exaltabitur in gloria.

Vers. Semper benedicam Domino.

Resp. Semper in ore meo laus ejus.

Vers. Cantate Domino et benedicite Nomini ejus.

Resp. Enunciate inter gentes gloriam ejus et omnibus populis admirabilia ejus.

Oremus. Largire nobis, misericors Pater, miserrimis peccatoribus eternam vitam propter Nomen sanctum Tuum, per Jesum Christum Dominum nostrum.

Hymnus Eucharisticus.

1.
Te Deum Patrem colimus,
Te laudibus prosequimur,
Qui corpus cibo reficis,
Cœlesti mentem gratia.

2.
Te adoramus, O Jesu,
Te, Fili unigenite,
Te, qui non dedignatus es
Subire claustra Virginis.

3.	4.
Actus in crucem factus es	Tibi, æterne Spiritus,
Irato Deo victima;	Cujus afflatu peperit
Per Te, Salvator unice,	Infantem Deum Maria
Vitæ spes nobis rediit.	Æternum benedicimus.

5.
Triune Deus, hominum
Salutis Auctor optime,
Immensum hoc mysterium
Ovante lingua canimus.
R. Amen.

Vers. In memoria æterna erunt justi.

Resp. Ab auditione mala non timebunt.

Vers. Corpora eorum in pace sepulta sunt, et nomina eorum vivent a generatione in generationem.

Resp. Sapientiam eorum narrabunt populi et laudes eorum enunciabit Ecclesia.

Oratio. Domine Deus, Resurrectio et Vita eorum omnium qui in Te confidunt, qui semper benedictus es in donis tuis et sanctis in operibus, immortales gratias agimus Majestati Tuæ pro *Gulielmo de Waynfleet*, Fundatore nostro, et pro omnibus Benefactoribus nostris, amplissimisque beneficiis tuis; quæ nobis per manus eorum tradidisti; Teque suppliciter obsecramus ut nos hisce donis tuis recte utamur ad Nominis tui honorem, ut una cum sanctis tuis æternæ gloriæ in cœlis participes fiamus, per Jesum Christum Dominum nostrum. *Resp.* Amen.

No. V.—ORIEL COLLEGE, OXFORD.
Grace before Meat.

Oratio. Benedicte Deus, qui pascis nos a juventute nostra et præbes cibum omni carni, reple gaudio et lætitia corda nostra ut nos affatim quod satis est habentes abundemus ad omne opus bonum, per Jesum Christum Dominum nostrum, cui, Tecum et Spiritu Sancto, sit omnis honos, laus, et imperium, in sæcula sæculorum. *Resp.* Amen.

APPENDIX IX.

Grace after Meat.

Domine Deus, Resurrectio et Vita credentium qui semper es laudandus cum in viventibus tum in defunctis; agimus tibi gratias pro *Edvardo Secundo*, Fundatore nostro, pro *Adamo de Brome*, præcipuo Benefactore, cæterisque Benefactoribus nostris, quorum beneficiis hic ad pietatem et ad studia bonarum literarum alimur; rogantes ut nos his donis tuis recte utentes, ad resurrectionis gloriam immortalem perducamur; per Jesum Christum Dominum nostrum. *Resp.* Amen.

No. VI.—Merton College, Oxford.

Grace before Meat.

Vers. Oculi omnium in te respiciunt, Domine.
Resp. Et tu das escam illis in tempore opportuno.
Vers. Aperis tu manum tuam.
Resp. Et implies omne animal benedictione.
Oratio. Benedicas nobis, Domine, omnibus bonis quæ de tua beneficentia accepturi sumus, per Jesum Christum Dominum nostrum. *Resp.* Amen.

Grace after Meat.

Quod corpora nostra, Deus, cibo potuque abunde refecisti, agimus tibi gratias, et Benignitati Tuæ quantum possumus maximas, simulque precamur ut animas nostras Verbo Spirituque tuo deinceps pascas, ut mala omnia fugientes, ea quæ placitura sunt Majestati Tuæ perfecte intelligamus, diligenterque meditemur, et ad ea præstanda toto impetu feramur per Jesum Christum Dominum nostrum. *Resp.* Amen.

Fidelium animæ, per Dei gratiam, requiescant in pace. *Resp.* Amen.

No. VII.—Corpus Christi College, Oxford.

Grace before Meat.

Nos miseri et egentes homines, pro hoc cibo quem ad corporis nostri alimonium sanctificatum es largitus ut eo recte utamur, Tibi, Deus omnipotens, Pater cœlestis, reverenter gratias agimus, simul obsecrantes ut cibum angelorum, panem verum cœlestem, Dei Verbum æternum Jesum Christum Dominum nostrum nobis impertiare, ut Eo mens nostra pascatur, et per carnem et sanguinem ejus alamur, foveamur, et corroboremur.

Grace after Meat.

Infunde, quæsumus, Domine Deus, gratiam tuam in mentes nostras; ut hisce donis tuis datis a *Ricardo Fox*, Fundatore nostro, cæterisque Benefactoribus nostris, recte in tuam gloriam utentes, una cum fidelibus defunctis in vitam cœlestem resurgamus per Jesum Christum Dominum nostrum. Deus pro infinita sua clementia, Ecclesiæ Suæ concordiam et unitatem concedat, Reginam nostram conservet, pacem regno universo populoque Christiano largiatur, per Jesum Christum Dominum nostrum.

No. VIII.—WADHAM COLLEGE, OXFORD.

Vers.   Benedictus sit Deus in donis suis;
Resp.   Sanctus in omnibus operibus suis.
Vers.   Adjutorium nostrum in Nomine Domini:
Resp.   Qui fecit cœlum et terras.
Vers.   Sit Nomen Dei benedictum:
Resp.   Ex hoc usque in sæcula sæculorum.
Vers.   Domine fac salam *Victoriam* Reginam.
Resp.   Exaudi nos cum invocamus te.

Oratio. Domine Deus, Vita et Resurrectis credentium qui semper es laudandus tum in viventibus tum in defunctis, agimus tibi gratias pro *Nicholas Wadhamo* armigero, et pro *Dorothea*, uxore ejus, Fundatoribus nostris defunctis aliisque Benefactoribus nostris, quorum beneficiis hic ad pietatem et studium literarum alimur; rogantes ut nos his tuis donis recte utentes, una cum defunctis resurrectionem gloriæ perducamur, per Jesum Christum Dominum nostrum. *R.* Amen.

No. IX.—ALL-SOULS' COLLEGE, OXFORD.

Appositis et apponendis benedicat Deus, Pater, Filius et Spiritus Sanctus.

No. X.—PEMBROKE COLLEGE, OXFORD.

Agimus tibi gratias Deus misericors, pro acceptis a bonitate tua beneficiis; enixe comprecantes ut serenissimam nostram Reginam *Victoriam*, totam regiam familiam, populumque tuum universum, tuta in pace semper custodias. *R.* Amen.

No. XI.—EXETER COLLEGE, OXFORD.

Grace before Meat.

Benedictus benedicat.

Grace after Meat.

Oratio. Gratias tibi agimus, omnipotens et æterne Deus, pro his atque omnibus beneficiis tuis. Conserves quæsumus Ecclesiam Catholicam, Regnum Britannicum, Reginam *Victoriam*, totamque progeniem regiam, desque nobis pacem in Christo æternam. *R.* Amen.

No. XII.—QUEEN'S COLLEGE, OXFORD.

Grace before Meat.

Benedic nobis, Domine Deus, et his donis, quæ ex tua liberalitate sumpturi sumus; per Jesum Christum Dominum nostrum. *R.* Amen.

Grace after Meat.

Vers. Benedictus sit Deus in donis suis.
Resp. Sicut et in operibus suis.
Vers. Adjutorium nostrum in Nomine Domini.
Resp. Qui fecit cœlum et terras.

Vers. Sit Nomen Domini benedictum.

Resp. Nunc, usque et in sæcula.

Oratio. Dignere, Domine Deus, largiri nobis omnibus te invocantibus propter Nomen Tuum sanctum vitam æternam. *R.* Amen.

Domine Deus, Resurrection et Vita credentium, qui semper es laudandus, tum in viventibus, tum in defunctis, agimus tibi gratias pro fundatore nostro *Roberto Eglesfield*, cæterisque nostris Benefactoribus, quorum beneficiis hic had pietatem et literarum studia alimur : rogantes ut nos, his donis recte utentes in Nominis Tui gloriam, ad resurrectionis gloriam perpetuam perducamur; per Jesum Christum Dominum nostrum. *R.* Amen.

Deus det vivis gratiam, Ecclesiæ, Reginæ, regnoque nostro pacem et concordiam, et nobis peccatoribus vitam æternam. *R.* Amen.

No. XIII.—Brasenose College, Oxford.

Ante Prandium.

Vers. Oculi omnium spectant in te, Deus.

Resp. Et tu das illis escas tempore opportuno.

Vers. Aperis manum tuam.

Resp. Et imples omne animal tua benedictione.

Mensæ cœlestis nos participes facias, Deus, Rex æternæ gloriæ.

Post Prandium.

Qui nos creavit, redemit et pavit, sit benedictus in æternum. Deus exaudi orationem nostram. Agimus tibi gratias, Pater cœlestis, pro *Gulielmo Smith* episcopo, et *Richardo Sutton* milite, Fundatoribus nostris ; pro *Alexandro Nowel* et *Jocosa Frankland* aliisque Benefactoribus nostris ; humiliter te precantes ut eorum numerum benignissime adaugeas. Ecclesiam Catholicam, et populum Christianum custodi. Hæreses et errores omnes extirpa. *Victoriam* Reginam nostram et subditos ejus defende. Pacem da et conserva per Christum Dominum nostrum.

Ante Cœnam.

Omnipotens et sempiterne Deus, sine quo nihil est dulce, nihil odoriferum, misericordiam tuam humiliter imploramus, ut nos cœnamque nostram benedicas; ut corda nostra exhilares; ut quæ suscepturi sumus alimenta, tuo honori, tuæque beneficientiæ accepta referamus; per Jesum Christum Dominum nostrum.

Post Cœnam.

Quod corpora nostra, Deus optime maxime cibo potuque abunde refecisti, agimus tibi gratias quantas, possumus maximas; simulque precamur, ut animas nostras verbo et Spiritu deinde pascas; ut omnia mala fugiamus; ut quæ sint tibi placitura perfecte intelligamus, diligenter meditemur, et ad ea præstanda toto impetu feramur; per Christum Dominum nostrum.

No. XIV.—BALLIOL COLLEGE, OXFORD.

Grace after Meat.

Vers. Benedictus est Deus in donis suis,
Resp. Et sanctus in omnibus operibus suis.
Vers. Adjutorium nostrum in Nomine Domini est.
Resp. Qui fecit cœlum ac terras.
Vers. Sit Nomen Dei benedictum.
Resp. Ab hoc tempore usque ad sæcula.

Tribuere digneris, Domine Deus, nobis omnibus bona facientibus ob tuum Sanctum Nomen vitam æternam. *R.* Amen.

Vers. In memoria æterna erit justus.
Resp. Et ab auditione mala nunquam timebit.
Vers. Justorum animæ in manibus Dei sunt.
Resp. Ne tangant eos instrumenta nequitiæ.

Oratio. Funde quæsumus, Domine Deus, in mentes nostras gratiam tuam ut tuis hisce donis datis a *Johanne Balliolo* et *Dervorguilla* uxore, cæterisque omnibus Benefactoribus nostris, rite in tuam gloriam utentes in vitam una cum fidelibus omnibus resurgamus ; per Jesum Christum Dominum nostrum. *R*. Amen.

Deus pro infiniti sua clementia Ecclesiæ unitatem et concordiam concedat, Reginam conservet, pacemque huic Regno populoque Christiano largiatur ; per Jesum Christum Dominum nostrum. *R*. Amen.

No. XV.—Worcester College, Oxford.

Grace before Meat.

Nos miseri homines et egeni, pro cibis quos nobis ad corporis subsidium benigne es largitus, tibi Deus omnipotens, Pater cœlestis gratias reverenter agimus ; simul obsecrantes ut iis sobrie, modeste, atque grate utamur. Insuper petimus, ut cibum angelorum, verum panem cœlestem, Verbum Dei æternum, Dominum nostrum Jesum Christum, nobis impertiaris : utque illo mens nostra pascatur et per carnem et sanguinem ejus foveamur alamur et corroboremur. *R*. Amen.

Grace after Meat.

Omnipotens et misericors Deus, qui donis tuis nos exsatiasti, effice ut quicquid per nos fieri aut prætermitti velis, deligenter observemus, mandata tua universa prompto atque fideli obsequio obeuntes, per Jesum Christum Dominum nostrum. *R*. Amen.

Vers. Domine salvam fac Reginam.

Resp. Et exaudi nos quando invocamus te.

Oratio. Agimus tibi gratias omnipotens et sempiterne Deus, pro *Thoma Cookesio*, baronetto, Fundatore nostro, cujus beneficio hic ad pietatem, studiumque literarum alimur : simul rogantes ut, his donis ad tuam gloriam recte utentes, una cum eo ad resurrectionis gloriam immortalem perducamur, per Jesum Christum Dominum nostrum. *R*. Amen.

No. XVI.—St. John's College, Oxford.

Grace before Meat.

Benedic, Domine, nos, et hæc tua dona quæ de tua largitate sumpturi sumus.

Pater noster qui es in cœlis, sanctificetur Nomen tuum, adveniat regnum tuum, fiat voluntas tua, sicut in cœlo sic etiam in terra; panem nostrum quotidianum da nobis hodie, et remitte nobis debita nostra, sicut et nos remittimus debitoribus nostris; et ne nos inducas in tentationem, sed libera nos a malo; qui tuum est regnum, potentia et gloria in sæcula sæculorum. *Resp.* Amen.

Grace after Meat.

Agimus tibi gratias omnipotens et sempiterne Deus pro his et universis beneficiis: dignare, Domine, misereri nostrum, et manere semper nobiscum, ut auxilio Spiritus Sancti, mandatis tuis sedulo obsequamur, per Jesum Christum Dominum nostrum. *Resp.* Amen.

Agimus tibi gratias omnipotens et sempiterne Deus pro *Thoma White*, milite, et Fundatore nostro defuncto, ac *Avicia* et *Joana* uxoribus ejus, quorum beneficiis hic ad pietatem et ad studia literarum alimur rogantes ut nos his donis ad tuam gloriam recte utentes, una cum illis ad resurrectionis gloriam immortalem perducamur per Christum Dominum nostrum. *Resp.* Amen.

Benedicamus Domino.

Deo gratias.

No. XVII.—Lincoln College, Oxford.

Grace before Meat.

Benedicas nobis, quæsumus te, et hisce creaturis in usam nostrum, ut illæ sanctificatæ sint et nobis salutares, ut nos inde corroborati magis apti reddamur ad omnia opera bona in laudem tui Nominis æternam. *Resp.* Amen.

Grace after Meat.

Æternæ Deus, bonorum omnium largitor, agimus tibi gratias pro electione, redemptione, conservatione, præsentique hac refocillatione; autque etiam pro *Ricardo Fleming* et *Thoma Rotheram* Fundatoribus nostris, cæterisque Benefactoribus quos excitare dignatus es ad eximia bona nobis præparanda; supplices te orantes ut eorum beneficia, quæ ad sempiternam donatorum memoriam vigent, complures alios ad eandem pietatem æmulandam excitare possint, et eorum quotidie memores non indigni reperiamur hac tanta benedictione, per Jesum Christum Dominum nostrum. Ecclesiam universam, Regem, totum hoc regnum Deus pro immensa sua bonitate conservet protegat et defendat, fidem nostram adaugeat, peccata remittat, afflictis solatium afferat, et pacem in Christo nobis sempiternam reddat. *R.* Amen.

No. XVIII.—Christ Church, Oxford.

Ante Cibum.

Nos miseri homines et egeni, pro cibis quos nobis ad corporis subsidium benigne es largitus, tibi Deus omnipotens, Pater cœlestis, gratias reverenter agimus; simul obsecrantes ut iis sobrie modeste, atque grate utamur. Insuper petimus, ut cibum angelorum, verum panem cœlestem, Verbum Dei æternum Dominum nostrum Jesum Christum, nobis impertiaris; utque illo mens nostra pascatur, et per carnem' et sanguinem ejus foveamur, alamur, et corroboremur. *R.* Amen.

Post Cibum.

[The Clerk reads from the Greek Testament.]

Omnipotens et misericors Deus, qui donis tuis nos exsatiasti effice ut quicquid per nos fieri aut prætermitti velis, diligenter observemus, mandata tua universa prompto atque fideli obsequio obeuntes, per Jesum Christum Dominum nostrum. *R.* Amen.

Vers. Domine, salvem fac Reginam.

Resp. Et exaudi nos, quando invocamus te.

Deus in cujus manu sunt corda regum: Qui es humilium consolator, fidelium fortitudo, protector omnium in te sperantium, da Reginæ nostræ *Victoriæ* populoque Christiano ut te Regem regum, et dominantium Dominum, agnoscant semper et venerentur, et post hanc vitam regni tui æterni fiant participes; per Jesum Christum Dominum nostrum. *R.* Amen.

Deus a quo derivatur omnis munificentia et bonitas, debitas tibi gratis agimus, quod felicis memoriæ *Regem Henricum ejus nominis octavum*, ad Ecclesiam hanc fundandam animaveris; et rogamus pro sancta tua misericordia, ut eum nos hoc tanto beneficio adjuti, ad laudem tui Nominis profecerimus, una cum omnibus qui jam in Domino dormierunt, beatam resurrectionem et æternæ felicitatis præmia consequæmur, per Jesum Christum Dominum nostrum. *R.* Amen.

No. XIX.—Jesus College, Oxford.

Ante Cibum.

Nos miseri et egentes homines pro cibo, quem ad alimoniam corporis sanctificatum nobis es largitus, ut eo utamur grati tibi Deus omnipotens, Pater cœlestis gratias reverenter agimus; simul obsecrantes ut cibum angelorum verum panem cœlestem Verbum Dei æternum Dominum nostrum Jesum Christum nobis impertiaris; ut illo mens nostra pascatur et per carnem sanguinem ejus foveamur, alamur et corroboremur. *R.* Amen.

Post Cibum.

Quandoquidem nos Domine, donis tuis, omnipotens et misericors Deus, exsatiasti, effice ut posthac quid per nos fieri aut secus velis diligenter observemus, atque illud animo sincero effectum præstemus, per Jesum Christum Dominum nostrum. *R.* Amen.

Vers. Domine salvam fac Reginam.

Resp. Et exaudi nos in die qua invocaverimus te.

Oratio. Deus, in cujus manu sunt corda regum, qui es humilium consolator et fidelium fortitudo et protector omnium in te sperantium, da Reginæ *Victoriæ* populoque Christiano triumphum virtutis tuæ scienter excolere ut per te semper reparentur ad gloriam, per Jesum Christum Dominum nostrum. *R.* Amen.

No. XX.—St. Edmund Hall, Oxford.*

Grace before Meat.

Benedic nobis, Domine Deus, et his donis quæ ex tua liberalitate sumpturi sumus; per Jesum Christum Dominum nostrum. *Resp.* Amen.

Grace after Meat.

Agimus tibi gratias, Deus et Pater, pro tot beneficiis, quæ nobis assidue et pro infinita tua liberalitate largiris, per Jesum Christum Dominum nostrum. *Resp.* Amen.

Fidelium animæ per misérecordiam Dei requiescant in pace. *Resp.* Amen.

No. XXI.—Trinity College, Cambridge.

Infunde, quæsumus, Domine Deus gratiam tuam in mentes nostras, ut his donis datis ab *Henrico Octavo* Fundatore nostro, Regina *Maria*, *Edvardo Tertio*, aliisque Benefactoribus nostris, recte ad tuam gloriam utentes, una cum illis qui in fide Christi decesserunt ad cœlestem vitam resurgamus, per Dominum nostrum Jesum Christum. *Resp.* Amen.

No. XXII.—St. Peter's College, Cambridge.

Agimus tibi gratias, omnipotens et æterne Deus, pro universis beneficiis tuis, pro viro recolendæ memoriæ Domino *Hugone de*

---

* From a MS. of the celebrated antiquary, Thomas Hearne, of St Edmund Hall, in the possession of the late Mr. Thomas Hearne Seymour, a connection of his, of Thame, Oxfordshire. The use of the latter clause is said to have been dropped only during the headship of Dr. George Thompson, in the early part of the present century.

APPENDIX IX.

Balsham, Fundatore nostro primario, cæterisque omnibus hujus Collegii Benefactoribus. Nobis vero famulis tuis tribue ut eorum donis ad Nominis Tui gloriam, et Ecclesiæ incrementum utentes, una cum illis atque omnibus qui in fide Christi decesserunt ad cœlestem vitam resurgamus, per Christum Dominum nostrum. *Resp.* Amen.

No. XXIII.—Benedictio Mensæ.*
(At the Religious House of Little Gidding.)

Ante Prandium.

Vers.   Oculi omnium in te sperant, Domine.
Resp.   Et tu das escam illorum in tempore opportuno.
Vers.   Aperis tu manum tuam.
Resp.   Et imples omne animal benedictione.
Gloria Patri.   Sicut erat.
Kyrie eleyson.
Christe eleyson.
Kyrie eleyson.
Pater noster, etc.

Oratio. Benedic nobis Domine Deus et his donis quæ ex tua liberalitate sumpturi sumus. Per Jesum Christum Dominum nostrum. *Resp.* Amen.

Benedictio. Mensæ cœlestis participes faciat nos Rex æternæ gloriæ. *Resp.* Amen.

Post Prandium.

Oratio. Agimus tibi gratias Dominus omnipotens Deus, pro universis beneficiis tuis, Qui vivis et regnas in unitate Spiritus Sancte Deus, per omnia sæcula sæculorum. *Resp.* Amen.

---

* Taken from a MS. volume of Occasional Services used at the Religious House of Little Gidding, which was some time in the possession of Lord Viscount Weymouth, and afterwards deposited either in the Bodleian, or in the library of St. John's College, Oxford.

Commemoratio Defunctorum.

Fidelium animæ per misericordiam Dei, requiescant in pace. *Resp.* Amen.

No. XXIV.—Graces used at St. John's College, Oxford, and afterwards at Lambeth, by William Laud, Archbishop of Canterbury.*

Before Meals.

O Lord, mercifully bless these gifts, and all temporall and spirituall gifts to our use and to thy holy service; and do thou have mercy upon and strengthen thy whole Universall Church, through Jesus Christ our Lord. *R.* Amen.

After Meals.

We thank thee, O Lord, for these and all thy gifts and blessings.

Make us to sit down at the Marriage-supper of the Lamb:

And give to the faithful, departed in the fear and love of thy Holy Name, a place of refreshment and light, through Jesus Christ. *R.* Amen.

No. XXV.—Winchester College.†

Ante Cibum.

Benedic nobis, Domine Deus, atque his donis tuis quæ de tua largitate sumus sumpturi, per Jesum Christum Dominum nostrum. *R.* Amen.

Post Cibum.

Agimus tibi gratias, omnipotens Deus! pro his et universis donis tuis quæ de tua largitate accessimus, qui vivis et regnas; et es Deus in sæcula sæculorum. *R.* Amen.

---

* From a MS. in the possession of the late Rev. Philip Bliss, D.D., Principal of St. Mary Hall, Oxford.

† The Psalms, Hymns, Prayers, Graces, and Dulce Domum, used by the scholars of Winchester College, Winchester, D. Nutt. 1845.

Te de profundis, summe Rex,
Jehovah, supplex invoco!
Intende voci supplicis;
Ad te precantim suspice.
Delicta si peccantium.
Severus observaveris,
Quis sustinebit impius?
Piusve quis non deficit?
At lenitas paterni tibi;
Hinc te veremur filii;

Te sustinemur unico
A lucis orto sidere.
Fiduciam tantamque spem
In te reponit Israel,
Tuo, Deus, qui sanguine
Peccata mundi diluis.
Deo Patri sit gloria,
Ejusque soli Filio;
Sanctissimo cum Spiritu,
In saeculorum saecula.

Omnipotens et aeterne Deus, qui tam es laudandus pro defunctis, etc. [*Ut in Grat. Act. post prandium in Coll. Nov.*, p. 279.]

APPENDIX X.

IN COMMENDATIONIBUS BENEFACTORUM.*

Ad cujusque termini finem commendatio fiat fundatoris, aliorumque clarorum virorum, quorum beneficentia Collegium locupletatur. Ejus hæc sit forma. Primum recitatur " Oratio Dominica," Pater Noster qui es in cœlis, etc.

Deinde recitentur tres Psalmi
{ Exaltabo te Deus meus Rex. Psalmus cxliv.
  Lauda anima mea Domine. Psalmus cxlv.
  Laudate Dominum, quoniam bonus. Psalmus cxlvi.

Post hæc legatur caput. Ecclesiastici xliv.

Hic finitis, sequatur Concio, in qua concionator Fundatoris amplissimam munificentiam prædicet: quantus sit literarum usus ostendat: quantis laudibus afficiendi sunt qui literarum studia beneficentia sua excitent: quantum sit ornamentum Regno doctos viros habere, qui de rebus controversis vere judicare possunt: quanta sit Scripturarum laus, et quantum illæ omni humanæ auctoritati antecedant, quantus sit ejus doctrinæ in vulgus utilitas, et quam late pateat: quam egregium et regium sit (cui Deus universæ plebis suæ curam commisit), de multitudine ministrorum verbi laborare, atque hi ut honesti atque eruditi sint, curare: atque alia ejus generis, quæ pii et docti viri cum laude illustrare possint.

* This form, taken from an original copy printed by Reginald Volfe, was issued by Queen Elizabeth's recommendation, having been sanctioned by Parker and several bishops of the Province of Canterbury.

APPENDIX X.

Hac Concione perorata decantetur:
Benedictus Dominus Deus Israel.

Ad extremum hæc adhibeantur:
Vers. In memoria æterna erit justus.
Resp. Ab auditu malo non timebit.
Vers. Justorum animæ in manu Dei sunt.
Resp. Nec attingit illos cruciatus.

Oremus. Domine Deus, Resurrectio et Vita credentium, qui semper es laudandus, tam in viventibus, quam in defunctis, agimus tibi gratias pro Fundatore nostro N . . . ceterisque Benefactoribus nostris, quorum beneficiis hic ad pietatem et studia literarum alimur : rogantes, ut nos his donis ad tuam gloriam recte utentes, una cum illis ad resurrectionis gloriam immortatem perducamur. Per Christum Dominum nostrum. *R.* Amen.

APPENDIX XI.

ANCIENT MONUMENTAL INSCRIPTIONS.

In the various ancient Monumental Inscriptions of our English forefathers still existing (though hundreds have been ruthlessly destroyed, or deliberately effaced) we find many interesting and remarkable memorials both of their faith and piety. Almost every important parish church affords specimens, which give the clearest idea of the relations which were believed to exist between the living and the departed; as well as of the deep interest which was taken by those still in the flesh in the faithful who, having gone forward, had passed through the Valley of the Shadow of Death to the region beyond.

The Monumental Inscriptions in England of the thirteenth and fourteenth centuries were as superior to those of the seventeenth and eighteenth centuries, both in brevity, good taste, and piety, as the calm and severe monumental effigies of the former era were to the grotesque and exaggerated examples of vitiated taste current in the latter period.*

---

* In West Wycombe church, Bucks, there is an inscription in which the persons departed, who are commemorated by the monument, are made to pray for their surviving children, thus:—" Richard East and Emma my wife, who deceased the xvij. of May, my wife the xx. of Iune, 1583. We lyved in wedlock leaving to the world, Rychard,

APPENDIX XI.

"Orate pro anima" was a sentiment and prayer in perfect harmony with the cold forms in marble which, with hands clasped as if in perpetual devotion and supplication, lay, as in sleep, facing the daybreak and morning sunshine, within the solemn chantry or hallowed aisles of our ancient churches. The inflated, pompous, and flattering inscriptions of more recent times were fitting accompaniments of the half-draped women in marble of a pagan age, who were represented as Fame or Victory upon the debased constructions of stone and alabaster, with urns, torches, and cherubs, which still disfigure our old cathedrals.

Though "Orate pro anima" was the most usual ancient mode of beginning an inscription, and later on, "Of your charity pray for the soul," etc., yet frequently the commencement ran as follows:—"In gracia et misericordia Ihu, hic requiescit corpus," etc.; and occasionally, more tersely, "Hic jacet corpus."* The terminations, always Christian,

Roberte, Hewgh, and Iohn East, our only children, whom the Lord bless and defend from all assayles of there enemies. Amen."

On the tomb of Robert Ingleton, in Thornton church, Bucks, the following unusual inscription occurs:—"Sit sibi propicia celi Regina Maria salvet eum Christi matris amore Deus." The spelling of the above and the following legends, often quaint, incorrect, sometimes inconsistent, and frequently unintelligible as regards single words, has been preserved by the author as it is found.

* Examples occur likewise, as follow:—"Placidè in Domino obdormiens;" "Obdormiat in Domino;"

"Pie in Domino requiescit;" "Hic requiescit in gracia et in misericordia Dei." "Hoc sub lapide justorum resurrectionem expectat," on the tomb of Elcock, Lord Mayor of York, at Christ Church in that city (Drake's "Antiquities of York," p. 321. London, 1736). "Hic in Domino requiescit Joannes Durhame" (Borley church, Essex); and "Hic jacet Magister Thomas Greenwoode, legum doctor, canonicus residentiarius istius ecclesie, qui obiit xi. die mensis Maii, an. Dom. 1421. Cujus anima in pace requiescat. 'Amen."—(York Cathedral.) Examples of a somewhat similar character exist, as follow :—"Here resteth in the hope of a

full of faith and hope, varied considerably, though the idea embodied in them was usually the same. Sometimes the ending ran thus:—" Whoose soule God pardon," or " Upon whose soule God have compacion," or " To whose soule God be pitiful," or " To whose soul God be merciful." Examples exist, but they are rare,* of—' On whose sowle, Crist Jhu, for his bitter passion, have infinite compasshion;" " Whom the Lord bless and defend from all assalyies of their enemyes;"† " On whom the greate God be pityful for Christes sake;" "To whom ye high and mercifull God grant the light of heaven and peace everlastyng;" " Whose soule the Lord God omnipotent pardon;" " God reward her soul with eternall salvation;"‡ and " Whose soules God bring to everlastyng life."§

Post-Reformation examples of definite prayer for the dead are provided in the Catena later on; ‖ here are added a few

blessed resurrection" (St. Katharine Cree, London); " Cujus animæ pax sit perpetua" (Thame church, Oxon); " Quorum animabus propitietur Altissimus, Amen."—(St. Bartholomew-the-Less, London. See Maitland's "History of London," vol. ii. book ii. p. 1071.) On a tomb to the memory of Richard Amherst and Dorothy his wife, who died July, 1654, in Pembury church, Kent, the inscription ends thus:—" Hoping for a joyfull resurrection at the coming of our Blessed Saviour;" and in the south chancel of Aylesford church in the same county, on Sir Paul Rycaut's monument, A.D. 1700, the prayer " Requiescat in pace" occurs. —(" Registrum Roffense," p. 791.)

* The following inscription is equally remarkable and rare:—

" Hic jacet Willelmus Talbot Miser et indignus sacerdos Expectans resurrectionem Mortuorum sub signo Thau."

† On the brass of " Richard East," West Wycombe, Bucks.

‡ On the brass of " Richard Manfeld Squer," at Taplow, Bucks.

§ On the monument of Sir John Saye and Dame Elizabeth his wife, at Broxbourne. (Clutterbuck's " Hertfordshire," vol. ii. p. 63.)

‖ My friend the Rev. J. T. Fowler, F.S.A., of the University of Durham, having examined the tombs of the churches in that city, reports specimens, full of Christian piety, showing how the older forms and better traditions, somewhat weakened and enfeebled, it may be, lingered on for some generations, notwithstanding the frequent debasement of taste and the widespread influence of pagan ideas. They might be extended to a great length. The following are curious examples, some being rare and peculiar, and others very considerably and generally followed :—

1. HOGSTON, BUCKS.—Elizabeth Mayne, deceased 24th August, 1599 :—

" Yet the reports of her good life, Among her friends remaineth :
Hir soule with God, the rest of hir This marble stone containeth."

2. THAME, OXFORDSHIRE.—On a monument on the chancel floor :—" In hope of ye Resurrection, under this tombe lyeth the body of Margaret wife of Gilbert Trowe," with a long and quaint prayer for her in verse.

3. ELSENHAM.—On the monument to Alice, wife of Dr. Tuer, the following expression is made use of :—" Her humble soul delivered from the downe-pressing birthen of this flesh. Oct. 7, 1619."

4. TITLEY, ESSEX.—Thoms Cecil, Rector. Ob. Jan. 29, 1627 :—

" Dum libris vivo, morior : sic vita mihi mors,
Nunc vitæ evoluo librum : sic mors mihi vita."

the existence of many with prayers for the departed inscribed on them ; e.g.—" R. I. P.," date 1827 ; "Eternal rest give to them, O Lord, and let perpetual light shine upon them," 1815 ; " R. I. P.," date 1805 ; " Requiescat in pace," date 1801 ; " May he rest in peace and rise in glory," date 1724 ; the same inscription in 1819, again in 1826 and 1827 ; " Requiescant in pace " in 1764, 1768, 1786, 1788, 1789, 1791, 1795, 1798, 1799. The above are taken from the Cathedral churchyard, St. Oswald's, St. Mary's, St. Margaret's, and St. Giles'. He also informs me that there are many similar inscriptions at Kirkthorpe, near Wakefield, and at Selby Abbey Church—the latter being of the seventeenth and eighteenth centuries.

"Whilst I live to my books I die: thus life to me is death.
Now I turn over the book of life: thus death is to me life."

5. SANDON, ESSEX.—On the monument to Anne, wife of Brian Walton, D.D., Rector, in the chancel, the inscription stands thus:—"Hæc lacrymarum valle, in cœlestem patriam emigravit feria prima Pentecost: Maii 25, anno Christi, 1649."

6. MOUNTNEYSING, ESSEX.—On a monument in the chancel, north wall, to "Joannes Prescot," the conclusion stands as follows:—" Migravit in lucem æternitatis, 19 Feb. A.D. MDCLVi."

7. THEYDON GERNON, ESSEX.—" Orate veniat regnum tuum," on the tomb of Dr. James Meggs, 1672.

8. CHRIST CHURCH, YORK.—" Hic requiescit in spe futuræ resurrectionis," on the tomb of William Richardson, in Christ Church, York, dated Dec. 29, 1680.

(Drake's " Antiquities of York.")

9. HOGSTON, BUCKS.—1680 :—" Hic requiescit a laboribus."

10. QUAINTON, BUCKS. (Chancel) :—" In spem beatæ resurrectionis, hic jacet corpus," etc. (A.D. 1691.)

11. NORTH WEALDE, ESSEX.—On a monument in the church-yard :—" Georgina Hellier, clericus, hic expectat resurrectionem, obiit 14 die Septembris, Anno Domini 1729, ætatis suæ 82."

12. DUNTON, BUCKS.—On the monument to the memory of the Rev. Samuel Clutterbuck, Rector :—" In the 66th year of his age, on the 9th day of April, being the solemn day of our Blessed Lord's Passion, he sweetly slept in the Lord."

13. A similar inscription is found in the church of St. Michael Belfry, York :—" Here lyeth the Body of that worthy and useful gentleman, Mr. Nicholas Blackbeard, who, after he had been Town clerk of this City twenty-five years, and with great prudence and faithfulness served his generation, sweetly sleepeth in the Lord, May 27th, 1671, æt. 59. Vixit post funera virtus."

14. SPELSBURY, OXFORDSHIRE.—On the tomb of Dame Dorothy Bathurst, wife of Sir Edward Bathurst, Baronet, which Dorothy died March 18, 1689, she is said to be "waiting for a blessed and joyfull resurrection."

15. STAPLEFORD, CAMBRIDGESHIRE.—"Willis Lee, borne at Batley in Yorkeshire, Vicar of this churche of Stapleford, 43 years, studious of the good of eyther place, nowe sleepeth heare waytinge for the blessed appearinge of Jesus Christ to judgment."

(W. Coles' Collections Brit. Museum, vol. i. fol. 41 [or 47].)

16. ST. MICHAEL'S, LONG STANTON, CAMBRIDGESHIRE.

"Quisquis eris, qui transieris, sta, pro lege plora,
Sum quod eris, fueramque quod es. Pro me precor ora."

17. ST. ANDREW-THE-GREAT, CAMBRIDGE.—Richard Humphrey:—

"Vide viator, quod sum.
Fui quod es.
Eris quod sum."

(Coles MSS. vol. ii. fol. 102.)

PRE-REFORMATION INSCRIPTIONS.

The following pre-Reformation inscriptions are added because of their uncommon character and form, being unlike those already cited, and as serving still further to illustrate the belief and practice of our forefathers:—

1. ST. NICHOLAS, OLAVE, LONDON.—William Read, Citizen and Fishmonger:—

"Who that passeth by this way,
For mercy of God, behold and pray
For all soules Christen, and for us,
One Pater Noster and an Ave,
To the Blessed Saynts and our Blessed Ladye
Saint Marye, to pray for us.
Qui pro aliis orat, pro se laborat."

(Maitland's "London," p. 1157.)

2. The following is a fifteenth-century example:—

> "We mey not prey, hertely prey yee,
> For our soulys Pater Noster and Ave;
> The sooner of owr Payne lesseyned be,
> Graunt us this Holy Trinity. Amen."

3. ST. MARTIN'S, LUDGATE, LONDON:—

> "Farewell, my friends, the Tyde abideth no man,
> Wee be departed frō hence, and so shall yee:
> But in this passage, the best song that we say can,
> Is *Requiem æternam:* Now Jesu grant it me :
> When we have ended all our adversitee
> Grant us in Paradise to have a mansion
> That schede His Blood for our redemption :
> Therefore we tenderly require yee
> For the souls of John Benson and
>   Anne, hys wyff,
>   of your charitie
> To say a *Pater Noster* and an *Ave*.

4. ST. MARTIN'S, VINTRY, LONDON.—Joannes Micolt and Joanna his wife:—"Quorum anime per Dei immensam misericordiam in Pace perpetua permaneant ac requiem possideant."

(Maitland's "London," p. 1133.)

5. "Jesu, for Thy mercy ther sowlys now save."—(Robert Reginald, in the church of Mancetter, Warwickshire.)

6. ST. LEONARD'S, FOSTER LANE, LONDON.—Robert Truppe's:—

> "Wherefore Jesu that of Mary sprong
> Let their souls thy Saynts among,
> Though it be undeserved on their syde,
> Yet, good Lord, let them evermore thy mercy abide;
> And of your charitie
> For their souls say a Pater Noster and an Ave.

(Weever's "Funeral Monuments.")

7. THEYDON, ESSEX.—"Before this tabernaculle lyeth buryed Thomas Greene, some time bayle of this towne, Margaret and Margaret hys wyves, which Thomas dyed the 8th day of July, MDXXXV. The which Thomas had wylled a prest to syng in this

church for the space of xx yeares, for him, his wyves, his children and all men's soules. And moreover he hath wylled one obyte to be kept the 8th day of July for the terme of xx yeares for the soules aforesaid, and at every time of the said obyte bestowed xxs. of good lawfule money of England."

CATENA OF INSCRIPTIONS

CONTAINING

PRAYERS FOR THE DEPARTED, FROM MONUMENTS IN CATHEDRALS AND PARISH CHURCHES, 1550—1870.

1550. OSSINGTON, NOTTINGHAMSHIRE.

" Of your charitie pray for the soul of Reynold Peckham, of Wrotham, in the county of Kent, esquire, which decesed the xxj day of July, in the yere of Our Lord God MCCCCCL. Whose soul God pardon."

1550. ST. ALKMUND'S, SHREWSBURY.

"Here lyeth George Pontesbury, who dyed the x day of October, Anno Dni. 1550. On whom the Lord, for Xt. Ihs. sake, have mercy. Amen."

1550. TWYFORD, BUCKS.

"Here lyeth buryed the Bodyes of Thomas Giffard, of Twiffard, in the coūtye of Buck', Esquyer, and Marie his Wyffe, Doughter of Wyllm Staveley, of Bignell, Esquyer, which Thomas decessyd the xxv. day of November, in the yere of oř lorde God MCCCCCL. On whose Soules Jhu have mercy. Amen."

1550. WING, BUCKS. (Inscription on a brass plate, defaced, date 1550.)

"I most hartely desyor you to pray
That I may have full resurrection at the Last Day."

1550. LITTLE DRIFFIELD, YORKSHIRE.

"here vnder lyeth Raufe buckton, of hamswell, in the Countie of yorke, Esquyer, and margaret his wyfe, yᵉ whiche Raufe deceessed the xxvij day of October in yᵉ yer' of oʳ lord god mᵗ vᶜ xl, and margaret deceessed the xvviij day of July in the yer' of oʳ lord god mᵗ vᶜ xlv. on whose soules and all Christen Jhu haue mercy."

1550.

In Thos. Gill's *Vallis Eboracensis*, or Hist. of Easingwold, 8vo. 1852 (p. 858), is engraved the brass of Thomas Magnus, Archdeacon of the East Riding, and Rector of Sessay, who died 1550; the inscription concludes thus: "whose soule god p̄don."

1551. HAWSTEAD, SUFFOLK.

On a tomb to the memory of two members of the Drury family, who died in 1551, the inscription concludes :—

> "From Fader and Moder in childhood he hath us take,
> Jesus on us have mercy wch. dyed for mannys sake."

1552. CHESHAM BOIS, BUCKS.

"All Christian people gyve thankˢ for the godly dep̄ture of Robert Cheyne, Esquier, who decessed the nynth daye of December, in the yere of oʳ lorde god a Thousand fyve hundredth fiftie two. Whose Soule we commende to Godˢ infinite mercy."

1552. ST. KATHARINE, COLEMAN STREET, LONDON.

> "I humbly do require all which pass this way,
> For Henry Webb, Esquire his soul devoutly to pray,
> Which Gentleman Usher was to King Henry the Eighth,
> And now lieth here buried, with Barbara his wife,
> Which the 5th of Feb. 1552 departed this Life.
> And the last day of March in like sort dyed he,
> The 1000 year of Our Lord God Five hundred, Fifty Three,
> On whose Soul, Jesus have mercy."
>
> (Maitland's "London," p. 1113.)

1553—1558. IPSLEY, WARWICK.

Nicholas Huband, Esq., & Dorothy his wife. " Upon whose soules God have mercy."

(Dugdale's " Warwickshire," vol. ii. p. 741.)

1556. NOWTON, SUFFOLK. (Chancel.)

"Pray for the sowle of Sr Richard Whytney, sometyme parson of Nowton and Ingham, who died 1556."

1556. ST. BARTHOLOMEW-THE-LESS, LONDON.

" Here lyeth now dead which late was quick
The comely corps of Anne Westwick,
Who died in childbed of her First,
Upon the fifth day of August:
Whose soule (doubtless) is long ere this
In Heaven with Christ in Joy and Bliss,
But yet for order of Charity
Upon her soul say Jesu hau mercy.
                    Anno Dom. 1556."

(Maitland's " London," vol. ii. book iii. p. 1,071.)

1557. SOUTHWICK, HANTS.

" Off your charitie pray for ye sowle of Anne Whyte, late the wyffe of John Whyte, of Southwick, Esq. . . . died 18 Nov., 1557. On whose soule and all cristen soules Crist have mercy."

1558. CHICHELEY, BUCKS.

"Hic jacet Anthonius Cave, Armiger quonda' Mercator Stapule Calicie, Dominus de Chicheley, qui obiit nono die Septembris, An. Dni. Millessimo xxxxxlviij. Cujus animæ p'picietur deus. Amen."

1558.

John Oldnall and Isabell his wife. Died 11 Aug. 1558. " Upon whose souls God have mercy."

(Dugdale's "Warwickshire," vol. ii. p. 795.)

1558. CLAWORTH, NORTHAMPTONSHIRE.

On a monument to members of the Fitzwilliam family, including Humphrey, William, Roger, & Edward, which Humphrey died June 30, 1558, the inscription concludes with— "whose souls God rest."

1558. ST. GEORGE'S CHAPEL, WINDSOR.

JOHN ROBYNS THE ASTRONOMER.

"Orate pro Anima Joannis Robyns, sacre theologie baccalaurii, nuper hujus regie capelle canonici, et quondam capellani tam regis Henrici octavi quam serenissime regine Marie, qui obiit 25° die Augusti, anno domini milessimo quingentesimo quinquagesimo octavo, cujus aminæ, ut in cœlo quiescat, Deus optimus, suam misericordiam, concedat."

560. ST. FAITH'S, LONDON.

"Stay and pray. Here lyeth buried the body of Margaret Robynson, late wyffe of Christofer Robinson, one of the proctors of Th'arches, who decessed the first day of May, Anno 1560, on whose soule and all Christan soules Jhu have mercy. Amen."

1560. DENHAM, BUCKS.

"Here lyeth the Body of Syr Leonard Hurst, sometyme parson of this Churche, who departed out of thys Transitory lyfe the last day of June, the yere of our Lord God a Thousand fyve hundredth and threscore. On whose Soule and all Christians Jesu have mer'. Ame'."

1560. HITCHAM, BUCKS.

"Pray for yᵉ soules of Thomas Ramsey and Margaret his wyf, which Thomas decessed the xxx day of Janyver, the yere of oʳ lorde M.DLX, on whose soules Ihu have mercy. Amen."

1562. CHESHAM BOIS, BUCKS.

"All Cheristian people geve Thanks to the Lorde for the Godly dep'ture of Wenefride, Doughter to the late lord Mordant, and Wyfe to John Cheyne, Esquyer, who decessed viijth

day of July, in the yere of o' lorde MCCCCCLXII. Whose Soule we comende to God' infinite mercy."

1562. CHESHAM BOIS, BUCKS.

"Of Roger Lee, gentleman, here lyeth the son, Benedict Lee, chrysome, whose soul Ihu pardon."

[There is no date on the brass inscription, but the record is entered in the Register of Burials, A.D. 1562. Roger Lee had married "Isabel, d' of John Cheyne, Eq^r.," and the Hon. Winefred Cheyne.—*Vide* previous inscription.]

1563. CRONDAL, HAMPSHIRE.

"Here under lyeth John Gyfford, esquyer, heyre apparent of Syr William Gyfford, knyght, who had to wyfe Elyzabethe, one of the dawghters of Syr George Throkmarton, knyght, and had by her issue fyve sonnys and viii daughters, and so changed this mortall lyfe the fyrst day of May, in the yere of our Lorde God 1563. On whose soule Jesu have mercy."

1564. MIDDLE, SHROPSHIRE.

"Here lyeth Buried in ye mercy of Jesus Christ the Body of Arthure Chambers, trew Patron of this Parish Church of Mydle, and Margret his wyfe; by her had issue one sonne and one daughter, wch Arther deceased the 19 of August, 1564, whose body and sowle god graunt a joyful resurection. Amen."

1566. COLESHILL, WARWICKSHIRE.

(MSS. Harl. No. 3,391.)

"Here lyeth the body of Sir John Fenton, Prest, Bachelar of Law, sometime Vicar of this Church, and Officiall of Coventrie, who deceassed the xvij. daye of Maye, 1566. Whose Soule Jhesus pardon. Amen."

(Dugdale's "Warwickshire," vol. ii. p. 1,015.)

1566. HARDMEAD, BUCKS.

"Of your Charitee pray for the Soul of Francys Catesby, of

Hardmede, Gent., the youngest son of Antonie Catesby, of Whiston, Esqr, decessid; which Francys decessid the xxi day of August, in the yere of our Lord God MDLvj. On whose Soule & all Christians God have Mercy. Amen."

1566. COLESHILL, WARWICKSHIRE.

"Here lyeth Isabell Ryddel, late the wife of Humfrey Ryddel, Baylie of Colshill, the only daughter of Edmund Parker, of Hartshill, which Isabell dyed the xxixth day of October, the yere of our Lord God MDCCCCLXVI. Whose Soul Jesu pardon."

(Dugdale's "Warwickshire," vol. ii. p. 1,015.)

1567. SOUTHWICK, HANTS.

"Here resteth in peace the bodys of John Whyte, Eq., and Katheryn (his first wife d. 1548). The said John decessyd the xix day of July, 1567. Whose soules Crist take to his mercy."

1568. NOWTON, SUFFOLK. (Chancel.)

"Orate pro anima Henrici payne, ar. quondā. Dñe huius manerii et patroni hujus ecclesie, qui obiit 25 die Julij, anno Regni Dñe Elizab. 26. et anno Dñi 1568."

1568. EAST WICKHAM, KENT.

"William Payne, yeoman of the Garde, deceesed xxv. Ianuarie, 1568. To whom God graunte a joyfull resurrexcion. Amen."

1569. WALTHAM ABBEY, ESSEX.

"Here under lyeth buryed nere to this piller the bodes of Thomas Cottle, Esquyer, and Magdalen his wyfe, who had esshue betweene them vi sonnes & iiij daughters, which Thomas deceassed the xxix. day of June, an° MCCCCLIX, and the said Magdalen, who was the causer of this Monument, deceassed the last day of Novemb^r, an° MCCCCXCI, whose bodes and soules god send a joyfull resurrection."

1569. DATCHETT, BUCKS.

"Here under this Tombe lyeth buryed in y² mercy of Ihu Christ, the body of y² Ladye Katheryn Barkeley, sometyme wyffe of S⁺ Mores Barkeley, Knyght, and Daughter to the Right Hon'ble William Blount, Lord Mountjoy, which Lady dyed y² xxiij. day of February, in the yere of o⁺ lorde God MCCCCCLIX.

> "Whose soule we wyshe as love doyeth bynde
> A place wyth Chryst in heaven to fynde."

1570. ST. DUNSTAN'S, LONDON.

"Here lyeth Clement Towne, whose Obit shall for ever be observed in this church, and his Mass always upon the day following, whose soule and His two wyfes' souls, Elisabeth & Elisabeth, and all their children's souls, Jesus take to His glorious mercy. Amen."

(Maitland's "London," vol. ii. book iii. p. 1,093.)

1571. ST. MARGARET, LOTHBURY, LONDON.

"Under this stone lyeth George Beaumon, Clerke & Doctor in Divinity, who departed this Life the 29 day of April, Anno Domini 1571; a man mercifull and good to the Poore; and borne in Kennigall in Cumberland; [to] whose Body and Soul God grant a joyful Resurrection."

1572. ETON, BUCKS.

"An° MDLXXii, August xviii Daye.

> "Under this stone lieth Thomas Smith, late a fellowe heare,
> And of Cambridge M⁺. of art°. of y² Kyngs Colledge theare,
> He did dep'te from earthlie life ye tyme above exprest,
> Whose soule we hope dothe now remaine in Abram's brest.

1574. ST. NICHOLAS, ROCHESTER.

"Under this stone lyeth buried the Body of Alice Williams . . . . deceased the xxx. of Marche, 1574. On whose soule God have mercy."

1574. ST. LAWRENCE JEWRY, LONDON.

Alice Blundell, died Nov. 21, 1574. "Unto whom God send (through Jhesus Christ) a joyful resurrection. Amen."

1574—1576. HILLESDEN, BUCKS.

"Here lyeth Alexander Denton, sone and Heyre to Thomas Denton, Esquire, and Marye his second Wife, one of the Daughters of Sir Roger Martyn Knight, which Alexander Deceased the 8 daye of Ianuarie, in th' yeare of Our Lorde God 1574, and Mary the 12 day of Iulie, in the yeere of our Lord God 1576, to whome our Lorde graunte a joyfol Resurrection : and erected at the charge of Mary Denton."

1578. ST. GILES', CRIPPLEGATE, LONDON.

Richard Roper lived 70 years and dyed the 28th day of September Anno Dom. 1578. Helen lived 65 years and Joane 2.

> "Good Helen, wife to me that was
> Prepare thyself with speed,
> That Thou and I, with this young maid,
> A plant of both our seed,
> May rest in One, and rise in Three,
> By power of Godhead's Might,
> When we with Angels shall assemble
> To Everlasting light."
>
> (Maitland's "London," p. 1103.)

1581. ST. NICHOLAS OLAVE, LONDON.

John Warre, died May 30, 1581.

"His body sleeps till angel's trump shall sound
God grant His soul at last with Christ be found."

1581. NORTH MUSCAM, NOTTINGHAMSHIRE.

"Here lieth the corpse of Thomas Smith,
Meat for worms to feed therewith,
Whose soule is gone to God on hie
Through Christ's merits & God's mercie,
Whose bodie I hope shall rise again,
And ever with Christ for to remain,
Deceased the second day of May,
Being in yeares of age thirty and three.
1581."

APPENDIX XI.

1584. RIPPLE, WORCESTERSHIRE.

In the midst of the chancel there was formerly a stone inlaid with brass. At the top was the figure of the Blessed Virgin, holding her Divine Child : below a man robed, praying. The inscription ran thus :—

"Thomas Bastard,* quondam hujus Ecclesiæ rector, qui obiit ultimo die Aprilis, A.D. 1584. Post tenebras spero lucem."

1592. SOLIHULL, WARWICKSHIRE.

"Here lieth the bodie of Henry Huggeford, late of Solihull, gent, deceesed the XIII. of November in the yeare of Our Lord God 1592. To whom the Lord grant a joyfull resurrection. Amen."

(Dugdale's "Warwickshire," vol. ii. p. 946.)

1601. BRAILES, WARWICKSHIRE.

"John Bishop, Patron of this church, who lived 92 yeares in good credit, and made an happie end ye third day off Aprill 1601. God grant him a glorious Resurrection. Amen."

1602. GRENDON, WARWICKSHIRE.

"John Chetwind & Margerie his wife. He died 1592, April 15. She died 1602, Dec. 20. Miserere mei Domine. Redemisti me in veritate. Amavi veritatem et dedit mihi Requiem. Nescit labi virtus ; miserere mei Deus."

(Dugdale's "Warwickshire," vol. ii. p. 1,106.)

1602. WITHYBROOKE, WARWICKSHIRE.

"Here lyeth the Bodie of Christofer Wright, of Pappisforde, Esq., who deceesed the first Day of December in the yeare of Our Lord, 1602. Whose soule God rest."

1602. CRENDON, BUCKINGHAMSHIRE. (North transept.)

"Here lyeth John Canon, deceesed Oct. 1, 1602. God give him reste eternall. Amen."

---

* Instituted Rector 1571, Regist. 32 Bull, folio 2 b.

1603. ILTON, SOMERSETSHIRE.

"Pray for the soule of Nycholas Wadham, which dep̃ted oute of this worlde in the yere of Our Lord, 1603. On whose soule IHU. have mercy."

1603. ST. MARTIN'S, OUTWICH, YORK.

"Joane Langley lyeth here, who yielded her soul to her Redeemer the last of April, 1603. May she rest in peace. Amen."

1604. YARDLEY, WORCESTERSHIRE.

"Here lieth Mr Henry Est, Eq^r, and Margery his wife, the which died the 13th day of April, Anno Dom. 1604. On whose souls God have mercy.

1606.

"Here lyeth the bodyes of William Riddel, of Blyth Hall, and Jone his wife, the which William departed this life the last day of August in the yeare of Our Lord God MDLviij. And the said Jone dyed the XIX. of August in the year of our Lord God MDLvi. whose soules Jesu pardon."

(Dugdale's "Warwickshire," vol. ii. p. 1,015.)

1606. BREWOOD, STAFFORDSHIRE.

"Here lyeth the bodys of Edward Gyfford, of White Ladyes, Eq^r, and Fraunces his wife, wch Edw. was 2^d Son of Sir Tho. Gyfford, of Chillington, K^t, and deceased the first of Ianuary, 1606, and Frances was eldest daughter & heire of Bartholomew Skerne, Esq., and deceased the . . . day of . . . On whose souls Jhesus have mercy."

1606. ST. DUNSTAN'S-IN-THE-WEST, LONDON.

William Crouch, Citizen & Merchant of London. Died, April 16, 1606.

[Conclusion—]

"Wherefore of God His mercy crave
Who hath of Mercy store,
And unto Him, commend my soule
(My friend) I crave no more."

(Maitland's "London," p. 1,096.)

1607. ST. MARY'S, NOTTINGHAM.

"Nicholas Kynnersley, Esquire, and his mother
Dear Amye, their corpes this stone doth cover,
They are now with Christ Jesus, in whom was their trust,
God grant them both at last to rise with the just.
A.D. 1607."

1609. BOURNE, CAMBRIDGESHIRE.

Erasmus Ferrers, 1609.
"Dulciter hic requiesco et adventum
Redemptoris mei expecto."

1610. TOPPESFIELD, ESSEX. (East side of chancel.)

"Ego, Richardus King, patria Herefordiensis, educatione Oxoniensis, professione theologus, officio capellaneus Jacobi Regis Serenissimi, et hujus Ecclesiæ Vicarius indignus, hoc in loco sacrosancte sponte depono et recondo corporis exuvias. Laus Deo, salus Ecclesiæ, et animæ meæ requies in æternam. Amen."

1611. ST. OSWALD'S, DURHAM. (Parochial Register.)

"Myles White, one of the singing men within the Cathedral Churche of Durham, and of the aige of LXXvij yeares, being a man of verie good . . . . was buried the xxiijrd daie of Iuli, 1611. Whose soule the lord Jesu grante mercye upon. Amen."

1612. WISTON, NEAR SELBY.

"Ora pro anima Gulielmi Hawkworth, qui obiit 29° die Julii, Anno Domini, 1612."

1613. WEST MALLING, KENT.

"Here resteth Ralph Adams, aged LI. yeeres, the which deceased May ye third, MDCXIIJ. Whose soul, God of his marcy, pardon for Ihesu's sake. Amen."

1615. DORCHESTER, OXON.

"Myles Parsons, aged 80 yeeres, lyeth buried here, who deceesed the iii. day of September, Aº Dni. 1615. To whom the Merciful God give peace and a joyfull rising for Xt. Ihs his sake. Amen."

1617. HEREFORD CATHEDRAL.

Bishop Benett, who died in 1617, has on a wooden tablet, signed "Georgius Benson," the following :—

"Deus illi semper amanti
Christum sit Christus dulce levamen."

1618. EDGBASTON, WARWICKSHIRE. (Flat stone, in the body of the church.)

"Humphrey & Anne Middlemore, and Frances Middlemore, there davghter, who dyed ye 4. December, Annº Dom. 1618. Whose sovl God Have mercy on. Amen."

(Dugdale's "Warwickshire," vol. ii. p. 897.)

1623. MORTEN MERHULL, WARWICKSHIRE. (Chancel.)

"Elizabeth, d^r of Stephen Harvy, of Milton Malsor, Northamptonshire, died July 3, 1623. Bone Jesu Qui hanc suscepti elatem Huic miserere."

(Dugdale's "Warwickshire," vol. 1. p. 495.)

1628. DASSET, WARWICKSHIRE.

"Peter Temple, of Stowe, Co. Bucks, Esqr. Deceased May 28, 1628. Whose soul God have in His Blessed Keeping. Amen."

1629. ST. MARY'S, LAMBETH. (South aisle, wall.)

"Elizabeth Baylie, late wife of John Baylie, obiit 24 June, Anno Dni. 1629. Ætatis suæ 25."

The inscription in verse thus concludes :—

"A husband's love, a father's pietye,
Dedicates this unto their memorie.
And when he hath his debt to Nature payd,
In the same grave himself will then be layd.
That all together when the Trump shall sound,
Husband, wife, children may in Christ bee found."

1630. POWDERHAM, DEVONSHIRE. (Coffin-plate.)

"Hic jacet sepultus ✠ Gulielmus Courtenay de Powderham, Miles, Catholicus Romanus et Confessor, qui obiit Londini in festo Sancti Johannis Baptistæ, Anno Salutis 1630, ætatis suæ 77°. Pro cujus anima intercedant Beata Virgo et omnes sancti."

1630. KIDDERMINSTER, WORCESTERSHIRE.

On a Tomb in memory of Sir Edward Blount, who died Nov. 13, 1630, the inscription concludes as follows.—

"Beatam vitam felici morte conclusit die 13° Novembris, Ann. Dom. 1630. Ætatis 76. R. I. P."

1633. BULKINGTON, WARWICKSHIRE. (Choir.)

"Hic jacet Robertus Cowper, nuper Vicar. de Bulkynton, qui obiit vices. die mensis Iulii, Anno Dom. 1633. Cujus animæ propicietur Deus. Amen."

1635. DRAYTON PARSLOW, BUCKS.

"Of your charitie pray for the soules of Benet Blackwelle and Agnes his wife, who died the xxx. day of Sept. MDCXXXV. With the children's soules Ihu have m'cy. Amen."

1639. IDBURY, OXFORDSHIRE.

The inscription to John Logan and his wife, in this church, A.D. 1639, ends thus :—

"Requiescant in pace. Amen."

1641. WITHYHAM, SUSSEX.

"Here resteth, hoping for pardon of his sins, and, in the end, a glorious resurrection through Christ Jesus, the corpse of Nathaniel How, who departed out of this transitorie life uppon the Feast of Our Lady's annunciation in the year of Our Lord God, MDCXLI. Orate pro anima sua, Viator."

1653. STAUNTON HAROLD.

On a Tablet of white marble is the following inscription :—

"In the year 1653, when all thinges sacred were throughout yᵉ nation, either demolisht or prophaned, Sir Robert Shirley, Barronet, founded this Church; whose singular praise it is to have done the best things in the worst times, and hoped them in the most callamitous. 'The righteous shall be had in everlasting remembrance.'"

Beneath the battlements of the chancel are also carved the following words in large letters:—

"Sir Robert Shirley, Baronet, Founder of this Church. On whose soule God have mercy."

1657. TEMPLE CHURCH, LONDON.

"For a sacred and religious remembrance of Charles Heath, Esq., a gentleman of this society, Amye Heath, his doleful wife, caused this stone to be laid. He died in the year of his age the 34th, of Christ 1657, by whom he expects a happy resurrection."

(Dugdale's "Origines Juridiciales," p. 174.)

1659. GREAT MISSENDEN, BUCKS.

"Hic jacet corpus Roberti Dormer de Peterly, armigeris, filii natu tertii Roberti Dormer, Baronis de Wing. Obiit die 23 Octobris, Anno 1659. Cujus animæ pptr. Deus."

1660. BLACKMORE PRIORY CHURCH, ESSEX. (Chancel.)

"Here lyeth the body of Simon Lynch, Rector of Runwell, (who for fearing God and the King, was sequestered, prosecuted, and persecuted to the day of his death by Gog and Magog, and left issue Elizabeth, Sarah, Symon, and Ithuel), unto whom the Lord be merciful. Who died the 16th June, 1660, aged 60 years."

1661. SEFTON, LANCASHIRE.

"Hic jacet corpus Dominæ Mariæ filiæ Domini Alexandri Barlow de Barlow, in comitatu Lancastriæ, equitis aurati, uxoris prænobilis domini Domini Carill, Vicecomitis Molineaux, quæ obiit 8 Idus Februarii Sanctæ Dorotheæ sacro. Anno Dni. MDCXLI. Cujus animæ misereatur Omnipotens Deus."

1664. SUNNING, BERKSHIRE.

"Hic jacet corpus Susannæ, uxoris Antonii Englefield de White-Knights, armigeris, quæ obiit secund. die Iunii, A.D. 1664. Ætatis vero suæ 65. Requiescat in pace. Amen."

1667. COUGHTON, WARWICKSHIRE.

"Here rests the corps of Ann Monson, widow of John Monson, the parents of the Lady Throcmorton, who at the age of L years resigned this transitory life for one eternal. Christ Jesus have mercy on her soule. Shee departed Aug. the XXIX. Day in the year of Grace MDCLXvij."

(Dugdale's "Warwickshire," vol. ii. p. 755.)

1668. ROUGHAM, NORFOLK.

"Here lys the bodie of Eliz. Peyton, the daughter of William Yelverton, Bart., and Ursula his wife, the heir of that family, who departed this life on the 15 of June, Anno Dom. 1668. In the day of judgment deliver her, O Lord. Piæ hic dormientis memoriæ Hoc monumentum imposuit I.B."

1668. EASINGTON, OXFORDSHIRE. (Floor of nave).

"Michael Dormer, esquire, died Nov. 14, 1668. God be merciful to him in the day of judgment. Amen."

1669. ST. NICHOLAS, FYFIELD, BERKS. (South porch).

"Here lyeth the Body of Anne, the wife of James Perrot, Gent.. who departed this Life May ye XXII. MDCLXIX. Requiescat in pace."

1671. SOLIHULL, WARWICKSHIRE.

"Here lyeth the body of Charles Waring, of Bury Hall, Gent., who died the eighteenth day of September, 1671. Cujus animæ propicietur Deus."

(Dugdale's "Warwickshire," vol. ii. p. 946.)

1672. ST. HELEN'S, WORCESTER.

"Mr. George Cocks, the youngest son of Sir John Cocks, Knight. He left this transitory world for one eternall at 18 years of age and 5 months. He deceased upon the 17th day of June, in the year of the Blessed Virgin's Son, the World's Redeemer, 1672. R.I.P."

1672—1675. BURSTON, BUCKINGHAMSHIRE.

"Here reposeth Arthur Hodges, and Mary his wife. He died Oct. 4, 1672. She died May 12, 1675.

"Whose souls God receive to favour and peace,
With joies to arise which never shall cease.
"Dominus Christus, miserere."

1675. ST. HELEN'S, WORCESTER.

On the tomb of Sir John Cocks of Cowle, Knight—

"Miseremini mei, miseremini mei, saltem vos, amici mei, quia manus Domini tetegit me."

1678. MERTON, WORCESTERSHIRE. (North wall of chancel).

"Thomas Tompkins, S.T.P. Died Aug. 20, 1678. Aged 87. Cujus corpus huc translatum Hic subtus quiescit."

1679. KEMSEY, WORCESTERSHIRE.

"Here lyeth the Body of William Acton, esquire, of Little Wolverton, in the parish of Stoulton, in the county of Worcester, the son of Thomas Acton, Esquire, of the same place, by Elizabeth his wife, daughter of John Weeden, Esquire, of Sarsden, in Oxfordshire. He married Barbara, daughter of John Vincent, Esquire, Bencher of the Society of Gray's-Inn, and had by her, one only child, William Acton, Esquire, now living: He died April 12, 1679. aged 39. Pray for his soul."

APPENDIX XI.

1680. ST. ASAPH CATHEDRAL.

"Exuviæ Isaaci Asaphensis Episcopi, in manum Domini depositæ, in spem lætæ resurrectionis per sola Christi merita. O vos transeuntes in domum Domini, domum orationis, orate pro conservo vestro, ut inveniat misericordiam in die Domini." (Bishop Barrow died at Shrewsbury June 24th, 1680, and was buried July 1st of the same year).

1684. MARSTON BUTLER'S, WARWICKSHIRE.

"William Woodward. Died Aug. 24, 1684." The inscription ends thus: "Abi, et ora pro anima sua, Viator."

1684. ASTWOOD, BUCKINGHAMSHIRE.

"Here under lieth the body of Samuel Cranmer, Esq. He was born at Aulcester, in the County of Warwick, about the year 1595, and died Ano. 1640. He descended in a direct line from Richard Cranmer, second son of John Cranmer, elder brother to Thomas, Archbishop of Canterbury. The antiquity of this Family is to be found in Parker's *De] Ant: Eccles: Britan*: and in Goodwin's *De Præsul: Ang*: etc. . . . . Here lyeth also Mary, his second wife. She was born at Hackney in August, 1604, and died in April, 1684. . . . . . Hoc posuit momentum Cæsar Woodals Cranmer, miles, in patris et matris sui memoriam, An. Dom. 1685, annoque primo Jacobi Secundi Regis. Defunctorum este memores ut in pace requiescant."

1685—1712. ILMINGTON, WARWICKSHIRE.

"Joan, wife of Richard Canning, of Foxcote, Died 27 April, 1685, and Apollonia, the wife of Francis Canning, Gent. Died 24 Jan., 1712. Requiescant in pace."

1686. TEMPLE GRAFTON, WARWICKSHIRE.

"Here lyeth the Body of Mrs. Ann Sheldon, the wife of

Blaze Sheldon, Gent. She deceased June y⁰ 6th, 1686, aged 57. Requiescat in pace."

1687. UPTON WARREN, WORCESTERSHIRE.

" Mrs. Elizabeth Flatebury, widow, died July 21, 1684. R.I.P."

1689. TAMWORTH, WARWICKSHIRE.

" Here lyeth interred the body of Clement Fisher, late of Wilncoat, gent., he maryed Ann, the daughter of John Savage, Senior, of Wilncoat, Gent. His second wife was Elizabeth, the daughter of Humphrey Arden, Gent., of the Family of Parkhall, in Warwickshire. God grant us a joyfull Resurrection. Amen. He dyed Sep. the 8, 1689. Aged 77."

(Dugdale's " Warwickshire," vol. ii. p. 1140.)

1695. BATH ABBEY.

"Here lies the body of Barkeley Carne, Gentleman, who dyed the 28th of Aprill, 1695. Cujus animæ prop'ietur Deus. Under this stone lyes also the body of Mary Carne . . . . . who dyed the 24th of May, 1696. Cujus animæ prop'ietur Deus."

1699. WHITCHURCH, BUCKS.

" Here lieth the Body of Thomas Scott, who lived at Crisloe, and departed this life on the 23rd day of April, 1699, aged 63 years.

" Since, Lord, thou hast been pleased
To call my body to the earth,
Do let my soul return to Thee
From whom it had its birth."
R. I. P.

1700. ST. MARY'S, ISLINGTON.

On a monument to the memory of William Taylor, who died . . . . . 1700—

" Sleep, then, blest man, till this Thy body be
Raised from the dust to immortality ;
That soul and body may, rejoined again,
With Christ, in perfect bliss, for ever reign."

1701. NORTHMOOR, OXFORDSHIRE.

The following inscription is cut upon an open railing, which was worked into the front of a gallery erected before the bell-loft or ringing-stage :—

> "Richard Lydall gave a new bell
> And built this bell-loft free;
> And then he said, before he died,
> Let ringers pray for me.
> 1701."

He did not die till 1721.

1702. KEMSEY, WORCESTERSHIRE.

"Barbara Vincent, widow of John Vincent, Esquire. Died Aug. 3, 1702, aged 84. Pray for her soul."

1702. CHESHAM, BUCKS.

"Here lyeth Ioyce, the wife of Edward Arundell, of Cornwall, Gent., and niece unto Sir Thomas Arundell, of Chesham. She died in London ye last of May, 1702, and desired to be buried here amongst her Relations. Requiescat in pace."

1704. KIDDERMINSTER, WORCESTERSHIRE.

"Here was laid the body of Capel Hanbury, Esq. May it rest, as he lived and died, in peace, in the 79th year of his age, 14th January, 1704."

1705. COSSEY, NORFOLK.

"Hic jacet Dnã. Elizabetha Englefeilde . . . . . vitam Christianam transactam Christiano fine conclusit . . . . . . Martii die 16. Anno Dni, 1705. Ætatis suæ 70. Requiescat in pace."

1705. OXBURGH, NORFOLK.

"I. H. S. Here lyeth ye Body of Jane, the wife of Richard Martin, who departed this life ye 1st day of February, 1705. May she rest in peace. Amen.

1711. SOLIHULL, WARWICK.

"Mary March, wife of William March. Departed this life the 2nd of June, Anno Dni. 1711. Requiescat in pace."

(Dugdale's "Warwickshire," vol. ii. p. 946.)

"Peter William March departed this life Jany. 4, 1718. Ætatis suæ 67. Cujus animæ propicietur Deus."

(Dugdale's "Warwickshire," vol. ii. p. 946.)

1712. KEMSEY, WORCESTERSHIRE.

"Thomas Vincent, Esq., Barrister-at-Law. Died Aug. 30, 1712, aged 62. Pray for his soul."

1713. UPTON WARREN, WORCESTERSHIRE.

"Here lies the Body of Mary Harrington, late wife to Charles Harrington, Esq., of Hytonhey, in Lancashire, and daughter of John Arden, who died Feb. 3, 1713, in the 25th year of her age. May she rest in peace. Amen."

1713. NEWLAND, GLOUCESTERSHIRE. (Gravestone, Churchyard).

"Here lyeth ye Body of Mary ye wife of John White, of Collford, who departed this Life ye 17 Day of September, 1713. Let her soul rest in peace."

1715. BRILL, BUCKS.

"Near this place lieth the body of Mary Belson, wife of Maurice Belson, of this parish of Brill, Esq., who died May 6, 1715. Her great charity to the poor has, we hope in the mercy of God, rendered her happy in heaven, and left her memory precious upon earth. May she rest in peace. Amen."

1716.

"Here lyeth the Body of Thomas Canning, gent., one of the younger sons of Richard Canning, of Foxcoate, within this parish, Gent., who marryed Mary, the daughter of Thomas

Sheppard, of Long Compton, Gent. He departed this life the 26 of July, 1716. Cujus animæ propicietur Deus."

On another inscription to persons of the same family there occurs " Cujus familiæ propicietur Deus."

(Dugdale's " Warwickshire," vol. i. p. 630.)

1717. WOOTTEN WAWEN, WARWICKSHIRE.

    Turberville Needham, gent. (mural monument).

" Corpus hic jacet, ut autem Spiritus in die Dñi. misericordiam consequatur tu interim adprecare, Viator Catholice, ut conservus tuus sempiterna requiescat in pace."

(Dugdale's " Warwickshire," vol. ii. p. 814.)

1717. UPTON, NOTTINGHAMSHIRE.

" Here lyes William Oglethorpe, who died Aug. 14, 1717. God be merciful to Him, give him rest, and grant him a joyfull resurrection to life everlasting."

1719. SPETCHLEY, WORCESTERSHIRE.

" Here lyeth the body of Thomas Berkeley, of Spetchley, Esq., who departed this life the 5th day of August, 1719, in the 67th year of his age. Requiescat in pace."

1719. WESTON UNDERWOOD, BUCKS. (Chancel floor).

" Here lies the Body of Nicholas Fortescue, Esq., descended from the Ancient Family of the Fortescues of Salden, in the County of Bucks, who departed this life on the 18th of October, Anno 1719.

> " Eighty-three years he lived—to die,
> Then died—to live eternally.

" Requiescat in pace. Amen."

1720. PERSHORE, WORCESTERSHIRE.

" Here lyeth the Body of Dame Margaret Hazelwood, beloved wife of Sir Thomas Hazelwood, Knight, of Wick, in this parish, who departed this life Jan. 17, 1720, aged 58. May she rest in peace."

1720. SUNNINGWELL, BERKS.

"John Denham, obiit June 4, 1720. Ætat. 60. Requiescat in pace.
"This peaceful grave my bones shall keep,
Until the judgment day;
Then raise me, Lord, from my long sleep,
And give life to this clay."

1721. KEMSEY, WORCESTERSHIRE.

"Margaret, the wife of William Acton, Esq., of Little Woolverton. Died Oct. 24, 1721, aged 40 years. Ora pro anima."

1722. SWAVESEY, CAMBRIDGESHIRE.

"Stay, traveller, and drop a tear for the sudden and unexpected Death of Dorothy Stacey, the wife of Berry Dodson, of this Parish, who (if the innocence of her life ye least spotted with faults, and her pious conversation can avail) joyfully waits for the blessed sentence. And in gratitude to her memory her disconsolate Husband hath placed this here. She dyed March ye 28, 1722, in the 25 year of her age. Requiescat in pace."

1725. KEMSEY, WORCESTERSHIRE.

"William Acton, Esq., of Little Woolverton. He Died July 16, 1725, aged 49. Pray for his soul."

1727. CLAWORTH, NORTHAMPTONSHIRE.

"Mary Dickenson, died Oct. 14, 1727.
"God Almighty raise her up again
At the Last Great day of all. Amen."

1727. HENGRAVE, SUFFOLK.

On the monument of Sir Thomas Gage, Baronet, who died Feb. 8, 1727, the inscription concludes with "R. I. P."

1728. CROWLAND ABBEY CHURCH, LINCOLNSHIRE. (South wall).

"Beneath lieth MARY, the Wife of ROBERT DARBY, who dep. this life Jan. ye 19th, 1728-9. AGED 80 YEARS. Cujus Animæ propitieiur [sic] Deus."

1729. MURSLEY, BUCKS.

"Hic jacet Maria Huddleston, filia Richardi Bostock Armigeri de Wixhall in Comitatu Salopiæ, Uxor Henrici Huddleston Armigeri De Lawston in Comitatu Cantabrigiæ. Obiit. Die 31° Augusti. Anno Dom. MDCCXXIX. Requiescat in pace."

1729. MURSLEY CHURCH, BUCKS.

"Hic jacet perillustris Dominus Franciscus Fortescue de Salden, Eques Auratus, in Comitatu Buckinghamiæ. Obiit die 9 Novembris, Anno Domini 1729. Anno ætatis 67. Requiescat in pace."

1729. GREAT MISSENDEN, BUCKS.

"Hon. Robert Dormer, died April 29th, 1729.

"He was beloved by rich and poor,
May his soul rest for evermore."

1729. HARLTON, CAMBRIDGESHIRE.

"Here lyeth the Body of John Smith, who died Nov. 29, 1729, aged 70 yeares. May he rest in peace and rise in glory. Amen.

"With speed amend and make no more delay,
And often think upon your dying day:
And pray to God your sins may be forgiven,
That so your soul may rest with Christ in Heaven."

1730. ELMEDON, WARWICKSHIRE.

"Anne Mayne died July . . . . 1730. God give her soul' rest and a joyful resurrection in the flesh. Amen."

1736. TOWERSEY, BUCKS.

"Roger North, yeoman, died Jan. 2, 1738, lieth here, whom God rest and raise up again at the last great day, through Jesus Christ our Lord. Amen.

"My time is come, my days are spent,
They were but short, they were but lent;
And now I have returned to dust,
God raise me up amongst the just."

1738. ALL SAINTS', WORCESTER.

Thomas Chetle, of the Wall House, Esq. Died May 5, 1738. "God give him peace and a joyfull resurrection in Christ Jesus. Amen."

1741. STOCK HARWARD, ESSEX.

"Here lieth the body of Elizabeth, the wife of Mr. John Mason, and daughter of Mr. Thomas Augier, who departed this life May y⁰ 24th, 1741, in the 26 year of her age. To whom God grant rest. Amen."

1748. POCKLINGTON, YORKSHIRE. (Churchyard.)
George Lee, Gent. . . . . . 1748.

> "For him whose corps reposeth here
> Pray we to Him who heareth prayer;
> Give, Lord, thy peace in Abraham's breast,
> Grant light divine, Eternal Rest.
> Thus all who pray, through Jesus' sake,
> Shall see His face when they awake. Amen.
>
> "The memory of y⁰ just is blest."

1748. HENGRAVE, SUFFOLK.

On the monument of Henry Jermyn Bond, and the Viscountess Gage. The former died Feb. 20, 1748. The inscription concludes with " R. I. P."

1750. ST. NICHOLAS', LIVERPOOL.

"Margaret Coates died June 27, 1750, aged 80 years.
> "Oh, may y⁰ glorious resurrection be
> Eternal happiness to thee and me."

1751. TISBURY, WILTSHIRE.

"Hic jacet Hubertus Hacon. Obiit Maii nono, Anno Dñi 1751. Requiescat in pace."

1753. ST. ANNE'S, MANCHESTER. (Churchyard.)

" ✠ Here lie interred the remains (which through mortality are at present corrupt, but which shall one day most surely be raised again to immortality, and put on incorruption), of Thomas Deacon, the greatest of sinners, and the most unworthy of Primitive Bishops, who died the 16th of Feb. 1753, in the 56th year of his age. And of Sarah, his wife, who died July 4th, 1754, in the 45th year of her age. . . . . . The Lord grant unto the faithful here underlying that they may find mercy of the Lord in that day."

1755—1762. SHERMANBURY, SUSSEX.

"Ες τουτο τις οριων
Ευσεβης ιστο.

"To the memory of the truly Rev^d. John Bear, D.D., Rector of this parish, and resident above 50 years, who died March 9, 1762, aged 88 years. A man of exemplary piety and learning, a public testimony of which the clergy gave in choosing him one of their Representatives in Convocation.

"And of Mary, his beloved wife, who died April 23, 1755, aged 80 years.

"The Lord grant unto them that they
May find mercy in the Lord in that Day.

"This monument was erected by her son, John Burton, D.D., 1767."

1757. NORTHFIELD, WORCESTERSHIRE.

"Ann Lloyd, wife of Thomas Lloyd. Departed this life Oct. 22, 1757, aged 40 years.

"Peace to her dear remains! May th' all-kind Power
Who heard our vows, and blest our nuptial hour,
Accept the tribute of my grateful heart,
And re-unite us where we ne'er shall part."
R. I. P.

1760. BLETCHLEY, BUCKS.

On a monument within the altar rails, in memory of Browne Willis, Esq., the celebrated antiquary, the inscription concludes thus :—

"Obiit 8 die Februarii, A.D. 1760. Ætatis suæ 78.
"O Christe Soter et Judex
Huic Peccatorum primo
Misericors et propitius esto."

1762. ST. NICHOLAS', LIVERPOOL.

"I. H. S. Here lieth the Body of Mary, wife of Joseph Roberts, who departed this life on the 17th day of February, 1762. Aged 36 years. Requiescat in pace."

1763. RICOT CHAPEL, NEAR THAME, OXFORDSHIRE. (Floor of nave.)

"✠In Memory of Sir John Collins, who died yᵉ 22nd of June, 1763, In yᵉ 74 year of his age. Requiescat in pace."

1763. TETSWORTH, OXFORDSHIRE.

"John Fettyplace, died Aug. 4, 1763, aged 47 yeeres.
"His body here in dust doth rest,
Sin caused that Earth claimed it as due,
God give him Peace in Heaven blest,
Christ give him Light, make all things new."

1763—1765. NORTON, DURHAM.

"To the memory of Timothy Mawman and Margaret his wife. He born Feb. 5, 1682, Died March 10th, 1763, aged 80. She born Oct. 10, 1679, Died Oct. 16, 1765, aged 86. God grant them a happy resurrection. Amen."

1765. THAME, OXON. (Churchyard.)

". . . . . Richard Striblehill . . . . died . . . .
1765, in the 40th year of his age.

"A friend to rich, a friend to poor,
God rest his soul for evermore:
And grant him, upon Abraham's breast,
A home of peace, a house of rest,
Through Christ who died, but rose once more,
Thus opening wide high Heaven's door,
That man might live for evermore."

APPENDIX XI.

1766. QUAINTON, BUCKINGHAMSHIRE. (Churchyard.)
"Ralph Robinson. Departed this life May 17, 1766.
> "We dye to live, who liv'd to dye,
> Through Jesus Christ; and so do I.
> So Lord whom I have loved best
> Grant me thy light and give me rest."

1769. HORTON, DEVON.
An inscription to the Pastons, Courtenays, Chichesters of Arlington and Throgmortons—one date on which is January 11th, 1769—contains the prayer, " Requiescat in pace."

1770. CLATFORD, HAMPSHIRE.
"Robert Hutchings, Gent. Died Ianuarie ye 7, 1770. Requiescat in pace. O Lord, raise me up again at the Last Day."

1770. ST. NICHOLAS', LIVERPOOL.
"I. H. S. Thomas Williams departed this Life 16th day of Dec., 1770, aged 60 years. Requiescat in pace. Amen."

1772. STOWE, SHROPSHIRE.
"John Baker, Gent. Born 16 Oct., 1698, died 18 Nov. 1772, aged 74.
> "He lived to thee, O God; in thee he dies,
> In trust of thee, O Christ, he hopes to rise,
> Life's sorrows o'er, Temptation's power is dead,
> And what was earthly fills this narrow bed.
> We who remain be instant in our prayer
> To ask the rest for him we hope to share.
> Lord Jesus, give new life for ever blest,
> Thy peace bestow, increasing heavenly rest:
> Grant to all faithful souls who hope in Thee
> Thy love to know, thy Face and Wounds to see.
> Amen."

1778. NEWLAND, GLOUCESTERSHIRE. (South Porch.)
"John Probyn, Esq., of Newland, died March 22nd, 1778, aged 70. On his soul God have mercy. Amen."

1774. MANCHESTER CATHEDRAL.

" ✠ Propitiare Domine animabus famulorum Tuorum qui nos præcesserunt cum signo fidei. Requiescant in pace.

"Here resteth the body of Mary, wife of Charles Bradshaw, who departed this life Oct. 10, 1774, age 24 years. And their daughter, Nov. 11, 1778, age 9 days. Mary, their daughter, departed this life, March 27, 1811, aged 39 years."

1780. BURTON-UPON-STATHER, LINCOLNSHIRE.

"In memory of Thomas Hollingworth, who departed this life April ye 5th, 1780, Aged 68 years.

"Let angels guard thy sleeping dust,
  Till Christ shall come to raise the just ;
  Then mayst thou wake with sweet surprise,
And in thy Saviour's image rise."

1782. ALGARKIRK, LINCOLNSHIRE.

"Mary Michaell, spinster, who died Nov. 19, 1782, aged 69. Fili Dei, miserere mei."

1784. ST. MARY'S THAME, OXFORDSHIRE. (Floor of Choir.)

"Here lies interr'd the Body of Ann, Daughter of the Rev^d. John Newborough, Vicar of this Parish, who died Octr. 6th, 1784. Requiescat in pace."

1787. ST. OSWALD'S, DURHAM.

"I. H. S. Here lies

"Henry Gelston, bereaved of life,
  Who had many troubles in his life,
  His flesh to rot, his bones decay,
The Lord have mercy on his soul, I pray.

"He died the 7th Day of Iune, 1787, aged 61 years."

1794. CATHEDRAL CLOISTER, SALISBURY. (East side.)

" ✠ To the Memory of The Rev. Richard Turner, who died on the 14th of May, 1794, aged 77 years. R. I. P."

APPENDIX XI.

1795. MISTLEY, ESSEX.

"In Memory of Elizabeth, the wife of Thomas Stafford, who departed this life May 16th, 1795. Aged 45 years.

> "I, Elizabeth Stafford, wish a happy resurrection to my ashes.
> While I was alive among mortals a little satisfied me,
> Now I am dead and alone in my grave I am content with less.
> I neither knew myself what I was, nor do thou inquire,
> Traveller, who ever thou art. If thou be pious pray for me,
> And pass on. Farewell—and live mindful of Death.
> Living I provided this epitaph—knowing I must die.
> The birth and life of mortals are nothing but toil to death."

1803. RAMSBURY, WILTSHIRE.

"In the hope of a glorious resurrection, through His Beloved Redeemer, Here resteth the Body of Ambrose Browne, who slept the sleep of death upon August 8, 1803.

> "Here sleepeth, Lord, a servant true,
>   By grace from Heaven blest;
> Thou mercy have upon his soul,
>   And grant him peace and rest."

1805. ST. MARY'S, DURHAM.

"1805, Jan. 1st, put a period to the cares of Robert Paxton, aged 56. He was dear to every friend of Integrity and Independence. His enemies were the enemies of Virtue. A widow's consolation for the loss of temporal happiness is an Hope that, with Him She may Rest in Peace and Rise in Glory."

1808. THAME, OXFORDSHIRE. (Floor, south aisle.)

"H. S. E. Richardi Smith, Arm. Com. Buck. Vice-prolegat. Obiit die xv°. Septembris. A.S. MDCCCviij. R. I. P."

1809. ST. OSWALD'S, DURHAM.

"Erected in memory of Mary Miller, Daughter of Ambrose

Miller of Shincliffe. Died 18th . . . . 1809. Aged 21 years.

> "Sleep here, fair saint, secure from mortal woes,
> And sheltering angels guard thy safe repose;
> Let pious Care each bold attempt restrain,
> That no rude hand thy sacred dust profane:
> Rest undisturb'd till Jesus bid thee rise,
> Then quit the tomb, and wake to endless joys."

1810. SPETISBURY, DORSETSHIRE.

"Ralph Southworth, died July 13th, 1810, aged 63.

> "O thou who here approachest, guest or friend,
> Pour forth one prayer, not heedless of thy end,
> That God in mercy to his eyes display
> The opening visions of eternal day."

1817. STOKE POGES, BUCKS.

On the monument of George Brooks, who died April 3, 1817, aged 76, the inscription concludes—"in humble hope that through the merits of his Redeemer he may obtain forgiveness of his sins, and be made partaker of the Kingdom of Heaven."

1817—1832. PENN, BUCKS.

On a tablet to the memory of Thomas Carter and his daughters, the former of whom died in 1832 and the latter in 1817, the inscription concludes with "Requiescant in pace."

1826. STOKE POGES, BUCKS.

"In Memory of Grace Elizabeth Falconer Fulman, who departed this life the 2th of April, 1826, aged 80 years. Requiescat in pace."

1830—1840. ST. ETHELBURGA'S, BISHOPSGATE. (South Aisle, Mural Tablet.)

"Sacred to the memory of Mr. Charles Johnson, late of the Parish of St. Botolph, Bishopsgate, who died Sep. 15, 1840, aged 61 years. Also of Elizabeth, his wife, who died Nov.

10, 1830, aged 50 years. Their remains, together with those of the three infant children, lie in the burial-ground of this church. In pace requiescant."

1838. TURRIFF, ABERDEENSHIRE.

"This tablet, erected by his surviving sister, is Sacred to the Memory of the Right Reverend Father in God, Alexander Jolly, D.D., Bishop of Moray, whose body sleeps in the churchyard of this parish, where he first exercised the ministerial office, having been pastor of this congregation from 1777 to 1788. He was afterwards removed to Fraserburgh, where he lived as priest and bishop forty-nine years, pointing out, by his faithful teaching, the way to heaven to those committed to his charge, and leading them in it by his bright example. Deeply learned in the ancient wisdom of the Church, he taught his flock to adhere to the old faith of Catholic and Apostolic Truth; while by a life of holiness, devotion, and self-denial, he gave to a declining age a pattern of the primitive piety. Living in a holy celibate, he renounced the world, without forsaking its duties: devoting his days and nights to preparation for heaven. He conversed with God in retirement, and was taken to his rest when no mortal eye was near to witness his departing moments, having been found on the morning of the Feast of St. Peter, 1838, calmly reposing in death. R. I. P. Born, 1756, ordained deacon, 1776, and priest, 1777. Consecrated, 1796."

1839. EASTRY, KENT. (Churchyard.)

"Thomas Mann, Eldest Son of Thomas and Elizabeth Mann, d. 28th June, 1839, aged 20 y^s.

"In love he lived, in peace he died,
In hope with God he shall abide."

1839. EVESHAM, WORCESTERSHIRE. (Churchyard.)

"In remembrance of Samuel Amos, who died May 3rd, 1862,

aged 80 years. Also of Maria, wife of Samuel Amos, who died May 29th, 1839, aged 56 years. R. I. P."

1841—1853. Thame, Oxfordshire. (East wall of Chancel.)*

"Hic jacet corpus Frederici Lee, Art. Mag., primum e Collegio S. Mariæ Magdalenæ, deinde Mertonensis, alumni, istius ecclesiæ per annos octodecim quondam sacerdotis, qui obiit die IV. Nov. anno salutis MDCCCXLI. Juxta portam meridionalem dormit Maria, uxor ejusdem, quæ obiit die Maii XXVII., A.S. MDCCCLIII. Quorum animabus et omnium fidelium defunctorum propitietur Deus. Amen."

1848. Cemetery, Lyme Regis, Dorset.

"Hic jacet Henricus Norrington, Presbyter Capellæ S. Mariæ apud Axeminster, qui obiit viii. Dei. A.D. MDCCCXLviij. Ætatis suæ anno XL. Jesu Domine miserere."

1854. St. Mary Magdalene College, Oxford. (Chapel.)

"Hic jacet corpus venerabilis viri Martini Josephi Routh, S. T. P. Rectoris Parochiæ de Tylehurst cum Theale et hujus Collegii Præsidis. Obiit die xxii. Decemb. Anno Domini MDCCCLIV. Ætatis suæ c. Cujus animæ propitietur Deus."

1859. West Hackney, Parish Church. (On a brass plate fastened to the inside of the stone pulpit.)

"✠ In memoriā Johan. Donnison notar. qui obiit xvi die Novemb. anno MDCCCLVIII. dni. et ætatᵉ. suæ LXVII. cui animæ propicietur Deus. Amen."

---

* Examples of Prayers for the Dead on monumental memorials have become so numerous and common during the last thirty years, that no attempt is made to chronicle them here. Some few representative specimens are alone given, to show their harmony in point of faith and sentiment with præ-Reformation custom.

1863. MICHAELCHURCH, SOMERSETSHIRE.

"Here lyeth the body of Sir F. W. Slade, of Maunsel, Bart., deceased 8 August, 1863. To whose soul may the Lord give peace. Amen. ✠ Jesu Mercy."

1866. HURSLEY, HAMPSHIRE. (Churchyard).

"Here rests in peace the body of John Keble, Vicar of this parish, who departed this life Maunday Thursday, March 29, 1866."

"Here rests in peace the body of Charlotte, wife of John Keble, who departed this life May 11, anno Domini 1866."

"Requiem æternam dona eis Domine et lux perpetua luceat eis."

1867. EASTRY, KENT. (Church.)

"In memory of William Boteler, Son of the above William Fuller Boteler. Born 23rd October, 1810. Died 6th July, 1867."

"Remember me, O my God, for good."

1870. CREECH ST. MICHAEL, SOMERSET. (Sanctuary.)

"In memory of Joseph Duncan Ostrehan, B.A., Vicar of this parish, son of Joseph Ostrehan, of St. Michael's, Barbadoes, Esq., who died September 11, 1870, aged 71. Also of Anne wife of the above, who was the fifth daughter of Robert Withy, of Broad-oak, in the county of Kent, Esq. She died March 21, 1870, aged 72. 'The Lord grant unto them that they may find mercy of the Lord in that day.'"

INDEX OF NAMES TO THE MONUMENTAL INSCRIPTIONS FROM 1550 TO 1870.

Name	Page		Name	Page
Acton, Margaret	326		Cave, Anthony	307
Acton, William	326		Chambers, Arthur	309
Acton, William	320		Chetle, Thomas	328
Adams, Ralph	315		Chetwind, John	313
Amos, Maria	336		Chetwind, Margerie	313
Amos, Samuel	335		Cheyne, Hon. Wenefride	308
Arundell, Joyce	323		Cheyne, Robert	306
Baker, John	331		Coates, Margaret	328
Barkeley, Lady Catherine	311		Cocks, George	320
Barrow, Bishop Isaac	321		Cocks, Sir John	320
Bastard, Thomas	313		Collins, Sir John	330
Baylie, Elizabeth	316		Cottle, Thomas	310
Bear, John	329		Courtenay, Sir William	317
Bear, Mary	329		Cowper, Robert	317
Beaumon, George	311		Cranmer, Mary	321
Belson, Mary	324		Cranmer, Samuel	321
Benett, Bishop	316		Crouch, William	314
Berkeley, Thomas	325		Darby, Mary	326
Bishop, John	313		Deacon, Bishop Thomas	329
Blackwelle, Benedict	317		Denham, John	326
Blount, Sir Edward	317		Denton, Alexander	312
Blundell, Alice	312		Dickenson, Mary	326
Bond, Henry Jermyn	328		Dodson, Dorothy	326
Boteler, William	337		Donnison, John	336
Bradshaw, Mary	332		Dormer, Hon. Robert	318
Brooks, George	334		Dormer, Michael	319
Browne, Ambrose	333		Dormer, Hon. Robert	327
Buckton, Ralph	306		Drury Family	306
Canning, Apollonia	321		Englefeilde, Elizabeth	323
Canning, Joan	321		Englefield, Susannah	319
Canning, Thomas	324		Est, Henry	314
Canon, John	313		Fenton, Sir John	309
Carne, Barkeley	322		Ferrers, Erasmus	315
Carne, Mary	322		Fettyplace, John	330
Carter, Thomas	334		Fisher, Clement	322
Catesby, Francis	309		Fisher, Elizabeth	322

APPENDIX XI.

Name	PAGE	Name	PAGE
Fitzwilliam, Humphry (and others)	307	Lydall, Richard	323
Flatebury, Elizabeth	322	Lynch, Simon	318
Fortescue, Francis	327	Magnus, Thomas	306
Fortescue, Nicholas	325	Mann, Thomas	335
Fulman, Grace E. F.	334	March, Mary	324
Gage, Sir Thomas, Baronet	326	March, Peter William	324
Gage, Viscountess	328	Martin, Jane	323
Gelston, Henry	332	Mason, Elizabeth	328
Giffard, Thomas	305	Mawman, Timothy	330
Gyfford, Edward	314	Mayne, Anne	327
Gyfford, Frances	314	Michaell, Mary	332
Gyfford, John	309	Middlemore, Anne	316
Hacon, Hubert	328	Middlemore, Frances	316
Hanbury, Capel	323	Middlemore, Humphrey	316
Harrington, Mary	324	Miller, Mary	333
Harvy, Elizabeth	316	Molineux, Viscountess	319
Hawkworth, William	315	Monson, Ann	319
Hazelwood, Dame Margaret	325	Needham, Turberville	325
Heath, Charles	318	Newborough, Ann	332
Hodges, Arthur	320	Norrington, Henry	336
Hollingworth, Thomas	332	North, Roger	327
How, Nathaniel	317	Oglethorpe, William	325
Huband, Nicholas	307	Oldnall, Isabel	307
Huddleston, Mary	327	Oldnall, John	307
Huggeford, Henry	313	Ostrehan, Anne	337
Hurst, Sir Leonard	308	Ostrehan, Joseph Duncan	337
Hutchings, Robert	331	Parsons, Myles	315
Johnson, Charles	334	Pastons, Monument of the	331
Jolly, Bishop Alexander	335	Paxton, Robert	333
Keble, Charlotte	337	Payne, Henry	310
Keble, John	337	Payne, William	310
King, Richard	315	Peckham, Reynold	305
Kynnersley, Nicholas	315	Perrot, Anne	319
Langley, Joane	314	Peyton, Elizabeth	319
Lee, Benedict	309	Pontesbury, George	305
Lee, Frederick	336	Probyn, John	331
Lee, Mary	336	Ramsey, Margaret	308
Lee, George	328	Ramsey, Thomas	308
Lee, William	303	Riddel, Jone	314
Lloyd, Ann	329	Riddel, William	314
Logan, John	317	Roberts, Mary	330
		Robinson, Ralph	331

Robyns, John	308
Robynson, Margaret	308
Roper, Helen	312
Roper, Richard	312
Routh, Martin Joseph . . .	336
Ryddel, Isabel	310
Scott, Thomas	322
Sheldon, Ann	321
Shirley, Sir Robert	318
Slade, Sir F. W.	337
Smith, John	327
Smith, Richard	333
Smith, Thomas	311
Smith, Thomas	312
Southworth, Ralph	334
Stafford, Elizabeth	333
Striblehill, Richard	330
Taylor, William	322
Temple, Peter	316
Tompkins, Thomas	320
Towne, Clement	311
Turner, Richard	332
Vincent, Barbara	323
Vincent, Thomas	324
Wadham, Nicholas	314
Waring, Charles	319
Warre, John	312
Webb, Henry	306
Westwick, Anne	307
White, Mary	324
White, Myles	315
Whyte, Anne	307
Whyte, John	310
Whytney, Richard	307
Williams, Alice	311
Williams, Thomas	331
Willis, Browne	329
Woodward, William	321
Wright, Christopher	313

APPENDIX XII.

JUDGMENT OF THE RIGHT HONOURABLE SIR HERBERT JENNER FUST, KNT., D.C.L., DELIVERED IN THE ARCHES COURT OF CANTERBURY IN THE CASE OF BREEKS *VERSUS* WOOLFREY, NOV. 19, 1838.

VERBATIM REPORT.

"THIS case was very fully and elaborately argued, and the Court thought it due to the arguments which were addressed to it, to take time to consider of its judgment, and to look into the authorities which were cited. It is a cause in which the office of the judge has been promoted by the Rev. John Breeks, vicar of the parish of Carisbrooke, in the Isle of Wight, against Mary Woolfrey, of that parish, widow, citing her to answer certain articles 'touching and concerning her soul's health, and for the lawful correction of her manners and excesses,' which is the usual style and language of the proceeding of the Court, 'and more especially for having erected, or caused to be erected, a certain tombstone, in the churchyard of the same parish, to the memory of Joseph Woolfrey, late of the parish, deceased, with a certain inscription thereon, contrary to the Articles, Canons, and Constitutions, as to the doctrine and discipline of the Church of England.'

"The cause is brought by letters of request from the diocese of Winchester (this Court having no original jurisdiction), the Chancellor of that diocese having referred the matter to this Court, as he had a right to do. The offence is one clearly of ecclesiastical cognizance, and it was not denied; nay, it was admitted that, if the inscriptions were of the character attributed to them in the citation, no person had a right to erect a tombstone with such inscriptions impugning the doctrine and discipline of the Church of England, and that a person so offending is liable to be punished, and the tombstone to be removed.

"The question then is, whether the inscriptions have been properly described in the citation; the additional offence laid in the articles, that the stone was erected without leave of the incumbent, does not, in my opinion, arise on the face of the citation; the question is therefore confined to the legality of the inscriptions. The inscriptions set forth in the articles being: 'Pray for the soul of J. Woolfrey,' and 'It is a holy and wholesome thought to pray for the dead' (2 Mac. xii. 46).

"This being a criminal proceeding, the burden of proving the charge lies on the promoter, and the clergyman of the parish is not an improper person to proceed in such a case; for to the incumbent belongs the superintendence of the church and churchyard, and it is his duty to take care that no inscriptions should be placed there which could be made the means of disseminating doctrines inconsistent with those of the established religion.

"The articles purport to state the law, and the facts to which the law is to be applied. The first article, with reference to the inscription, alleges that, by the Twenty-second Article of the Church of England, agreed upon in 1562, it is declared that, 'the Romish doctrine concerning purgatory, pardons,' and other things therein mentioned, is 'a fond thing vainly invented, and grounded upon no warranty of Scripture, but rather repugnant to the Word of God.' That all persons erecting, or causing to be erected, in the churchyard of any parish any tomb or headstone, containing any inscription contrary to the doctrine and discipline of the Church of England and to the Articles of the said Church, the persons so doing ought not only to be peremptorily monished immediately to remove the same, but also be duly corrected and punished; and this proposition has not been denied by the other side. The second article sets forth the facts that, notwithstanding the premises, Mrs. Woolfrey did erect a tomb or headstone, with the inscriptions before-mentioned, which it alleges to be contrary to the doctrine and discipline of the Church of England, and to the Articles, Canons, and Constitutions thereof, and particularly to the said Twenty-second Article; that due notice has been given to her to remove the same, but that she refuses so to do. The third article annexes a copy of the inscriptions, and the articles conclude with praying that she be peremptorily monished to remove the stone, and be canonically corrected and punished, and condemned in the costs.

"The law, then, principally relied on is the Twenty-second Article, although there is a general reference to other Articles, Canons, and Constitutions of the Church, and it is competent to the promoter to refer to the other Articles, and reference was made in the argument to the Thirty-fifth Article on the Homilies, the first book of which was published in the reign of Edward VI., and the second in that of Elizabeth, and particular reference was made to the Seventh Homily on Prayer.

"In the argument in support of the articles, it was argued that the Twenty-second Article, in declaring that the Romish doctrine of Purgatory is repugnant to the Word of God, did in effect declare that the offering of prayers for the dead was also opposed to the Word of God, as constituting part of the doctrine of Purgatory, for that the two were so intimately blended together that it was impossible to separate the one from the other; consequently that an inscription inviting passers-by to pray for the soul of the deceased, and containing the passage from the Maccabees, was an illegal inscription.

"The point, then, upon which the whole question turns is,

whether prayer for the dead is so necessarily connected with the doctrine of Purgatory as to form a part of it? It is no doubt true that the doctrine of Purgatory includes the practice of praying for the dead; but it does not necessarily follow that the converse of the proposition is true—that is, that prayers for the dead necessarily constitute a part of the doctrine of Purgatory as held by the Romish Church. If that point could be made out, there would be an end of the case, and the Court would be bound to monish the party to remove the stone, and to punish her with ecclesiastical censure, and with costs. This was the point to which the counsel directed their arguments, and many authorities were cited, to some of which the Court will presently advert.

"The counsel very properly abstained from entering into the theological part of the question; and it would not be proper for the Court to take upon itself the duty of inquiring whether the doctrine of Purgatory, as received by the Romish Church, is or is not supported by any warranty of Scripture. The law, that is the Twenty-second Article, has expressly stated that that doctrine is 'grounded upon no warranty of Scripture, but is rather repugnant to the Word of God,' and by this law I am bound to govern myself.

"The question then, shortly, is this—Is praying for the dead involved in the doctrine of Purgatory? Now, with a view to deciding that question, the first thing to determine is, What is the doctrine of Purgatory as received in the Romish Church? This may be best ascertained by a reference to the decrees of the General Councils, and to authors who have written on the subject. As far as I have been able to learn, it does not appear that there was any declaration of this doctrine of Purgatory by any General Council until that of Florence, in 1438, which contained the first allusion to the doctrine. This was followed up by a decree of

APPENDIX XII.

the Council of Trent, in 1563, which was a year after the Articles of Religion were set forth by royal authority in this country.

When I state that no mention was made of the doctrine of Purgatory in any General Council previous to that of Florence, I do not mean to say that the doctrine was not received at an earlier period; it would appear, according to the best authorities to which the Court had access, that the notion of Purgatory was first introduced about the fifth or sixth century. Bishop Tomline, in the second volume of his 'Elements of Christian Theology,' states that 'the practice of praying for the dead began in the third century; but it was not till long afterwards that Purgatory was ever mentioned among Christians. It was at first doubtfully received, and was not fully established until the papacy of Gregory the Great, in the beginning of the seventh century.' The doctrine then so introduced, and which is declared by the Twenty-second Article of our Church to be repugnant to the Word of God, is thus described in the 'Catechism of the Council of Trent:' 'Est Purgatorius ignis quo piorum animæ ad definitum tempus cruciatæ expiantur, ut eis in æternam patriam ingressus patere possit, in quam nihil coinquinatum ingreditur.' It was also a part of that doctrine that the pains of Purgatory may be alleviated or shortened by the prayers of the living, by masses, and by thanksgivings. This doctrine being declared by the Church of England to be without warranty of Scripture, the question is, Whether prayer for the dead falls under the same condemnation?

"Now the first argument that suggests itself against this supposition is, that the prayer for the dead is a practice of a much earlier date than the introduction of the doctrine of Purgatory. It clearly appears that the practice of praying for the dead prevailed amongst the early, if not the earliest, Christians, who at that day had no notion of the doctrine of Purgatory. It would be a waste of time to travel through all the authorities which might be referred to to prove not only the prevalence of the practice of praying for the dead long prior to the introduction of Purgatory, but also that the prayers by the primitive Christians for the souls of the departed were offered with a different intention from those who profess the Romish religion. The object of such prayers with the latter was to relieve the souls of the departed from the pains of Purgatory; that of the former was, that the souls might have rest and quiet in the interval between death and the resurrection, and that at the last day they might receive the perfect consummation of bliss; but certainly such prayers had no reference to a state of suffering, in which the souls were supposed to be during the intermediate time. With reference to this point, it will be right to state one or two passages from authors on this subject. Bishop Taylor, in his 'Dissuasive from Popery' (in the tenth volume of Bishop Heber's edition), says: 'There are two great causes of their mistaken pretensions in this article from antiquity. The first is, that the Ancient Churches in their offices, and the Fathers in their writing, did teach and practise respectively prayers for the dead. Now, because the Church of Rome does so too, and more so—relates her prayers to the doctrine of Purgatory and for the souls there detained — her doctors vainly suppose that whenever the holy fathers speak of prayer for the dead, they conclude for Purgatory; which vain conjecture is as false as it is unreasonable; for it is true the fathers did pray for the dead—but how? 'That God should show them mercy, and hasten the resurrection, and give a blessed sentence in the great day.' But then it is also to be remembered that they made prayers, and offered for those who, by the confession of all sides, never were in Purgatory; even for patriarchs and prophets, for the apostles and evangelists, for martyrs and confessors, and especially for the Blessed Virgin Mary. And he cites authorities—Epiphanius, St. Cyril, and others. 'Upon what account,' he adds, 'the fathers did pray for the saints departed, and, indeed, generally for all, it is not now seasonable to discourse; but to say this only, that such general prayers for the dead as those above reckoned, the Church of England never did condemn by any express articles, but left it in the middle. But,' he adds, 'she expressly condemns the doctrine of Purgatory, and consequently all prayers for the dead relating to it.' And in vol. ix., p. 58, he shows that, though the ancient fathers of the Church did sanction prayers for the dead, they did not even know the Romish doctrine of Purgatory. Again, Archbishop Usher, whose opinions upon the subject have been recently reprinted in the 'Tracts for the Times,' says: 'Our Romanists do commonly take it for granted that Purgatory and prayers for the dead be so closely linked together, that the one doth necessarily follow the other: but in so doing they greatly mistake the matter; for howsoever they may deal with their own devices as they please, and link their prayers with their Purgatory as they list, yet shall they never be able to show that the commemoration and prayers for the dead used by the ancient Church had any relation with their Purgatory.'

"Without reference, then, to any other authorities, which are numerous on the point, it is clear that prayers for the dead are not necessarily connected with the doctrine of purgatory, since they were offered up by the Primitive Church long antecedent to the doctrine of Purgatory being received by the Church of Rome.

"But it was said, that, whatever might have been the case in the early ages with respect to the practice of praying for the dead, the Church of England had taken a different view of the subject; and with reference to what had taken place in the earliest time of the Reformation, and subsequently, that though prayers for the dead were not considered, in the first instance, contrary to the principles of the Christian religion, yet that in later times they had been considered as opposed to the principles and doctrines of the Church, as had been shown by the alterations made at different times in its Liturgy.

"In the Primer of Henry VIII., in the Burial and Communion Services, such prayers were used, and in the 'Formula of Faith,' in the time of Henry VIII., prayers for the dead were enjoined as a 'pious and proper work.'

"In the First Prayer Book also of Edward VI., prepared by persons of great eminence and learning, called together by the King to consider the alterations necessary to be made in the public service of the Church, in consequence of the progress of the Reformation of the established religion, such prayers were retained. It is not immaterial to see the manner in which this Prayer Book had been compiled, and I cannot refer to more satisfactory authority than the Act of Parliament by which the book was established, namely, the 2nd and 3rd of Edward VI., chapter 1, which is entitled, 'An Act for Uniformity of Service and Administration of the Sacraments throughout the Realm,' in the preamble of which it is stated that 'with the intent that a uniform, quiet, and godly order should be had, his Highness had appointed the Archbishop of Canterbury, and certain of the most learned and discreet bishops and other learned men of the realm, to consider and ponder the premises, and thereupon having as well eye and respect to the most sincere and pure Christian religion taught by the Scripture, as to the usages in the Primitive Church, should draw and make one convenient and meet order, rite, and fashion of common and open prayer and administration of the sacraments to be had and used in his Majesty's realm of England and Wales;' and with reference to these principles the First

Prayer Book of Edward VI. was drawn up, and in this book prayers for the dead were inserted, although in some degree different from those in the Primer of Henry VIII. Such prayers, therefore, were not considered by those learned persons as connected with the Romish doctrine of Purgatory. But the Second Prayer of Edward VI. was afterwards drawn up, in which these prayers were omitted, and it was argued that they were inconsistent with the doctrine of the Church, as then established, and various authors were referred to to show that they were omitted on that account; and several writers do take that view of the subject. But it is agreed that there is no express prohibition of such prayers; it must, therefore, be shown that they were prohibited by necessary implication. It appears, however, from writers and historians, that these alterations in the Liturgy in the Second Prayer Book of Edward VI. were acceded to principally at the instance of Calvin and Bucer, though on what grounds precisely I have not been able to learn. But there is one authority at least to show that it was not because, in the opinion of the majority of the persons employed in its revision, they were inconsistent with the doctrines of the Church of England.

"The Act of Parliament by which the Second Prayer Book of Edward VI. was established—the 5th and 6th of Edward VI., chapter 1, also entitled 'An Act for the Uniformity of Service and Administration of Sacraments throughout the Realm'—in its recital, which must be taken to express the sentiments of the majority of the legislature, states: 'Where [whereas] there has been a very godly order set forth by the authority of Parliament for common prayer and the administration of the sacraments, to be used in the mother tongue within the Church of England, agreeably to the Word of God and the Primitive Church,' adopting the words of the former Act, which enjoined 'a regard to the religion taught by Scripture, and to the usages of the Primitive

Church,' 'very comfortable to all good people desiring to live in Christian conversation and most profitable to the estate of this realm, upon the which the mercy, favour, and blessing of Almighty God are in nowise so readily and plenteously poured as by common prayer, due using of the sacraments, and often preaching of the Gospel, with the devotion of the hearers,' and it goes on to state that 'yet notwithstanding a great number of people do wilfully abstain and refuse to come to their parish churches, and other places, where common prayer, the administration of the sacraments, and the preaching of the Word of God is used,' and in the fifth section it sets forth, 'and because there hath arisen in the use and exercise of the aforesaid Common Service in the Church heretofore set forth, divers doubts for the fashion and manner of the administration of the same, rather by the curiosity of the ministers and mistakers, than of any other worthy cause, therefore, as well for the more plain and manifest explanation thereof, as for the more perfection of the said order of Common Service, in some places where it is necessary to make the same prayers and fashion of service more earnest and fit to stir Christian people to the true honouring of Almighty God,' and it goes on to set forth that the King and Parliament had caused the Book of Common Prayer 'to be faithfully and godly perused, explained, and made fully perfect.' This Act was repealed by the 1st of Mary, which was itself repealed by the 1st of Elizabeth, chapter 2, which restored the 5th and 6th of Edward VI. Now up to this period of time, it seems that at least there was not any express prohibition of prayers for the dead, nor any notion that they implied a necessary belief in the doctrine of Purgatory, though in consequence of professors of the Romish religion taking advantage of the practice as an argument to support their own doctrine of Purgatory, it was thought proper that the form of prayer should be altered, and those prayers omitted in the public

APPENDIX XII.

service of the Church as not being enjoined (which is admitted) or sanctioned by any warranty of Scripture.

"The authorities seem to go no further than this, to show that the Church discouraged prayers for the dead, but did not prohibit them; and that the Twenty-second Article is not violated by the use of such prayers. The ground on which the Church consented to the omission of these prayers could not, perhaps, be better stated than by Mr. Palmer, in his 'Origines Liturgicæ,' to this effect:—

"'When the custom of praying for the dead begun in the Christian Church has never been ascertained. We find traces of the practice in the second century; and either then or shortly after it appears to have been customary in all parts of the Church. The first person who objected to such a prayer was Aerius, who lived in the fourth century; but his arguments were answered by various writers, and did not produce any effect in altering the immemorial practice of praying for those at rest. Accordingly, from that time, all the Liturgies in the world contain such prayers. Some persons will, perhaps, say, that this sort of prayer is unscriptural, that it infers the Romish doctrine of Purgatory, or something else, which is contrary to the will of God, or the nature of things. But when we reflect that the great divines of the English Church have not taken this ground, and that the Church of England herself has never formally condemned prayers for the dead, but only omitted them in her Liturgy, we may, perhaps, think that there are some other reasons to justify that omission.' And then this learned writer proceeds to state the probable reason of the omission of these prayers in the Liturgy of the English Church —namely, that they might be abused, to the prejudice of the uneducated classes, to the support of the Roman Catholic doctrine of Purgatory. I am, therefore, of opinion, that in this case there has been no violation of the Twenty-second Article of the

Church, so as to call for punishment by ecclesiastical censure. The Twenty-second Article does not prohibit prayers for the dead, unless so far as they necessarily involve the doctrine of Purgatory; and the inscription has not been shown to be a violation of that Article.

"But it is said that other Articles of the Church have been violated, and reference was made to the Thirty-fifth Article, which is to this effect: 'That the Second Book of Homilies contained a godly and wholesome doctrine, and necessary for these times, as doth the former Book of Homilies, which were set forth in the time of Edward VI.; and therefore we judge them to be read in churches by the ministers diligently and distinctly, that they may be understanded by the people.' And it is said, in the Seventh Homily *On Prayer*, the practice of praying for the dead is declared to be an erroneous doctrine; and therefore as the Homilies are directed to be read in churches, for the edification of the people, it must be necessarily inferred that they are forbidden and prohibited by the Church of England. Now, if this were clearly so, it would seem somewhat extraordinary that many divines of the Church should, in the face of these Articles and of the Homilies, have fallen into the error of believing the Church of England had not prohibited prayers for the dead, but merely discouraged them; but it is still more extraordinary that, considering the violent disputes which had occurred with respect to this point, there had been no express prohibition of the practices in the Articles of 1562. If it had been the intention of the Church to have forbidden the practice, surely there would have been an express and distinct prohibition of it.

"In looking to the Homily it must be considered what was the purpose for which it was composed—viz., to discourage the practice of praying for the dead as connected with the doctrine of Purgatory; but in no part of the Homily is it declared that the

APPENDIX XII.

practice of praying for the dead is unlawful—merely that it is useless: that prayers for the dead could have no effect in altering the condition of the dead, and that in the Word of God we have no commandment to do so; and referring to St. Chrysostom and St. Cyprian, it is said, 'Let these and such other places be sufficient to take away the gross error of Purgatory out of our heads; neither let us dream any more that the souls of the dead are anything at all holpen by our prayers.' It seemed clearly to have been the intention of the composer of the Homily to discourage the practice of praying for the dead; but it does not appear that in any part of the Homily he declares the practice to be an unlawful one. But supposing he had been of opinion that such prayers were unlawful, it is not to be necessarily inferred that the Church of England adopted every part of the doctrines contained in the Homilies. If it had been the opinion of the framers of the Articles and Canons of the Church that prayers for the dead were opposed to the Scriptures, they would have expressly declared their illegality. On this part of the case, then, I am of opinion that there has been no violation of any of the Articles of the Church. No other Articles have been referred to specifically to make out the proposition that the Church considered prayers for the dead an illegal practice.

"But it was urged in this case, that the person by whom the tombstone was erected being a Roman Catholic, it must be supposed that the invitation contained in the inscription, to pray for the dead, has a necessary reference to the doctrine of Purgatory as received by the Church of which she is a member; and that the inscription must be taken in a Roman Catholic sense, because the quotation from the Maccabees was taken from the Roman Catholic version of the Bible, and not from that authorized by the Church of England. Now I do not think this argument sufficient to authorize me to put any other construction on the inscription than the words will bear, according to their plain meaning. It is true that the version does not agree with the English translation (in fact, in one translation, there is not a 46th verse in the 12th chapter of Maccabees); but the question is not whether the version is correct or not, but whether the meaning is or is not inconsistent with that contained in the English version? Now it is impossible to read the English version and not see that the sense of the quotation is the same in both; and that the reconciliation spoken of by Judas meant a reconciliation of the dead, with a view to the resurrection. Whether the doctrine is taken from the text according to the Romish or English version, the question is, Whether it is a violation of the Articles, Canons, and Constitutions of our Church? That is the view I must take of the case, sitting here as an ecclesiastical judge. If anything arose from the circumstances of the party being a Roman Catholic, or from the sense in which the words of the inscription are understood by the Romish Church, it should have been specifically pleaded, for the Court has no judicial information of the existence of a Roman Catholic Bible.

"I shall conclude this part of the case with one observation—What has been the practice of eminent divines of the Church of England? It was correctly stated in the argument that an inscription was placed on the tombstone of Bishop Barrow, in the cathedral of St. Asaph, in 1680, to this effect: 'O vos transeuntes in domum Domini, in domum orationis, orate pro conservo vestro, ut inveniat misericordiam in die Domini.' It is not possible to conceive that Bishop Barrow would have suffered such an inscription to have been placed upon his tomb if he had believed that it was contrary to the doctrine and discipline of the Church to which he belonged.

"I am, then, of opinion, on the whole of the case, that the offence imputed by the articles has not been sustained; that no authority or canon has been pointed out by which the practice of praying for the dead has been expressly prohibited; and I am accordingly of opinion, that if the articles were proved, the facts would not subject the party to ecclesiastical censure, as far as regards the illegality of the inscription on the tombstone. That part of the articles, therefore, must be rejected.

"The other branch of the case is subject to different considerations, viz., the erection of the stone without the consent of the incumbent, which is an ecclesiastical offence. It has been suggested in the argument, that the proceeding on this branch of the case should have been in the civil form, by monition; but it seems to me that this is the proper form of proceeding. I am not aware of any case in which a different form has been followed. But this offence was not specified in the decree, or citation, served on the party. The only ground of illegality on the face of the citation consisted in the inscription; the erecting, or causing to be erected, a monument without the leave of the incumbent, is a distinct and separate offence, which should have been set forth in the citation, in order that the party cited might know what she was called upon to answer. I am clearly of opinion that, according to the law and practice of the Court, the citation was insufficient to raise the question whether the consent of the incumbent had been obtained or not; and, on this part of the case, likewise, I am of opinion that the articles are inadmissible. The Court, therefore, on this view of the case, is bound to reject the articles altogether, and to dismiss the party, and with costs."

APPENDIX XIII.

A FUNERAL SERMON.*
OUR DUTY TO THE DEPARTED.

"Have pity upon me, have pity upon me, O ye my friends, for the hand of God hath touched me."—*Job* xix. 21.

THERE is always something very solemn and touching in contemplating Death. It works so many changes, turns the course of so many hopes and desires, alters plans, frustrates anticipations, makes a few rough places plain, and many smooth ways rugged, that men cannot fail to remember the hour when it pleased God to terminate the day of probation of some well-loved relative or friend, and to summon him to the particular judgment-bar of his Redeemer and Judge. Men cannot fail to remember the day, because the course of their own lives, still realities to themselves, was altered by the influence; and those who were left behind were rudely reminded of the change by the startling contrast between the past and the present. The voice loved and welcomed, the sound of the footfall known so well, the hand with its kindly grasp and the heart with its beat of sympathy, are silent and still. The well-used chair is vacant; the open book unread; the familiar room tenantless.

* Preached at All Saints', Lambeth, on Sunday, 10th September, 1871, upon the death of the Rev. J. A. Johnston, Vicar of St. John's, Waterloo Road, who departed this life, August 29, 1871.

APPENDIX XIII.

Here, in this vast city, we, as Christian men and women, have lost much, because no longer the departed lie, sleeping their last sleep, round our sacred sanctuaries. It was well to be reminded continually that life is fleeting and transitory; to be told with the expressive power of deeds done before our natural eyes—the solemn act of burial—that this is but our time of probation, a short life in comparison with that which continues for ever and ever beyond the grave; and that here we have no continuing city, but seek one to come. It was well when Holy Church, as at the font and at the altar, stood by, in the persons of her ministers, to commend the bodies of the faithful to the earth, as they had commended their souls into the hands of a merciful Creator; and pointed with strong confidence to the sign of the Crucified as a token of light in a day of separation and mourning and woe. It was well, when men went up to the House of Prayer, to adore Three Persons in One God, and to ask favours and graces for themselves, that they saw on either side of the pathway, where the shadow of the cross fell, memorials of the silent dead, with a simple prayer that mercy might be shed from on high in the great day of the Lord. These beautiful and touching sights bade the faithful not selfishly to pray for themselves alone, nor realize their own wants exclusively, but to remember in their sacrifices and orisons the friends of old, who had been called away from this transitory world to the place of departed spirits, and to put into actual practice the consoling doctrine of the Communion of Saints. With holy Job, the friend passed from sight and ken seemed to cry out to them in his need, "Have pity upon me, have pity upon me, O ye my friends, for the hand of God hath touched me."

Yes: Death is solemn indeed, and should frequently be made the subject of holy meditation. Our ancestors in times gone by, and not long gone by either, were accustomed, when writing their last wills and testaments, to affirm as the first and chief reason for their so doing: "Forasmuch as there is nothing more certain than death, and nothing more uncertain than the hour and day thereof"—a sentiment which it would be well for all of us ever to keep in our minds; so that while we have time we may strive to love God, and do good unto all men, especially unto those who are of the household of faith.

Now the faithful departed, as you well enough know, form an important part of the One Family of God. Those who have gone before us in the sleep of peace belong to you not solely or chiefly because of affinity or relationship, but because both you and they have partaken, by the mercy of our Father in Heaven, of a new nature in Christ. Though we miss them from our side in the daily warfare which we, left behind, are still called upon to wage; though they are no longer here, going in and out, in daily work or common worship, yet have they as true and real an existence as when they lived on earth, and are one with us in God, who is the Father of all. Doubtless, as in the case of the rich man and Lazarus, they are permitted either directly or by some inscrutable agency, to know what is happening in the world; interested in those left behind, sorrowful when sin has the dominion, rejoicing when grace triumphs, anxiously waiting for the full fruition of the joy of all the ransomed, and longing for the beautiful breaking of the everlasting day, when that joy in its full perfection shall for ever reign supreme.

For this, therefore, it follows that though death has both its solemn and sorrowful side, it has likewise another—a side from which to the eye of Faith may be seen the dark cloud's silver lining. He, who took man's nature upon Him in the pure womb of the ever-blessed Virgin, fought the battle of life, agonized and died for us men dead in trespasses and sins; and by His own inherent power, as God, rose again on the first Easter Day for our salvation. He went down alone to the way of the passage of Jordan. His feet touched the cold waters in the valley of the shadow of death. Through the dark river he passed, reaching the Heavenly Canaan beyond, on the confines of His own home where enshrouded dwells the Eternal in unapproachable majesty. Thither to the land of Paradise He bore the message of redemption by Himself completed, and of death by death overcome. Then the prison-bars were unloosed and the doors flung open that the prisoners might rejoice because of Calvary, and in due course obtain the consummation of their hopes in Him. As Zechariah of old, prophesying in the Name of the Lord, had declared—"I will bring the third part through the fire, and will refine them as silver is refined, and will try them as gold is tried: they shall call on my Name, and I will hear them: I will say, It is my people: and they shall say, The Lord is my God." *

Yet now, until the great day for the restitution of all things, they wait for the full realization of the loving-kindness of God,— those, that is, who have died in His faith, fear, and favour. Not yet have they attained to the vision of the King in his beauty. Safe and surely secure from temptation, they are, it may be, paying a penalty, if it be still unpaid, because of the sins and frailties of this mortal life; waiting God's will and work until it shall please Him in a time accomplished to unfold the glories of the city of peace. For themselves, therefore, we may believe that they desire to be remembered by those still in the flesh when the life-giving Eucharist is offered, and the mingled voices of our worshippers here rise to God's throne. "Have pity upon me, have pity upon me, O ye my friends, for the hand of God hath touched me." Need this Christian lesson be further set forth, or more closely applied as regards those whom, whether recently or more remotely we have loved and lost?

On the present occasion, as you know, we have specially to

* Zechariah xiii. 9.

remember one who was with us so lately, known to many, respected and regarded by all, the Vicar of an adjoining parish, closely connected with this by his office,* whose almost sudden death has caused sorrow, and a deep feeling of loss to not a few. Making no noise in the world, and courting no popularity, at the same time unflinching in his statement of Divine Truth, yet owning no enemies, he was a warm and sincere supporter of the Catholic Revival, with boldness, zeal, and discretion. Six weeks ago and he, we might have held, had still many years of life and usefulness before him. Burdened, however, by the anxieties—never adequately realized except by those who have to bear them—of a large London parish, with constant toil of mind and body, he nevertheless appeared in ordinary health and spirits. But such was only an appearance. Unremitting in labour, steady, regular, sometimes with help, frequently with little sympathy expressed, and sometimes single-handed, he had here worked in his sacred office for nearly a quarter of a century. And this had naturally told upon the constitution of one who was keenly sensitive and never so physically strong as he seemed. So that when the attack came, and he lay prostrate, there was little or no power to enable him to rally. The light it is believed had for some time been burning low, and yet it burned lower still and so went out.

Not here would we lift the veil before the chamber of death to declare more than that as a pure and self-denying Christian priest he had lived, and as a pure and self-denying Christian priest he died. One, erewhile a respected fellow-worker with myself here, ministered tenderly to the dying, and then gave him our Lord's Body and Blood,—blessed viaticum for the soul in its passage through the gate of death. Calm, recollected, patient, forgiving, suffering

---

* The Vicar of St. John's, Waterloo Road, is the *ex-officio* patron of the Church and Vicarage of All Saints', Lambeth.

APPENDIX XIII.

keenly, but keen in faith, the spirit of the sick man passed upward to the God who gave it. And Death was there.

For ourselves the warning is momentous, the lessons pertinent and marked. "One shall be taken and another shall be left." "The night cometh when no man can work." What is our case that the good and merciful God has left us with the day of grace upon us, while He has called some far more deserving of his goodness and mercy away? Why is it that shroud and shell and coffin have been ordered for others, borne away from their old homes, and that our frames still glow with life and strength and health? O beloved, let us each point the moral for himself; in solemn earnest and hearty intention let us all prepare to meet our God.

But no more for ourselves. What has been said will suffice. Ours be not self-contemplation and selfishness, but true Christian charity. Let us ever remember the departed. With some, their memories soon fade and are forgotten; with others they remain green and fresh through the summer and autumn of a long life, even into the chill and loneliness of its winter-time and close. So be it with all gathered here. Though others may forget and mention not their names, let no return of their anniversary remain unused and unhonoured by us. As the hart desires the water-brooks, so do the souls of those departed in Christ long for Almighty God. To Him they cry out of the deep. As we turn over the sacred books they used in their lifetime, as we linger in the homes dearer to us because they were *their* homes too, when we go to visit the graves where their bodies rest, away from the dust and turmoil of this vast city, in a sleeping-place where the grass grows green and the sunshine falls; or when in dull November, year by year, All Souls' Day comes round again, with its hallowed associations and loving duties, let us always remember the departed and pray, "Lord, thy kingdom come." "A little while," as he remarked on his death-bed, whose memory and worth are before us to-day, "A little while, and this separation shall be ended." And when it is ended there shall be a break and a parting nevermore, for God shall be all in all.

Lord, have mercy on the departed and hasten Thy coming. Christ, be merciful to the dead, and raise them up again at the last day. Lord, be merciful to him whom we love, taken from us. And though links be broken here, because of our sins, do Thou, O pitiful and most merciful, because of the Passion on Calvary, hereafter bind them and us together again in Thyself, when and as Thou willest, for ever and evermore. Amen.

INDEX.

"Abraham's Bosom," the Term, 66.
Active Intercommunion, 92.
All Souls' College, Oxford, Graces used at, 285.
Ancient Monumental Inscriptions, 298.
Angelic Operations on Earth, 5.
  ,, Operations on Individuals, 6.
Anglo-Saxon Customs regarding the Dead, 81, 82, 83, 84, 87.
  ,, Psalter, 82.
Allatius on Prayer for the Dead, 33.
All Souls' Day, 102.
Anniversaries, Mass on, 225.
Anniversary of the Dead, The, 100.
Anthologium, The, 49.
Apostolical Constitutions contain Prayer for the Dead, 67.
Aquinas, St. Thomas, on Divine Love, 18.
Articles of 1536, The Ten, 139.

Balliol College, Oxford, Graces used at, 287.
Beads, Forms of Bidding the, 274.
Beadsmen, Office of, 101.
Bede's History, 81, 83, 87.
Bond created by the Sacraments, 7.
Brasenose College, Oxford, Grace used at, 286.
Bucer's Arguments against Prayer for the Dead, 153.
  ,, Influence in England, 146.
Burial of the Dead, 13.
  ,, Service, Character of the, 149.

Calvin's Influence in England, 146.
Care for the Dead amongst the Ancients, 12.
  ,,   ,, under the Patriarchs, 24, 25.
Catacombs, Inscriptions from the, 20, 21.

Celebratio Cœna Domini in Funeribus, 272.
Chantries, Suppression of the English, 138.
Chantry, The Perpetual, 100.
Charity and its Fruits, 92.
Church Militant, The, 18.
  ,, Patient, The, 18.
  ,, Property, Sir H. Spelman on, 139.
  ,, Triumphant, The, 18.
Commemoration of the Dead a most ancient Tradition, 65.
Communication of Good Works and Offices, 19.
Communion of Saints, 146.
  ,, with the Father, 3.
  ,, with the Son, 3.
  ,, with the Spirit, 4.
  ,, with the Angels, 5.
  ,, between the Faithful, 7.
  ,, in the Eucharist, 8.
  ,, Service in King Edward VI.'s First Prayer Book, 270.
  ,, St. Paul on, 9.
  ,, unaffected by Death, 9.
  ,, of Saints perfect in Heaven, 9.
  ,, Fruits of, 11.
  ,, Reality of Spiritual, 11.
"Communionem Sanctorum," The Clause, 8.
Constitutions, Apostolical, The, 67.
Corpus Christi College, Oxford, Graces used at, 283.

Daily Mass for the Dead, 226.
Daniel's Codex Liturgicus, 49.
Day of the Lord, The, 46.
Dead, Baptism for the, 44.
  ,, Burning of the, 13.
  ,, Burial of the, 13.
  ,, Care for the, 12.

INDEX.

Dead, Embalming of the, 13.
  ,, Office for the, 228.
  ,, Matins for the, 236.
Death of Bishops and Abbots publicly announced, 87.
Denzinger's Ritus Orientalium, etc., 49.
Departed Spirits, The Place of, 42.
"Dirige," Use of the term, 96.
Doles at Funerals, 98.
  ,,   The Use of, 83.
Döllinger on Purgatory, 16.

Early Christian Writers, Vagueness of, 89.
Egyptians, Mythology of the, 13.
Eleemosynary Institutions, Dr. Stephens on, 138.
Enoch's Translation, 22.

First Prayer Book of Edward VI, 142, 143, 144, 270.
Form of Bidding the Beads (various), 274.
Funerals, Use of the Cross at, 82.

"Gospellers" of the Reformation Era, 151.
Gough Missal, The, 275.
Grace at All-Souls' College, Oxford. 285.
  ,, Pembroke College, Oxford, 285.
  ,, Queen's College, Oxford, 285.
  ,, St. Edmund Hall, Oxford, 292.
  ,, St. Peter's College, Cambridge, 292.
  ,, Religious House, Little Gidding, 293
  ,, Lambeth under Abp. Laud, 294.
  ,, Winchester College, 294.
  ,, Lincoln College, Oxford, 289.
  ,, Christ Church, Oxford, 290.
  ,, Jesus College, Oxford, 291.
  ,, St. Mary Magdalene College, Oxford, 281.
  ,, Oriel College, Oxford, 282.
  ,, Merton College, Oxford, 283.
  ,, New College, Oxford, 277.
  ,, University College, Oxford, 277.
  ,, Trinity College, Oxford, 280.
  ,, Trinity College, Cambridge, 292.

Grace at Corpus Christi College, Oxford, 283.
  ,, Wadham College, Oxford, 284.
  ,, Brasenose College, Oxford, 286.
  ,, Balliol College, Oxford, 287.
  ,, Worcester College, Oxford, 288.
  ,, St. John's College, Oxford, 289.
Graces used at the Colleges of Oxford and Cambridge, 277.
Gregorian Sacramentary, The, 62.

Hades, The Greek, 13.
Hearse in Beauchamp Chapel, 97.
  ,, at Tanfield Church, 97.
  ,, Use of the, 96.
Hebrew Ritual of the Spanish Jews, 36.
Hell, Our Lord's Descent into, 42.
  ,, a Place for the Lost, 90, 91.
Hilda, Abbess of Whitby, Death of, 87.
Holy Communion at Funerals, 271.

In Commendationibus Benefactorum, 296.
Indulgences, Pope Leo X. and, 134.
  ,, farmed by Dominicans, 135.
  ,, Augustinians, 135.
Inhumatio Defuncti (*secundum usum Sarum*), 197.
Intercommunion between Saints on Earth and Saints in Heaven, 8.
Intercession, The Duty of, 184.
Invocation of Angels still practised in England, 6.
  ,, Saints, 19, 103.

Jesus College, Oxford, Graces used at, 291.
Jewish Grave-stones in the Crimea, 33.
  ,, Catacomb at Rome, Inscriptions in the, 34.
  ,, Inscription in Germany, 37.
  ,, Belief in the Resurrection, 29.
  ,, Prayers for the Dead, 33, 34, 35, 36, 37.
  ,, Monumental Inscriptions, 33, 34, 37.
Josephus on Prayer for the Dead, 32.

Laud, Archbishop, 155.

INDEX.

Liber Festivalis, Bidding Prayer from the, 275.
Limbus Infantium, 90.
    „ Patrum, 90.
Lincoln College, Oxford, Graces used at, 289.
Littledale on Prayers for the Dead, 16.
Liturgia Romana Vetus, 62.
Liturgy of St. Ignatius, 57.
    „ the Monophysites, 57.
    „ the Syro-Jacobites, 57.
    „ St. Gregory Abulfaragius, 58.
    „ St. Cyril, 58.
    „ Alexandria, 58.
    „ St. Basil, 59.
    „ St. Celestine, 59.
    „ St. Dionysius, 59, 63.
    „ Michael of Antioch, 59.
    „ John Bar Madan, 59.
    „ St. James of Botna, 60.
    „ Malabar, 60.
    „ the Church of Abyssinia, 61.
    „ St. Peter, 62, 63.
    „ St. Xystus, 63.
    „ the Mozarabic, 62.
    „ St. James, 50, 58.
    „ St. James (Rattray's Version), 51.
    „ Christians of St. Thomas, 50.
    „ St. Mark, 52, 61.
    „ St. James, Brother of our Lord (corrupt), 53.
    „ St. Clement, 53.
    „ the Scotch Episcopalians, 52.
    „ St. Clement (Jacobite), 54.
    „ the Apostolical Constitutions, 54.
    „ St. John Chrysostom, 55.
    „ the Nestorians, 56.
    „ the Apostles, 56.
    „ Theodore of Mopsuestia, 57.
    „ of the Church of England, 142, 145.
Loving Cup, Use of the, 85.
Luther's heretical notions, 151.

Maccabees, The Books of, 30.
Magdalene College, Oxford, Graces used at, 281.
Mai, Cardinal, De Papiri Vaticani, 14.

Maitland on the Reformation, 151.
Mamachi's Origines Christianæ, 82.
Manual, The York, 275.
Manuale Sarisburiensis, 96.
Martyr's (Peter) Influence in England, 146.
Mass of Requiem, 94.
    „ of the Holy Trinity, 95.
    „ of our Lady, 95.
Mass-penny, The, 96.
Masses for the Dead, after Salisbury use, 220.
Mediæval Rites of Sepulture, 97.
Merton College, Oxford, Grace used at, 283.
Missa in Cemeterio, from Abp. Ecgbert's Pontifical, 269.
Missa pro Defunctis secundum Ritum Romanum, 211.
Missal of Leofric, 82, 86.
Monasteries, Suppression of the English, 136, 137.
    „ Spoliation of the English, 137.
Month's Mind, The, 99.
Mythology of the Egyptians, 13.

Nestorian Service for Burial of a Priest, 57.

Obit, The, 99.
Office for the Dead (after the Roman Rite), 228.
Officium Defunctorum, 95.
One Family of Christ, The, 18.
Onesiphorus, Prayer for, 45.
Order for the Burial of Infants (according to the Roman Rite), 263.
Oriel College, Oxford, Graces used at, 282.
Origen on Prayer for the Dead, 69.

Paradise, 90.
Pembroke College, Oxford, Graces used at, 285.
Penitent Thief, The case of the, 40, 41, 42.
Perpetual Chantry, The, 100.
"Placebo," Use of the Term, 95.
Prayer of Oblation, 147.
Prayer, St. Thomas Aquinas on, 182.
    „ Bishop Hammond on, 183.
Prayers for the Dead, 155.
    „   „ Reasons for, 185, 186, 187, 188.
    „   „ Council of Florence on, 188.

INDEX.

Prayers for the Dead, Bishop Alex. Forbes on, 188.
,, ,, Gerson, Chancellor, on, 189.
,, ,, Malcolm M'Coll on, 190, 193.
,, ,, in Consecration Service (A.D. 1620), 158.
,, ,, Bishop Overall on, 160.
,, ,, Bishop Cosin on, 160, 161, 162.
,, ,, Bishop Buckeridge on, 162.
,, ,, Bishop de Dominis on, 167.
,, ,, in Consecration Service of St. Peter's College, Cambridge, (A.D. 1632), 163.
,, ,, Bishop W. Forbes on, 164.
,, ,, Herbert Thorndike on, 165, 167.
,, ,, Last Century Examples of, 178.
,, ,, Last Century Bidding Prayer containing, 179.
,, ,, taught by the Mediæval Church, 92, 93.
,, ,, Bishop Wilson on, 176.
,, ,, rejected by Burnet, Hoadley, and their school, 176.
,, ,, rejected by the Puritans, 176.
,, ,, taught by the Church of England, 177, 178.
,, ,, Dr. Samuel Johnson on, 179.
,, ,, Bishop Heber on, 179.
,, ,, Bishop Barrington on, 180.
,, ,, Bishop Legge on, 180.
,, ,, Bishop Kaye on, 180.
,, ,, Bishop Wilberforce on, 180.
,, ,, Bucer's arguments agst., 153.
,, ,, universal in earliest Christian era, 15.
,, ,, in the time of Judas Maccabeus, 14.
,, ,, Dr. Brett on, 165.
,, ,, in special service for King Charles's Martyrdom, 168.
,, ,, Bishop Gauden on, 169.

Prayers for the Dead, Bishop Jeremy Taylor on, 169, 170.
,, ,, Bishop Ken on, 171.
,, ,, Jeremy Collier on, 172.
,, ,, Joseph Bingham on, 174.
,, ,, Charles Wheatley on, 175.
,, ,, Bishop Gunning on, 175.
,, ,, Bishop Smallridge on, 175.
,, ,, [Archbishop Sheldon on, 156.
,, ,, Bishop Blandford on, 156.
,, ,, Bishop Andrewes on, 157, 158.
,, ,, Archbishop Bramhall on, 157.
,, ,, Archbishop Usher on, 157.
,, ,, Dr. Hammond on, 157.
,, ,, Bishop Hickes on, 157.
,, ,, Bishop Beveridge on, 156.
,, ,, Hamon L'Estrange on, 156.
,, ,, John Johnson on, 156.
Pre-Reformation Inscriptions, 303.
Prison House, The, 39.
Processional, The Salisbury, 274.
Proctor on the Burial Service, 148, 149.
Progression after Death, 47.
Pseudo-Origen on Prayer for the Dead, 69.
Purgatory, St. Paul on, 106.
,, Anglican Documents on, 141.
,, Early Opinions concerning, 105.
,, St. Clement of Alexandria on, 109.
,, Origen on, 109, 110, 111.
,, St. Hilary on, 111, 112.
,, St. Gregory Nazianzen on, 112.
,, St. Ephrem Syrus on, 112.
,, St. Jerome on, 113.
,, St. Augustine on, 113, 114.
,, St. Paulinus of Nola on, 114.
,, St. Cyprian on, 115.
,, St. Chrysologus on, 115.

Purgatory, St. Gregory of Nyssa on, 115.
   „ Venerable Bede on, 117.
   „ St. Catherine of Genoa on, 118—189.
   „ Seven Conceptions of, 118, 119, 120.
   „ The Synod of Bethlehem on, 120, 121.
   „ Chrysanthus, Patriarch of Jerusalem, on, 122.
   „ Four Opinions regarding, 107.
   „ Council of Trent on, 123, 128.
   „ Thirty-nine Articles on, 123.
   „ Dr. J. M. Neale on, 126.
   „ Cardinal Fisher on, 129.
   „ Barnes, the Benedictine, on, 129.
   „ Christopher Davenport on, 129.
   „ Dr. J. H. Newman on, 129.
   „ Professor Klee on, 108.
   „ Archbishop Usher on, 107.
   „ Dr. Deacon on, 106.
   „ Bishop A. P. Forbes on, 106.
   „ Dr. F. W. Faber on, 106, 124.
   „ Dr. Döllinger on, 16.
   „ Cardinal Wiseman on, 130.
   „ Tracts for the Times on, 130.
   „ Societies for the Relief of Souls in, 130.
   „ Current Anglican Conception of, 131.

Queen's College, Oxford, Graces used at, 285.

Raising of the Spirit of Samuel, The, 26, 29.
Reformation, Controversies at the, 154.
   „ Reaction to the, 144.
   „ Rev. W. Maskell on the, 155.
Relaxation of Sin hereafter, 18.
Religious House at Little Gidding, Graces used at the, 293.
Renaudot on the Antiquity of Prayers for the Dead, 65.
Resurrection of the Body, 22, 23, 29, 32.

Rich Man and Lazarus, The Case of the, 40.
Rites of Burial, 96.
   „ the Church of Durham, 150.
Rituale Ecclesiæ Dunelmensis, 83.
Runic Inscription at Lancaster, 84.

Sacramentarium Leonianum, 62.
Sacramentary, The Gregorian, 62.
Sacrilege, Bishop South on, 138.
St. Ambrose on Prayer for the Dead, 74.
St. Augustine on Prayer for the Dead, 75, 76, 77, 78.
St. Chrysostom on Prayer for the Dead, 71, 72, 73.
St. Cyprian on Prayer for the Dead, 69.
St. Cyril on Prayer for the Dead, 70.
St. Edmund Hall, Oxford, Graces used at, 292.
St. Ephrem on Prayer for the Dead, 78, 79.
St. Epiphanius on Prayer for the Dead, 70.
St. Gregory on Prayer for the Dead, 75.
St. Peter's College, Cambridge, Graces used at, 292.
St. Thomas Aquinas on the Punishment for Sin, 91.
Saints, Invocation of, 19.
   „ A Technical Term, 2.
   „ The Assembly of the, 2.
Salisbury Processional, Bidding Prayer from the, 274.
Samuel, Raising the Spirit of, 26, 29.
Sanctified, The, 1.
Second Prayer Book of Edward VI., 147.
Sects at the Reformation, Increase of, 152.
Sepulture, Use of the Cross in, 82.
Seven Masses for the Dead, The, 99.
Soul Mass, The, 94.
"Soul Shot," Use of the Term, 82.
Spirit, The Work of the Holy, 4.
Spirits, The Place of Departed, 42.
Spiritual Bonds unbroken by Death, 21.
Story of Imma and Tunna, Bede's, 86.

Tartarus, The Latin, 13.
Tertullian on Prayer for the Dead, 68.
   „ „ Oblations for the Dead, 67.
Tetzel, John, and Indulgences, 134.
Thanksgiving after Meat, 85.

Theodore, Archbishop, on Mass for the Dead, 95.
Thorpe's Homilies of the Anglo-Saxon Church, 81.
Trinity College, Oxford, Graces used at, 280.
" " Cambridge, Graces used at, 292.

University College, Oxford, Graces used at, 277.
Use of the Cross at Funerals, 82.
" " in Sepulture, 82.
" Loving-cup, 85.

Use of the Hearse, 96.

Venial Sins, 16.
Vigilia Mortuorum, 95.

Wadham College, Oxford, Graces used at, 284.
Winchester College, Graces used at, 294.
Witch of Endor, The, 26.
Worcester College, Oxford, Graces used at, 288.

York Manual, The, 275.

THE END.

www.ingramcontent.com/pod-product-compliance
Lightning Source LLC
Chambersburg PA
CBHW030342230426
43664CB00007BA/505